The New York Times
ESSENTIAL LIBRARY

Children's
Movies

The New York Times
ESSENTIAL LIBRARY

Children's Movies

A Critic's Guide to the Best Films
Available on Video and DVD

PETER M. NICHOLS

TIMES BOOKS

Henry Holt and Company   New York

Times Books
Henry Holt and Company, LLC
Publishers since 1866
115 West 18th Street
New York, New York 10011

Henry Holt® is a registered trademark of
Henry Holt and Company, LLC.

Library of Congress Cataloging-in-Publication Data

Nichols, Peter M.
    The New York Times essential library : children's movies :
a critic's guide to the best films available on video and DVD /
Peter M. Nichols.—1st ed.
        p. cm.
    Includes index.
    ISBN 0-8050-7198-9
    1. Motion pictures for children—Catalogs. 2. Video recordings
for children—Catalogs. I. Title: Children's movies.
II. New York times. III. Title.

PN1998.N7329 2003
791.43'75'083—dc21
                                        2003051130

Henry Holt books are available for special promotions
and premiums. For details contact: Director, Special Markets.

First Edition 2003

Printed in the United States of America
1   3   5   7   9   10   8   6   4   2

To Jenny, Ana, and Jeff

Contents

Preface

For this book the term *children's movie* is considerably broadened. To be sure, many of these films were made primarily for children, but most of them reach out to a larger family audience. Some—*High Noon, Groundhog Day, Lawrence of Arabia*—don't meet most people's definition of a children's movie at all.

Few of these films are good for simply parking the kids in front of on a rainy afternoon. They are chosen to give children up to the age of twelve or so a taste of various genres and eras. All are generally suitable for children, all or most are highly entertaining, but they are also meant to give kids a feel for what the movies have been about over the decades. Many will require some thought and are better watched with grown-ups on hand to help set the context. Everybody should have some fun in the bargain.

A couple of these films go back to the 1920s and the silent era, and about twenty of them are in black and white. Kids hate black-and-white films until they start watching an entertaining one—*King Kong, Bringing Up Baby, To Kill a Mockingbird*—whereupon they tend to forget about the lack of color. The notion of old movies makes many kids cringe, but as organizers of sleepovers can tell you, give these films a chance and they earn rapt audiences.

One challenge for a handicapper of children's movies is to set an appropriate age level. In my experience parents object to sex and extreme violence, but often they seem most adamant about obscenity. Judgments vary widely. There are other questions of appropriateness. Will kids understand a film and will it interest them? As with questions about sex, violence, and profanity, opinions skew all over the age brackets. For example, some family film guides consider the screwball comedy *Bringing Up Baby* suitable for age six, while other guides recommend the film for ages twelve and older.

Keep in mind that there is a high parental death rate in many movies intended for children. In films from *The Lion King* to *The Black Stallion,* children lose parents, often violently, as a way of being forced to establish their own identities and begin independent adventures in new situations. Children watching these films certainly appreciate young counterparts on-screen who shake adult control and take on freedom, but it can be traumatic, to say the least, to watch them lose their mothers or fathers and sometimes both.

Parents should also be aware of shifts in the rating system introduced in 1968 by the Motion Picture Association of America. Films released before that year are unrated, of course, unless in unusual instances when they have been rated for distribution on video. A large number of movies in this book carry a PG rating, which should be reassuring to many parents. Remember, though, that the PG-13 rating wasn't adopted until 1984 after Steven Spielberg campaigned to establish a new category for films (some, like *Raiders of the Lost Ark,* his own) that weren't offensive but could frighten children with their levels of violence and intensity.

As a result, a movie like *The Bad News Bears,* which has plenty of strong and spirited profanity, was given a PG, for parental guidance, when it was released in 1976. Today it undoubtedly would be given a PG-13.

It's dangerous to assign any one age to a film. Many movies in this guide seem right for about ages eight and up, but parents could well disagree. Every family has its own standards. Whenever there is doubt, it's vital for parents to watch the film before showing it to their children.

Finally, if you'll permit a plug for a format, watch these films on DVD whenever possible. Only a few of these titles are unavailable on disc (*The African Queen,* for example). DVD provides by far the better image, and the extra features often explain why these films are bellwethers of their genres.

The New York Times
ESSENTIAL LIBRARY

Children's
Movies

1. ABBOTT AND COSTELLO MEET FRANKENSTEIN

Bud Abbott, Lou Costello, Bela Lugosi, Lon Chaney Jr., Glenn Strange, Lenore Aubert, Jane Randolph

DIRECTED BY CHARLES T. BARTON

1948. 83 minutes. Black and white. No rating

That title needs a little expanding upon. Chick (Bud Abbott) and Wilbur (Lou Costello) meet Frankenstein all right (more accurately, Frankenstein's monster), but their main challenge is Dracula, played to the hilt by that Dracula of movie Draculas, Bela Lugosi. Wolfman, portrayed by Lon Chaney Jr., is also a threat. Frankenstein's creation does put in an appearance, of course. Boris Karloff declined the role in this film (he was sick of it), but there is little falloff with Glenn Strange, a huge man and by all accounts one of the sweetest people ever to disappear under monster makeup.

When the film opened in Australia, the three creatures proved so upsetting that they were cut out of it almost entirely—which must have left very little movie. Kids today will love them all, and that includes little kids, once they realize it's all a spoof. Abbott and Costello should please them, too, though some of their patter, honed over years of vaudeville and radio routines, could confuse them. Costello: "I work sixteen hours a day." Abbott: "A union man only works eight hours a day." Costello: "I belong to two unions." You have to be at least seven to follow that.

In this scenario both Dracula and Frankenstein have been brought from Europe to the McDougal House of Horrors, run by the obnoxiously curt McDougal (rousingly played by Frank Ferguson, an extremely busy character actor who reportedly appeared in thirteen movies in 1948 alone). One day Wilbur, a McDougal shipping clerk, gets a call from a man named Talbot (Chaney) who warns them that

Dracula and the monster are on the way and must be stopped. Talbot would stop them himself, but he turns into Wolfman when the full moon comes out, which in this flick is every night.

It seems that Dracula wants the simplest of human brains (Wilbur's) to install in the monster. In true Abbott and Costello fashion, only Wilbur lays eyes on Dracula, the monster, and Wolfman. Chick, the straight man, always arrives seconds too late to see anything. The kids will be amused by the old pivoting dungeon wall trick with Wilbur spinning in and out of perils that Chick just misses.

Wild chases ensue through some impressive sets at Universal. Prior to 1946 the studio was churning out a movie a week—Abbott and Costello comedies, Deanna Durbin musicals, Maria Montez exotica, horror movies, serials, shorts, cartoons—but later the studio decided to go highbrow with films like *Hamlet,* with Laurence Olivier, which won the Oscar in 1948. By then, though, Universal needed money and again turned to Bud and Lou.

On the set Costello liked to spray seltzer, start food fights, and set fire to things. The production is said to have laid out $3,800 for pies to throw. In the view of some on the film crew, the real monsters were Abbott and Costello. The movie was directed by Charles T. Barton, a former vaudeville performer himself who made almost every kind of movie imaginable. His recollections of Costello, passed along on the DVD, are of a hotheaded tyrant. Abbott had epilepsy and a drinking problem that often incapacitated him by 4 P.M. Otherwise, they were pros who got the job done.

Lugosi was already famous, but he had grave money problems and badly needed the work. On the set, the constant clowning irritated him, but he worked hard, seemed to enjoy himself, and lent good support and tutelage to the rest of a cast not accustomed to working with vampires. Chaney was renowned himself. His father, the silent star Lon Chaney, had played the hunchback of Notre Dame and the deformed creature in *Phantom of the Opera,* among many roles, but he died before he might have portrayed Dracula in Tod Browning's talkie in 1931. (The role went to Lugosi.)

Chaney Jr. played about every name monster, including Frankenstein's and the Mummy, during a career that ran some 150 films. His drinking reportedly far exceeded Abbott's, though he always rallied on the set. Being Wolfman was an ordeal, requiring staying stock-still during hours of time-lapse photography as the transformation from man to monster progressed. "I didn't relish putting glue all over his face when he was a little high," a makeup woman says on the disc.

After the huge success of this movie in 1948, Bud and Lou went on to "meet" about everybody: the Killer (played by Karloff, who didn't object to appearing with the boys as long as it wasn't as Frankenstein), the Invisible Man, Captain Kidd, Dr. Jekyll and Mr. Hyde, the Mummy, the Keystone Kops.

In 1948 the monster horror tradition of Dracula and the like was about to give way to the atomic age and the giant bugs and aliens of the 1950s. *Meet Frankenstein* was described as a cross between American folklore and Transylvanian burlesque. Chaney said that good horror involves thought and feeling, and that Abbott and Costello ruined it by making it funny. Perhaps, but horror is no more immune to parody than anything else, and here a good, silly time dresses up in not a bad-looking production.

Dracula and the rest are hardly threatening to even the very small ones. To make sure, brief them beforehand and while you're at it tell them where all this fits in the monster parade over the decades.

2. THE ADVENTURES OF ROBIN HOOD

Errol Flynn, Olivia de Havilland, Claude Rains, Basil Rathbone, Alan Hale

DIRECTED BY MICHAEL CURTIZ AND WILLIAM KEIGHLEY
1938. 102 minutes. No rating

"In our hearts Theseus continues to slay the Minotaur, Beauty charms the Beast, and Robin Hood steals from the rich to aid the poor," wrote the British critic Damian Cannon in a recent re-review of Michael Curtiz's film. Robin ran around Sherwood Forest, of course, but in 1938, Curtiz had Errol Flynn bounding about Bidwell Park in Chico, California. A couple of years earlier Flynn raced through Curtiz's *Charge of the Light Brigade* in Chico, about a hundred miles north of Sacramento. Obviously it was a good town for an action film.

More than sixty years later, *The Adventures of Robin Hood* is still a first-rate film for kids and families—fresh, vibrantly colorful, full of life. In 1938, Warner wanted a rollicking costume adventure to add punch to a lineup of films severely restricted by the production code, which was enacted in 1930 and strictly enforced by 1934. Some good clean fun in the woods and at the court of the leering, insidiously evil Prince John (Claude Rains), albeit with some swordplay and more than a hard knock or two, was innocent enough.

"It seems almost ungrateful, churlish perhaps, even to mention the total lack of consequence on display," Cannon wrote. That's a roundabout way of saying no one seems to get hurt. "Chests are struck by longbow arrows, yet there's no blood, heads are tapped by swords and the loser topples, even traitors are only banished and not beheaded. Perhaps this is legacy of our gory age, making one sensitive to the inherent dichotomy."

Sanitized violence is common in movies deemed suitable for kids, of course, but here it's performed in high style. As the dashing, good-natured Robin, Flynn leaps and soars and defies Prince John and John's hatchet man, Sir Guy of Gisbourne (Basil Rathbone), who is so ruthless he's kind of funny. Robin of Locksley has been the subject of nearly thirty movies over the decades. The great Douglas Fairbanks was Robin in the 1922 silent film, and, for some actual bloodshed, Kevin Costner was in Sherwood's treetops in the quite dark and violent *Robin Hood: Prince of Thieves* (1991), which isn't a bad movie but certainly isn't for small children.

Curtiz's film is by far the best of them, a stew of ancient Robin Hood stories, ballads, and even parts of Sir Walter Scott's *Ivanhoe,* which also dealt with Norman oppression of the Saxons. With no worries about historical accuracy, it also borrows from an operetta in which Robin and Sir Guy vie for Maid Marian (Olivia de Havilland), adding the necessary romantic ingredient.

We begin in the 1190s. On his way back to England from the Crusades, Richard the Lionheart (Ian Hunter) is detained by the Austrians, giving John an opportunity to seize the throne. In the forest beyond John's walls, Robin Hood, a Richard loyalist, puts together a rebel band featuring two of history's renowned recruits, the rotund Friar Tuck (Eugene Pallette) and Little John (Alan Hale), who sends Robin cartwheeling into a stream in the famous duel with staffs.

Apart from the derring-do, this Robin Hood stays relaxed about himself. He treats everyone fairly and honestly and doesn't mind when the laugh is on him. His feelings are plain and direct, his convictions deeply held. But this is primarily a film of action and flourish. Trumpets proclaim everything, blown in great blasts at every opportunity and especially at the tournaments Prince John designs to lure Robin from hiding and into imprisonment. Robin and his men are forever sneaking into these affairs, sometimes shrouded in monk's robes. Not one to avoid an archery contest, Robin taunts John with his laughing disdain and narrowly escapes. Flynn is perfect for this kind of thing, a big Peter Pan at the head of his Lost Boys.

Teach the kids a new word: *swashbuckler*. The Fairbankses, father and son, were great swashbucklers, as was Burt Lancaster. A natural athlete with a big personality, Flynn might be the greatest swashbuckler of them all. In another case of Hollywood envisioning somebody else for a part, Jack Warner wanted James Cagney, whose performance in *A Midsummer Night's Dream* (1935) put Warner in mind of Fairbanks's old Robin. Cagney certainly could have summoned plenty of attitude for verbal tiffs with John, but it would be hard to imagine him flying through the woods quite like Flynn. Anyway, Cagney got into a row with Warner over money and quit the studio.

Flynn had just made *Captain Blood* (another good swashbuckler for kids seven and up) and *Charge of the Light Brigade*. Curtiz directed both of those films, which also starred de Havilland, who is about as fresh and beautiful as one could want. (Note her horse in *Robin Hood*. Later Roy Rogers named it Trigger.) Flynn made eight films with de Havilland and twelve with Curtiz, who was Jack Warner's action man and one of the most versatile and prolific of the studio directors of the '30s and '40s (*Yankee Doodle Dandy, Mildred*

Pierce, and *Casablanca*—see page 54—his one Oscar amid four nominations). As with Howard Hawks and Preston Sturges, Curtiz's career tailed off after the war, though artistically he never equaled the other two.

For *Robin Hood,* he shared the director's credit with the workmanlike William Keighley, who was brought in because of his experience with full, three-strip technicolor. Later, Jack Warner wanted livelier action and assigned Curtiz. Nominated for best picture, *Robin Hood* lost the Academy Award to Frank Capra's *You Can't Take It With You.* It did win Oscars for editing and art direction. If kids grumble about grungy old movies, the colors here remain beautifully textured. "They just don't make movies with this level of tonal saturation anymore, and that's the truth," Mr. Cannon wrote.

Bloodless as it is, there is still a good deal of violence. Some small children might be bothered. Otherwise, we have a clean bill of health, with no big scares or traumas.

3. THE AFRICAN QUEEN

Humphrey Bogart, Katharine Hepburn

DIRECTED BY JOHN HUSTON
1951. 105 minutes. No rating

This is a grand film for kids who are getting acquainted with the movies. The special effects are antiquated, but there is plenty of action (shooting rapids and the like) and a story that thrives on natural excitement without digital pumping up. Children will relate to opposite types being thrown together in German West Africa at the start of World War I. Charlie Allnut (Humphrey Bogart), an unkempt and reluctant steamer captain, drinks his gin mixed with the dark waters of the Ruiki River. Rose Sayer (Katharine Hepburn), a starchy spinster missionary, looks as if she'll pass out with consternation. Together they battle the bush, the Germans, and, until they fall in love at the helm of a thirty-foot scow, each other.

With Rose at the tiller, the wheezing old craft slides downstream on its supposedly impossible journey through rapids and over waterfalls to a lake and a confrontation with the German warship the *Louisa*. Behind the scenes it was still the great old days of Hollywood, albeit on wild and remote locations in the Belgian Congo and Uganda. On-screen young viewers encounter a few "screen legends," as reflected in the title of Hepburn's book about the experience, *The Making of the African Queen: Or How I Went to Africa with Bogart, Bacall and Huston and Almost Lost My Mind.*

Actually the resilient, outspoken Hepburn kept her wits about her very nicely, but there were some dangerous, trying moments laboring in the jungle. Bogie was splendid to work with, she wrote. Ten years earlier he became famous as a trapped killer in *High Sierra* and as the hard-boiled detective Sam Spade in *The Maltese Falcon,* also directed by John Huston. Charlie Allnut, by contrast, is a fine children's character. As Rose steers the boat, Bogie does some terrific monkey and hippo imitations, almost falling down laughing at himself.

Kids can develop soft spots for supposed tough guys. In *Casablanca* (1942), children of about ten or so should meet Bogie as the noble, world-weary saloon keeper Rick Blaine. Bogart's characters often wanted no part of the situations they found themselves in, but got involved anyway because of principle and a sense of responsibility. In *The African Queen* it's Rose's idea to blow up the *Louisa* with homemade torpedoes. Charlie thinks it a foolish idea, but sees it as his duty to help her accomplish the mission and persists even after she becomes discouraged. "Never say die. That's my motto!" Allnut tells Rose enthusiastically. One could almost say we have Bogie in his family-movie mode.

Hepburn's Rose warms as her repressed standoffishness gradually gives way to Charlie's openness and honesty. By this time Hepburn was midway through a film career that would include four Oscars (for *Morning Glory, Guess Who's Coming to Dinner, The Lion in*

Winter, and *On Golden Pond*) and eight more nominations, one of them for *The African Queen.* The daughter of a prominent New England family, she never bothered with the Hollywood crowd, preferring a small, more erudite circle. Some described her as arrogant. In any event, she didn't appear to be the best match for a shoot in the jungle.

"We lived in bamboo bungalows," she told Bogart's son, Stephen. "Half the time we didn't know what we were eating, and we didn't want to know. I found a snake in my toilet." She and the rest became quite ill. But her own account is full of enthusiasm and anticipation for the project, which began with her insistence on authentic period clothing she dug up in the Museum of Costume in London before the troupe decamped for the Congo.

As she tells it in her book, foremost in her mind at that point was how she would get along with the fabled John Huston. "Well, maybe he's great," she wrote. "But he makes me uneasy. I feel all hands and feet and I simply can't imagine being directed by him. Frankly, I think he's one of the overly masculine boys who fascinate themselves and the New York critics by being great guys, and, oh well, I hope I'm wrong."

Army cavalryman, magazine editor, painter, expatriate hobo wandering Europe, hunter, Greenwich Village actor, boxer, Huston made his first mark as a filmmaker with *The Maltese Falcon* in 1941 (a fine introduction to film noir for children of eleven or twelve). By the time they all got together in Africa he and Bogie had also made *The Treasure of the Sierra Madre* (1948), which won Huston Oscars for direction and screenplay, and *Key Largo* (also 1948). As an actor, of course, we remember Huston as the jaded, silkily lethal Noah Cross in *Chinatown* (1974).

"Handle him with care," Hepburn wrote about Huston. When they met in London, Hepburn had seen *The Asphalt Jungle* (1950), one of Huston's best, and had some complaints about that film. "Felt it to be a bit sloppy from the script angle," she wrote in her book. "Told him so in an effort to jolt him. He just smiled and said, 'Is that so, dear? Interesting.'" One can hear the slow, sleepy, viperous Huston delivery. "He put one constantly on the defensive," she wrote, "as I was always in the position of exposing my point of view and getting a perfectly blank reaction."

Hepburn worried about the *Queen* script, too, which was adapted from C. S. Forester's book, but it would be turned into one of the film's strong points by Huston and the critic, screenwriter, and novelist James Agee. In London and later in Africa, she was also distressed at Huston's long absences from the project. Primarily he was off shooting elephants. For that part of the tale, consult the movie about the movie, *White Hunter, Black Heart,* with Clint Eastwood as Huston.

The African Queen was Hepburn's first experience with Bogie. "A generous actor," she wrote. "And a no-bunk person. He just did it. He was an actor who enjoyed acting. Knew he was good. Always knew his lines. Always on time. Hated anything false."

Hepburn and most everybody else had intestinal problems in the jungle. Huston and Bogie didn't, presumably because they lined themselves with alcohol. "He and Huston would be a great team," she wrote. "They drank more than plenty. I'm a great one on good habits of life, so you can imagine what went through my mind as I looked at them. Sorry pair."

After a while, though, she developed a close relationship with Huston, whom she found kind and attentive and anxious to please. There was the matter of his directorial style. At one point he decided that the straitlaced Rose should lighten up and adapt a smile like Eleanor Roosevelt's. "You know, thinking ahead of our story," he said to Hepburn. "And thinking of your skinny little face—a lovely face, dear. But skinny. And those famous hollow cheeks. And that turned-down mouth. You know, when you look serious, you do look rather, well, serious."

Huston recommended a "society smile," like Mrs. Roosevelt's. "That is the goddamnedest best piece of direction I have ever heard," Hepburn wrote. "I was his from there on in."

Early in the film the Germans burn an African village, which will disturb some young children. But this is a fine film for children from the age of eight. Rose and Charlie have begun to have sex, but this is kept very circumspect. There is no profanity.

4. APOLLO 13

Tom Hanks, Bill Paxton, Kevin Bacon, Gary Sinise, Ed Harris, Kathleen Quinlan

DIRECTED BY RON HOWARD
1995. 135 minutes. PG

Ron Howard's film about the ill-fated 1970 moon mission does a fine job for kids. The long, big buildup to the flight may try the patience, but as technicians literally stand on the astronauts' shoulders to strap them tightly enough into their seats, all systems are go. By far the best scene is the blastoff, with its graphic power and vibrations, sheets of ice peeling off the rocket, and crushing G-forces distorting faces.

Later an ominous little bang in the capsule signals a crisis that aborts the flight and begins a harrowing battle to get back alive. Flat-out devotion to authenticity carries this film as surely as mission commander Jim Lovell (Tom Hanks) manually performs the maneuver that brings the crew through a blazing reentry into the earth's atmosphere. Drained by three dark, frigid days in a crippled lunar module, he has thirty-eight seconds to get the job done. The real Jim Lovell had fourteen seconds, but Howard says that if he stuck to every little detail NASA fed him in preparation for shooting he would have gone crazy. What's more, the film would have become more a tech manual than an often riveting, inspirational tale of Americans coming through under extreme duress.

It took Hanks, a great space enthusiast in real life, to fiddle with verb tense and contribute to the roster of deathless English utterances. Lovell actually said, "Houston, we've had a problem." Hanks makes it "we have a problem," and so it stands. From ground level the film checked out with John Noble Wilford, who won a Pulitzer Prize covering the space program for the *New York Times*. "The ambiance is just right," he wrote, "down to the Houston parties, the smoke-

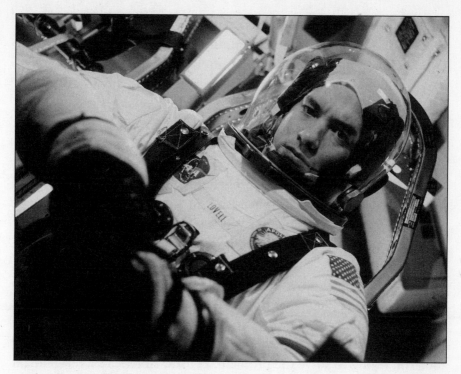

Apollo 13 (Used by permission of Universal Studios Home Video)

clouded intensity of engineering meetings, the astronauts in their casual Ban-Lon shirts, and flight controllers with their short haircuts, narrow ties, and shirt pockets lined with plastic pen holders."

As it is, some critics wondered what happened to artistic imagination, but this is one of those instances when imagination yields to execution and unabashed emotion without too much sacrifice. Kids will soak it up, though the more cynical among them could have a problem with all the earnest enthusiasm. Straining violins usually carry the load in these situations, but here it is the trumpet, the long-stemmed kind that sounds from the ramparts and from afar. With all due respect to Uncle Sam, God himself takes a hand.

Much of the drama is on the ground. As Lovell's wife, Marilyn, Kathleen Quinlan's sole job is to put on dewy expressions of adoration for her guy. That and clean up the kids' rooms, hold potluck suppers for the Houston astronaut gang, get plucky with aggressive media crews setting up camera towers in the Lovell front yard, and ultimately keep herself together come crunch time during the mission's long ride home. One can almost imagine Quinlan getting her face ready for another day of veneration in front of the cameras. But that's all right. Ham-fisted with its sentiments, the movie still does a good job with personal and professional relationships and the daily ruck and roil of the suburban household.

Otherwise we are locked into events with the factuality of a documentary. (In fact, fragments of documentary are woven in here and there.) To prepare, Hanks and other actors moved in with astronauts living in Houston. Does this result in acting, or is it mimicry? Whichever, the characters are no less captivating for young viewers caught in the grip of a white-knuckle crisis. "If it doesn't work we aren't going to have enough power left to get home," Jack Swigert, played by Kevin Bacon, says. Simple as that.

The strongest themes of this film—and its best lessons for kids—are fortitude and persistence. No matter what goes wrong, and it's practically everything, the *Apollo* crew and ground control never lose focus on trying to solve the problem. Hanks, America's Everyman, is especially steadfast as Lovell. In the command center, mission director Gene Kranz, portrayed by Ed Harris, lights up. The cigarette is startling in such a setting. In the film, technicians have heated discussions. NASA consultants advised Howard to calm things down. The real command center never got agitated.

For the ride home, the crew transfers to the lunar-landing module, which will expend less power than the main capsule. On the DVD of the film, Tom Kelly, former chairman of Grumman, explains that in places the module was a fraction of an inch thick. "Three layers of Reynolds wrap," he says. "You could easily put your foot through it." Before reentry, they transfer back to the capsule and Lovell and Swigert have a brief shouting match. That never happened, but Howard added it to break up the bland equanimity.

In the film, the most interesting astronaut stays back in Houston. A measles outbreak grounded Ken Mattingly, who hadn't contracted the disease but might have come down with it aloft. When an onboard explosion vents the oxygen supply and damages other systems, Mattingly, played by Gary Sinise, climbs into a simulator in

Houston and figures out every step the crew has to take to conserve every last wisp of power.

The movie does a terrific job with the heart-stopping four-minute wait for the capsule to reestablish contact after entering the earth's atmosphere. Previous missions took no longer than three minutes. In real life Marilyn Lovell was told there was a less than 10 percent chance the mission would return. As the three-minute mark passes, eyes fall and we feel the dread flood in. Finally, the parachute appears, voices crackle, and there is a roar of relief in Houston. On one hand kids get a fitting climax to a fine action film. They can also appreciate three men who never gave up, did their best with what they had, and accepted their lot with grace and courage. The right stuff, as they say.

Violence isn't an issue. Swigert's very active sex life earns a brief glimpse, but nothing to impair family viewing. Nor is the mild profanity a deterrence in a film that is best for ages seven and up.

5. BABE

Babe the gallant pig, James Cromwell, Magda Szubanski, Fly the feminine sheepdog, Rex the macho sheepdog, Maa the very old ewe

DIRECTED BY CHRIS NOONAN
1995. 89 minutes. G

From the very first scene we know there's something outstanding about Babe, the meek, unfailingly civil piglet who goes on to fame in Chris Noonan's film, adapted from the novel *Babe the Gallant Pig*, by the Australian writer Dick King-Smith. In a dark and forbidding breeding shed, suckling pigs watch their sleek, well-fed elders being

Babe

led off to trucks by large men in high rubber boots. The pigs are resigned. This is what pigs do unquestioningly in life on their way to what they suppose is pig paradise. Only Babe is aware of the impending loss. "Good-bye, Mom," he says.

So here we have still another children's film kicking off with matricide. But don't be too alarmed. Very young viewers (six is a reasonable age to begin) will shake this off relatively quickly in light of fast-moving developments. Into the barn strides Farmer Hoggett (James Cromwell), a very tall man (six foot seven) in search of a very little pig to take home to his property in the Australian countryside. As Babe is dangled before him, "There was a faint sense of common destiny," says the narrator (Roscoe Lee Browne).

Cromwell typically plays nasty high-ranking officials in films like *L.A. Confidential, The General's Daughter,* and *Space Cowboys,* but here he is absolutely splendid as a dry, wise sheep farmer who at first envisions Babe on his dinner table but later hatches a far-out scheme to send the pig where no pig has gone before.

Kids will immediately take to Babe and Hoggett's farm. A pig among pigs, Babe breaks the mold. To begin with, he has no sense of territory and tries to walk into Hoggett's house, a privilege reserved for cats and dogs. Having no idea what pigs are good for, he is unaware of what Hoggett has planned for him come Christmas. On the Hoggett platter will be either Babe or a duck. The duck is fully informed on that score and is trying to pass himself off as a rooster.

All around the barnyard, role-playing, status-conscious creatures would make George Orwell proud. The movie was the brainchild of Dr. George Miller, an Australian physician and filmmaker best known for the *Mad Max* films, which are a long way from Hoggett's farm. "I love the story as much for its subtext as for its surface plot," he said when the film came out. "It's about prejudice on a farm where each animal has its place. Into this biased world comes a pig with an unprejudiced heart who takes all other creatures at face value, and by treating all the other animals as equals, he irrevocably changes their lives forever."

What role, other than becoming a main course, is there for a sweet little pig who treats everybody with kindness and respect despite the disdain shown those of his lowly function? The answer to that is nothing short of revolutionary, and it begins with Babe's extreme adaptability and game willingness to stretch parameters, as it were.

As a sheep farmer, Hoggett employs two border collies, Rex and Fly, who tend the flock in the fields. Needing to fit in somewhere, Babe respectfully asks to be adopted by Fly, the female collie, whose own pups have been given to others. In the sheep community, Babe's warmth and concern affects Old Ewe, queen of the flock, and the two become confidants. These liaisons come into play after Babe sounds the alarm that rustlers are trucking off much of the flock. "The little porker is a watch pig," notes the thoughtful Hoggett. Later, of course, the trust between pig, dogs, and sheep will have its payoff as Babe gets the sheep to do his bidding. Hoggett was right about the little porker. He makes a fine sheepdog.

For kids it's a perfect lesson in tolerance, respect, and civil behavior. Sheep traditionally regard dogs as wolves, and dogs think of sheep as stupid. In the field, brisk aggression helps the dogs intimidate sheep to run this way or that. Babe, on the other hand, has to ask the sheep nicely.

Pig and duck and dog and sheep bare their souls. "The animal characters are so real that I felt we could best serve the story by using live animals," Miller said. "Animation was never considered." Employing a menagerie, the film took eighteen months to prepare and six months to shoot, all in an Australian village eighty miles south of Sydney. Forty-eight piglets got their big chance, trained in teams of eight. How does one train a piglet? Each species responded to a different sound. For pigs it was a clicker. "At the beginning, so much seemed impossible," said Noonan. "I was honestly afraid that we'd be chasing animals all over the place and not be able to give the film the look and emotion we wanted."

But even the most talented porker or fowl wasn't entirely up to some of the more intricate moments. Animatronic stand-ins were remote-controlled, packed with computers, and encased in sleek, incredibly detailed coats with every hair and feather in place. "Up to now, our animatronics never had to be exact matches with other animals," said the head of Henson's Creature Shop in Queensland. "That multiplied the difficulty factor by ten."

The clones do the talking, their lip movements synchronized by puppeteers and computers. It is a film of simple eloquence. "I wanted people to quickly abandon the idea that they were watching animals and just accept them as normal beings," Noonan said. "That meant treating them as actors and moving them so that the camera could operate around them as it normally does with humans. We tried to create performances from them that clearly communicated an emotion."

His film lost the best picture Oscar to *Braveheart*. Susan Sarandon's performance in *Dead Man Walking* earned her a nomination that year. "Thank heaven I'm not competing against that pig," she said.

Babe's success as a "sheepdog" inspires the startlingly porcine Mrs. Hoggett (Magda Szubanski) to use his fame to raise some much needed revenue in Babe: Pig in the City, *a 1998 sequel directed by Miller. Try that one if you like, but it is darker, more convoluted, and less effective than the original. The pig belongs down on the farm and environs. Even small children will appreciate the reasons nice piglets don't have to finish last. The animals are terrific, and so is Hoggett. Yes, there is violence when Rex attacks Fly, and this could upset small children. There is no sex or profanity.*

6. BACK TO THE FUTURE

Michael J. Fox, Christopher Lloyd, Lea Thompson, Crispin Glover, Thomas F. Wilson

DIRECTED BY ROBERT ZEMECKIS
1985. 116 minutes. PG

Asked to label his film, Robert Zemeckis responds, "Comedy adventure science fiction time travel love story." Michael J. Fox, its star, says, "Action comedy coming-of-age film . . . musical." Their point

Back to the Future
(Used by permission of Universal Studios Home Video)

is that here we have a grab bag of ideas hammered together into an original that could have come out of Doc Brown's garage workshop along with the DeLorean that takes Marty McFly (Fox) back to 1955.

Zemeckis and his cowriter Bob Gale came up with the concept, which Gale basically describes as: "What if you went to high school with your parents?" Or, as the worried Marty puts it, "My mom has the hots for me!" Time-traveling back three decades, the teenaged McFly encounters his mother, Lorraine Baines (Lea Thompson), who is then a teenager herself in high school. Lorraine comes on strongly to Marty. He is horrified at the situation, but she has no notion that the boy she falls for will be her son thirty years later.

That aspect is worked through with enough dexterity that it needn't concern young viewers, who will take to this film and its two sequels starting at about age eight. But the mom-son pairing did worry Disney when Zemeckis was pitching the film in the early '80s. Other studios were standoffish, if not precisely for that reason. By that time Zemeckis had a flaky reputation and two small, entertaining features that hadn't made much of an impression at the box office, *I Wanna Hold Your Hand,* about teenagers trying to wangle tickets for the Beatles' first appearance on *The Ed Sullivan Show,* and *Used Cars,* about the sales wars under the fluttering plastic pennants. In a time before Zemeckis hits like *Who Framed Roger Rabbit* (1988, see page 296), *Back to the Future* didn't strike anyone as the hottest property. "We couldn't sell it to save our lives," Zemeckis says in a commentary on the DVD.

There was one booster: Steven Spielberg. "He was the only guy who got it," Zemeckis says. You may well ask what further boost one needs beyond Steven Spielberg, but at the time Zemeckis was making the rounds trying to sell his film, Spielberg wasn't quite secure enough about his own status to throw his influence behind an iffy proposition. So they agreed to wait awhile until Zemeckis had a hit, which turned out to be *Romancing the Stone* (1984). Eventually Spielberg served as executive producer of *Back to the Future,* which helped Zemeckis fend off numerous studio intrusions and "brilliant ideas." For example, when the Universal executive in charge of the film actually insisted it be called *Space Man from Pluto,* Spielberg was on hand to write a note saying that everybody on the set had a good laugh over that and were grateful for the fellow's sense of humor.

Zemeckis set most of *Back to the Future* in the 1950s because he wanted Marty McFly to invent rock 'n' roll, but also because a seventeen-year-old's parents would have been that age themselves back then. In the '50s, Zemeckis says, teenagers became a kind of ruling entity in this society. He also wanted to demythicize, gently and humorously, traditional parental claims that they had it harder than their kids and weren't prone to vices. Not only is Marty startled by Lorraine's advances, he is abashed to see that she is a smoker.

Marty, of course, must bring together Lorraine, one of the most popular girls at school, and his nerdy Milquetoast of a father (Crispin Glover) so they will marry and eventually bring him into being (all the while backing out of Lorraine's clutches). Securing such an unlikely union requires an operator, as it were, swift of tongue and adept at turning around even the most hopeless situations. Zemeckis always wanted Fox, who was very fine as the glib, striving, right-wing misfit among liberals on the television series *Family Ties*. Universal wanted Eric Stoltz, who in fact was cast as Marty but had no flair for comedy and was let go after months of shooting and an expenditure of $4 million.

Fox worked from 10 A.M. to 6 P.M. on *Family Ties* and from 6 P.M. to 2 A.M. on *Back to the Future*. Asked why he kept such an insane schedule, he answered, "Because I said I would." Zemeckis also has high praise for Thompson and Glover in the roles of Marty's parents, who begin as teenagers but turn into lumpy middle-aged folks. Going from seventeen to their late forties was a tough jump for young actors, Zemeckis says.

Christopher Lloyd needs no aids as the wild-eyed and wilder-haired inventor Doc Brown, who devises the DeLorean that takes Marty to the past and back to the present. Doc is a cross between Albert Einstein and Leopold Stokowski. Zemeckis says that he felt no need to explain how Marty met Doc. It just seemed natural that a bright, involved kid would gravitate to an inventor cooking up all kinds of crazy things in his garage.

The garage element is vital to the film because from that chaotic little workshop comes a wondrous invention concocted not by government or a corporation but by a freelancer obsessed with his dreams. The nature of his invention is important, too. There must be a couple of hundred movies about time travel, and like many of them this one has a seat-of-your-pants feel. Zemeckis and Gale at first conceived a refrigerator-like machine, but they worried that young viewers would go out and lock themselves in a fridge. Zemeckis decided the device had to be mobile so it could get back in case of trouble.

In 1986 the *New York Times* film critic Vincent Canby complained about "gigantism" in high-tech special effects. Zemeckis and Gale had succumbed to that tendency themselves when they wrote *1941* for Spielberg, Canby wrote, but with *Future* had created "an especially satisfying time-machine fantasy. The human comedy isn't allowed to take second place to the film's technology, which is fairly fancy. The special effects are never more arresting than the comic tale of its young hero."

Zemeckis manages some nice touches. Marty's 1980s down vest is taken for a life preserver in the 1950s. Ronald Reagan is on the marquee of the town's movie theater. Now the guy is president. Someone wants to know who is vice president. Jerry Lewis? Back then a label on clothing usually indicated one's own name. To Lorraine, then, Marty is Calvin Klein.

While testing the DeLorean in the wee hours in the parking lot of the Twin Pines mall, Doc Brown is gunned down by terrorists. This being the 1980s, they are Libyan. The scene is very violent and will upset young children. Some sexual innuendo is thrown about but kept modulated, which is just as well if you are Marty and obliged to go to a lover's lane with the girl who is to become your mother. There is no profanity.

7. THE BAD NEWS BEARS

Walter Matthau, Tatum O'Neal, Vic Morrow, Joyce Van Patten, Jackie Earle Haley, Erin Blunt

DIRECTED BY MICHAEL RITCHIE
1976. 102 minutes. PG

A lot of parents will be angry with this selection. When the film starts on DVD, we are given a long look at the rating assigned by the Motion Picture Association of America. "PG," it says, "some material may not be suitable for children." The rating box pauses for all to contemplate, pregnant with what it says and what it doesn't. This is 1976, remember, and there is no PG-13 rating as yet. As is true with all but a handful of movies, the studio (Paramount in this case) has not requested an updated evaluation for the video era.

Here is a curious case of one of the better kids' movies running a risk of being judged not fit for kids. The reason is profanity. In this observer's experience with describing movies to parents, bad language is the one unpardonable sin. Violence isn't good, certainly, but blood can flow and few make much fuss. Actual sex is forbidden, of course, but movies aimed at adolescents are full of suggestiveness. A few obscenities, on the other hand, and indignation is at a boil.

Here's hoping a moderate amount of obscenity—including racial slurs—doesn't rule out this highly enjoyable movie for your family, because kids will love it and so will you. On the Web, a critic notes that with all its profanities *The Bad News Bears* wouldn't be made today. Even without the obscenities it wouldn't be made today; it's much too fresh and original. Michael Ritchie's film—let's give it a PG-13 right here and now—may be the seminal movie about a hopeless kids' team being taken in hand by an equally hopeless adult with a therapeutic outcome for both. It is far and away the best film of this kind. The picture has been aped so often over the years that it's hard to fight off a feeling that you don't want to sit through this kind of movie again. Resist that inclination.

No coach has slouched from the depths like Morris Buttermaker (Walter Matthau), and no team has bumbled quite like the nine- to thirteen-year-olds wearing the uniform of Chico's Bail Bonds. We have blond kids and Mexican kids, a black youngster who'd like to be Hank Aaron, a typical overweight kid, an asthmatic.

Buttermaker is a former minor league pitcher who never reached the majors but struck out Ted Williams twice during spring training. He now cleans swimming pools in Southern California and has been hired to coach by a distracted father who has no time for his son. Every kid in Buttermaker's charge has a problem, from obesity to crippling inferiority complexes to debilitating arrogance. Buttermaker's most visible difficulty is alcoholism. (Yes, there is drinking, too—a lot, to be honest.)

We first realize we're in for something special when the sloshed Buttermaker crashes over the curbstone and rolls up to the ball field in a great old Cadillac convertible with the trunk lid removed to allow better access to a tangle of pool-cleaning vacuums and hoses. On the back seat is a cooler loaded with beer. From now on, Buttermaker will never be without a cold one, even on the field as he desultorily imparts the basics of the game to downtrodden, skeptical little boys who instantly identify him as a loser and, more important, as someone who cares not a whit about them and is merely going through the motions.

Matthau, who died in 2000, made an art of the shambling, lovable reprobate in films from *The Odd Couple* to *Grumpy Old Men*, both with Jack Lemmon. In *Bears* one recognizes innumerable elements copied in movies ever since. Take the parents of the players. Though their kids belong to an elaborate league that opens its season with marching bands, many parents show little individual interest in their kids. Some root lovingly from the stands. Others live up to the cliché and get nasty and abusive if a game goes the wrong way or their child doesn't perform up to expectations. An opposing coach (Vic Morrow) slaps his pitcher, who also happens to be his son.

One of the best things about this film, though, is that the kids rally and work through their situation with a good deal of self-reliance. Buttermaker is there for guidance, but he's no paragon, and the kids have to figure out most things for themselves. In some ways, they seem more adult than the parents.

In what has become time-honored fashion, thanks in no small measure to this film, Buttermaker's indifference gradually turns to caring about the team. Obliged to forfeit their first game after falling twenty runs behind in the first inning, the Bail Bonds club starts to improve after the addition of an earthy twelve-year-old pitcher named Amanda (Tatum O'Neal). Buttermaker coached Amanda when she was nine and had a great fastball and a sharply breaking curve. Now she wants ballet lessons, braces for her teeth, and looks forward to wearing a bra. She isn't happy to see Buttermaker, whom she calls Boilermaker and still blames for not marrying her still-single mother and providing Amanda with a nuclear family. No more baseball for her, or so she tells Buttermaker, so go vacuum the bottom of the Pacific Ocean.

"You were great when you were nine, but girls peak athletically at about that age," Buttermaker tells her. That does it. Back on the mound, Amanda takes the team to the championship game.

O'Neal began her career three years earlier playing a brash nine-year-old opposite her father, Ryan O'Neal, in Peter Bogdanovich's

Paper Moon. With her fresh good looks, husky voice, and nicely brash manner, she almost steals *Bears* from Matthau.

At the end, a very nice thing happens. With the game tied, Buttermaker benches his better players and gives the poorer ones a chance to play. So the team loses. The boys regard Buttermaker as if he's lost his mind, but they get the point that there are more important things than winning. Buttermaker heads for the cooler. Beers all around.

We've discussed the language. Aside from a scuffle or two, there is no violence. Amanda's distress over her family situation may bother some children. Nine seems a sensible starting age, but parents will decide.

8. THE BEAR

Tchéky Karyo, Jack Wallace, André Lacombe

DIRECTED BY JEAN-JACQUES ANNAUD
1988. 94 minutes. PG

The Bear is a fine family movie, but don't expect a Disney dog-and-pony show. Jean-Jacques Annaud was after a different kind of animal film. While he was making *Quest for Fire* (1981), about man's survival and development 80,000 years ago, he became interested in how mammals communicate through attitudes and behavior without the use of language. "I was astonished that I hadn't seen any fiction film based on this material, where an animal would be the star of a psychological drama," he wrote. "So I decided to do an entertaining, commercial adventure and psychological film that would have a bear as hero."

Bears would convey feelings and attitudes. For a story line, Annaud adapted a 1916 novel called *The Grizzly King,* by James

The Bear
(Used by permission of Columbia TriStar Home Entertainment)

Oliver Curwood, a hunter who later became a naturalist. Curwood based his book on a true story of a hunter in British Columbia who wounded a bear and then dropped his rifle over a cliff. The bear returned and was about to kill him, but left him alone.

Much the same happens in *The Bear,* fleshed out by a back story or two and abetted by a supporting cast of heroes and heavies, animal and human. Two professional hunters (Tchéky Karyo and Jack Wallace) use sparing dialogue to explain hunterly and ursine behavior we might not figure out ourselves. At first they seem to be simple, no-nonsense types bent on stacking up as many bear carcasses and skins as possible. Later, perhaps in keeping with the naturalist streak in Curwood's hunter, they have a change in attitude.

In the first of two primary story strands, they pursue and wound a huge male brown bear, a stupid and possibly fatal mistake that could cost the younger hunter his life. The other part of the movie takes place entirely away from humans and involves a bear cub who, having just lost his mother in an avalanche, attaches himself to the wounded male. Thus the little one joins the ranks of many movie offspring (more than twenty of them in this book) who are forced to establish identity and begin their own adventures after the death or disappearance of a parent or parents.

As many viewers know, male bears are cannibalistic and often eat the young of other bears. We wonder what will happen when this one and the cub cross paths in a mountain meadow. The little one wants to be friends; he also needs someone to show him how to get something to eat. A first meeting goes badly, when the grouchy, exhausted grown-up snarls and swats at the cub. But he is in no shape to give chase. Bleeding heavily, the big bear rolls around trying to seek relief from the bullet in his body and finally settles into the cool mud of a streambed. The cub cautiously makes a second approach, moves to the gaping hole in the side of the bear, and begins to lick the wound. By now it is apparent that the two need each other, and a rare bond is formed.

At that point the film becomes a chase. The hunters bring in a pack of dogs and track the big bear up into the high crags. The little one scrambles along, with his friend helping if and when he can. All along we sense communication between them. Later the big bear has his showdown with the hunter who shot him. Trapped on a pinnacle without his weapon, the man trembles with terror, sobbing and pleading for mercy. The film does a good job with him and his older partner, who begin as one-track characters but gradually grow enough in their views to respect the animals and come to a kind of mutual understanding with them as they pack up and leave the high country.

Annaud shot the film entirely outdoors in the Dolomite Mountains in northern Italy. Prior to this film he had made *Black and White in Color,* which won the Oscar as best foreign film in 1976, and *The Name of the Rose* (1986) in addition to *Quest for Fire.* On the strength of that record he commanded a big budget and took plenty of time to plan and coordinate a movie that would eventually return $120 million at the box office, a large sum for the late '80s.

The Bear can be harrowing, maintaining such a realism that many times you wonder how they did it. The animals needed no script, but every scene was plotted by storyboard. A crew of two hundred went to the Dolomites. A couple of animatronic bears went along for the fight scenes, but live bears did all the rest. A bear named Bart played the big male. To act as though he had been shot, Bart had to walk on three legs, with the fourth leg tucked under him. The filming couldn't proceed until he learned how and performed on cue. It took three years.

Three trainers worked with Bart and his stand-ins, eleven with the cub and his alternates, three with the puma, three with the dogs, three with the hunters' horses. There were two veterinarians, a zoological adviser, a wild grizzly consultant, and a falconer. When the cub's mother is killed she is snuffling around a hive at the base of a rock pile, which collapses. The 900,000 honeybees were flown in from Germany.

The film is good for children of all ages, but they should be gently let in on the fact that there's no cuddly tale in store. Many scenes could be upsetting: the mother's death, the wounding of the big bear, horses badly mauled when the bear circles and attacks the hunters' camp while they are off chasing him. A statement notes that no animals were injured during filming. Some scenes—a puma stalking the cub, for example—are just scary. This being a realistic story, we have some sex, with the big bear mounting a passing female (the camera discreetly turning elsewhere, but the microphone recording the noises). And there is some drug consumption, with the little one getting stoned on some mushrooms. We could almost say they're only human.

9. BEAUTY AND THE BEAST

With the voices of Robby Benson, Paige O'Hara, Richard White, Jerry Orbach, David Ogden Stiers, Angela Lansbury, Bradley Pierce, and many others

DIRECTED BY GARY TROUSDALE AND KIRK WISE

1991. 84 minutes. G

Don Hahn, the film's producer, calls this film the "last of the red-hot fairy tales." Disney had already rallied Snow White, Cinderella, and the Sleeping Beauty during its first great era of feature animation, which ran from the late '30s through the '50s. By 1959, when *Sleeping Beauty* was released, the studio had lost some of its zest for the genre and had moved into television and live action films. Arriving in 1991, *Beauty and the Beast* landed in the middle of Disney's prolific second era of animated features, which began with *Who Framed Roger Rabbit* in 1988 and ran through *The Little Mermaid* (1989), *Aladdin* (1992), and *The Lion King* (1994) before yielding to the current era of computer-generated features that began with *Toy Story* in 1995.

Disney considered using computers for *Beast,* but after three months of effort about all the digital department could manage was a wire-grid chicken leg. So the film stuck to traditional hand-drawn animation until the climactic ballroom scene. At that point a couple of years had passed (an exceptionally fast time for the making of an animated feature), and *Beast* storyboarders felt that improved computer imagery would give Belle and the Beast the feel of live action as they swept across the dance floor. Otherwise, we can be thankful for a gloriously rich late example from the old school of animation.

Walt Disney first considered *Beauty and the Beast* in the 1930s, but typically he was given to periods of long rumination. By the late '40s he couldn't have been all that anxious to venture into material adapted so brilliantly by the French poet and playwright Jean

Cocteau in his *La Belle et La Bette* (1946). Considered one of the best films ever made, Cocteau's live action adaptation generally makes fascinating surrealistic departures from the fairy tale narrative. Kids shouldn't miss this film either, but do Disney's first.

Beast has Greek, Italian, and African origins. Hahn also mentions parallels with such shunned perceived monsters as the phantom of the opera and the hunchback of Notre Dame. Disney followed the French version of the story, written in 1756, about a young woman named Belle who agrees to take her father's place as a prisoner in the great castle of a beast who falls in love with her and is later transformed into a prince when she returns his love. The prince is a bland fairy tale hunk and a definite letdown compared to the beast, who is an arresting, conflicted combination of bull, gorilla, bison, and wolf.

Before he reveals a gentler side, the beast's gruff demeanor could alarm the littlest ones, but probably not for long. By 1991 *Roger Rabbit* had shown that children were ready for more grown-up material. Furthermore, *The Little Mermaid* proved that adults could enjoy animated features along with their kids. One lure was the music of Alan Menken and the lyrics of Howard Ashman. Cocteau said that for his "Beast," music wasn't to accompany "but cut across it so that when film and music come together, it seems as though by the grace of God." By contrast the songs of Menken and Ashman not only stay in step with the film but introduce and explain story elements and drive the narrative.

The pair had introduced the approach in their first Disney collaboration, *The Little Mermaid* (see page 164), and with that film and *Beauty and the Beast* they lifted the animated feature onto the plane of a Broadway musical. Indeed, Frank Rich, theater critic of the *New York Times,* called the film the best Broadway musical comedy score of 1991. While that was certainly a comment on the state of the theater, it also was startling acknowledgment that an animated film could have such appeal to adults.

But there was much more to this elevation than the music. For all its sentiment, which is never overdone, *Beast* stays lean, swift, and dry-eyed. Hahn says there was a need to get Belle and the beast together quickly and this led to a tightening of exposition. Belle's brains and independence are set up quickly in the "I want song," the Broadway term for a number that lets the heroine establish what she's after in life. John Canemaker, head of animation studies at New York University's Tisch School of the Arts, notes the characters' multidimensionality. Belle has a cool unflappability that moves her beyond the kiddie realm. When she first spies the beast, she recoils but instantly recovers and carries on as if nothing has happened. The beast, too, is a complex and formidable sort, capable of rage, despair, and tenderness.

On the DVD, Hahn talks about resisting extraneous asides and using "smash cuts" to keep the narrative moving. Before its release, Disney took a bold step and showed the movie unfinished at the New York Film Festival. In theaters adults flocked to the movie as well as kids. "It was almost as if everybody wanted to regard it as live action," Hahn says on the DVD. And so it came to pass that on the evening of March 30, 1992, *Beauty and the Beast* was up for an Oscar as best picture, the first animated film to find itself in that position (and the last, since animation now has its own category).

Jonathan Demme's *The Silence of the Lambs* won most everything that year, but in the song category *Beast* had three of the five nominations and was essentially competing against itself. The winner, "Beauty and the Beast," was sung by Angela Lansbury, the voice of Mrs. Potts. A four-time Tony winner on Broadway, Lansbury was unsure about the number at first. "Alan Menken sang it on a tape, which he sent me," she said in an interview. "I thought it had a rock rhythm, which isn't my style. He said he didn't care how I did it." Doing it her way, she recorded the song in one take.

Ashman died of AIDS in March 1991 shortly before *Beast* opened. He was ill during the filming, and everybody involved gathered daily at a hotel near his home in Fishkill, New York, to work out the songs. They also decided to make household objects of Mrs. Potts (a teapot), Lumiere (a candlestick with the voice of Jerry Orbach), and others who served the beast during his original incarnation as a prince. One wonders what Cocteau would have made of that idea, but it doesn't damage the most sophisticated of fairy tales, one that teaches us that beauty comes from within.

When first encountered in the castle, the beast's anger and threatening behavior could frighten the little ones. Soon they will see him in a different light, but they may need help getting by these early stages. Belle's pompous would-be suitor, Gaston, turns murderous and the beast is fatally stabbed atop his own ramparts. That's all for the good, of course, but it is violent. With a little forewarning, children from ages four or five should enjoy themselves.

10. BEETLEJUICE

Michael Keaton, Alec Baldwin, Geena Davis, Winona Ryder, Sylvia Sidney, Catherine O'Hara, Jeffrey Jones, Glenn Shadix

DIRECTED BY TIM BURTON
1988. 92 minutes. PG

You have to take this movie Tim Burton's way, or don't bother with it at all. Kids will get it, which is fortunate; many critics didn't when the film opened. No plot, they said, sophomoric humor, but not all of them agreed. "The story is bland and the movie is slow to get going, but with crazy comedy you settle for the moments of inspiration, and this picture has them," Pauline Kael wrote in *The New Yorker*. "The young director, Tim Burton, takes stabs into the irrational and the incongruous; the film's blandness is edged with near genius (and some great special effects)."

Burton, of course, was the quirky loose cannon who broke the bonds of Disney, where he had some basic training as an animator, to direct *Pee-Wee's Big Adventure* (1985), a live action cartoon about a nine-year-old in an adult's body. With *Beetlejuice* we see him ratcheting up his style prior to his quantum leap into the big time with *Batman* in 1989.

All he is really getting at, if anything, is that life after death is just as mundane as it was before, only with different problems. As dead people, for example, what do you do when you're stuck in your old house for 125 years before being allowed full entry to the afterlife (especially if you detest the new owners)? How do you deal with bureaucracy after death? (If you think that goes away, it doesn't.) How do you get anybody to pay attention to you as a ghost? (Forget cutting eyeholes in $300 designer sheets.)

The movie works as a Burtonesque blast of Americana gone completely nuts twelve highway toll stations out in rustic Connecticut. Later in Burton's career we are in similarly bizarre waters in *Edward Scissorhands* (see page 81), but there we at least have a core and "arc" (Hollywoodese for beginning, middle, and end). This time we latch on to things as they fly by: death, ghosts, a goth kid obsessed with the dark side, interior design, possibilities for the "world's leading supernatural research center and amusement park." It's all very visual. Children can grab hold at about age ten, maybe a little younger.

Looking for some establishing shots of a small village, Burton found nothing Connecticut enough in Connecticut, so he chose a village in Vermont. In the film, Adam and Barbara Maitland (Alec Baldwin and Geena Davis) are deliriously happy renovating their precious big old white house when Adam drives their Volvo through a covered bridge and into a creek. Returning home damp and bedraggled, they cannot see their reflections in the mirror and find a *Handbook for the Recently Deceased*.

In death as in the flesh, the Maitlands like to hang out in the attic, where Adam can work on his weird scale model of their village. From up there they recoil in horror at the new owners from New York City, Charles and Delia Deitz (Jeffrey Jones and Catherine O'Hara). A harried developer, Charles is looking for little more than a bucolic change of pace. The crazed Delia, a creator of unspeakably bad sculpture, wants nothing less than to make the house her Manhattan annex, and so she imports her designer, Otho (Glenn Shadix).

Soon Delia and Otho are flouncing around the place complaining about lack of "organic flow-through," decrying L.L. Bean, deploring an indoor outhouse of a bathroom, and spray-painting the walls with notes about their own design plans. At first, the Maitlands try to flee, but being dead they are confined to the house. For them Burton's countryside has become a desert riddled with giant sandworms, forcing them back inside. Desperate for advice on how to get rid of the Deitzes, the Maitlands consult their handbook, which leads them to a kind of emergency center for the deceased.

Naturally there is a waiting room with a rude receptionist. "We just did the big one two months ago and already you want help," she tells the Maitlands, reminding them they are on a voucher system and it's best not to waste them. Burton is a student of film history (witness *Ed Wood*) and fond of bringing actors from past eras into his films (for example, Vincent Price in *Edward Scissorhands*). Here he uses Sylvia Sidney, whose career dates to the late 1920s, as Juno, the Maitlands' caseworker in the land of death.

Because of budget limitations, Burton shot the special effects at the same time as the live action, which is rarely done and made his crew uncomfortable. The waiting room is a virtual special effect by itself, full of characters with shrunken heads, a woman who has been sawed in half, and other specimens. Juno has no quick fix for the Deitz problem, but she heartily recommends against hiring an otherworldly troubleshooter named Betelgeuse (pronounced Beetlejuice), played with maniacal intensity by Michael Keaton.

Burton thrives on characters like Betelgeuse, and on actors like Keaton, whom he would cast as the caped crusader in *Batman*. With spiky hair and a gravelly voice, Betelgeuse is a cross between a fireworks display gone wrong and a downed high-voltage wire. He describes himself as the "afterlife's leading bio-exorcist" and a Harvard Business School graduate who survived the Black Plague. The trouble is that besides being intolerably crass, he is impossible to get rid of.

The Maitlands eventually engage Betelgeuse, but their only reliable ally is the Deitzes' morose camera-packing teenage daughter, Lydia (Winona Ryder). The black-clad Lydia is thought by some to be Burton's representative in the proceedings. In any event, she is the only living person who can see the Maitlands. Shown a space in the house that might work as a photography darkroom, she replies, "My whole life is a darkroom." Well, so she says. Lydia feels closer to the Maitlands than to her parents, and at one point she does plan to throw herself out the window to join the Maitlands in death, but in a nice Burtonesque touch, she turns into a "normal" high school kid by film's end.

Burton is good at playing with the excruciatingly ordinary. The Maitlands have no chance of getting rid of the Deitzes, especially after Charles learns that there is money to be made by promoting the place as a haunted house. Betelgeuse's madly inspired ways to scare them off only strengthen their intent to turn the property into a kind of theme park with a display depicting fifty great moments from the paranormal and an insect zoo. "My father never walks away from equity," Lydia says.

This isn't a film for small children, who could be disturbed and confused by many of the images and goings-on. Among older preadolescents and adolescents, though, the movie was so wildly popular that it too became a theme park attraction. There are some sexual references and a few obscenities.

11. BIG

Tom Hanks, Jared Rushton, Elizabeth Perkins, Robert Loggia, John Heard, Mercedes Ruehl

DIRECTED BY PENNY MARSHALL
1988. 104 minutes. PG

"I remember thirteen being all elbows and knees," Tom Hanks told the *New York Times* correspondent Aljean Harmetz after *Big* was released in 1988. "The girls had already grown up. I started the role with the point of view of a newborn giraffe. They have spindly heads and look geeky when they run." When it comes to impressing girls their age, thirteen-year-old boys usually are out of luck. "If they try to act older, it's like a drunk trying to act sober," Hanks said.

At a carnival, a device called Zoltar issues a card granting thirteen-year-old Josh Baskin (David Moscow) one wish. Josh has a crush on a girl who prefers boys who can drive. Josh wishes he could be that old. After a stormy night he swings out of bed on the long, hairy legs of Tom Hanks. Zoltar has outdone himself. Josh is now thirty-something. Clothes don't fit, and there are amazing anatomical discoveries. Thinking he's an intruder, his mother (Mercedes Ruehl) chases him out of the house with a knife. Later when the little Josh doesn't reappear, she assumes he's been kidnapped.

Expulsion from home is a good development, however, because it forces Josh to live new adventures as a man in the outside world. A surburban kid, he goes to New York and takes a hotel room for $19 a night in an area where the gunfire in the streets is louder than in *The French Connection* on the television screen. This frightens him and he curls up and cries. His only link to his prior adolescence is his redheaded, smart-mouthed friend Billy (Jared Rushton), who at first takes the adult Josh for some kind of pedophile, but finally becomes convinced that he really is Billy's old skateboarding, video game–playing pal.

Billy visits Josh regularly in the city and helps him apply for a job at a toy company by suggesting that Josh's previous job experience as a paper boy be upgraded to "circulation" on the application. As a kid in a man's body, especially a kid adept with gadgets and games, Josh goes far and fast in the toy business, and he pulls adults along in his wake. "Of course, identity switching is nothing new, and comedies have always relied on it in various forms," the critic Janet Maslin wrote in the *New York Times*. Often in the past a different guise let a character learn about other people and experiences. The '80s were more self-centered. "When an '80s character changes age or sex or personality," Maslin wrote, "the device is used mostly as a means of letting the hero find out more about himself."

In *Big*, by contrast, others learn from Josh. Calcified adults are enthralled by a child in a man's body. For some reason they can't identify, Josh is beyond the usual pressures. "Even if the grown man's secret boyishness is treated as something he must hide from others, it becomes a source of enchantment for everyone he meets," Maslin wrote.

Impressed by Josh's creativity and guilelessness, his boss (Robert Loggia) makes him director of development. Josh can sit in his office and fiddle with games and toys all day. "A lot of what makes *Big* appealing is the caliber of Tom Hanks's performance, the genial style of Penny Marshall's direction, and the screenplay's wittier touches," Maslin wrote in her review of the film. "But a lot of it is also the sight of Mr. Hanks really enjoying himself by playing with toys." On the verge of a major career, Hanks was thirty-one, the son of a mother who remarried three times and a father, an itinerant cook, who moved Tom and his brother and sister up and down the length of California. In elementary school, Harmetz wrote, he was the class clown.

As Josh Baskin, he strove for innocence. "You would go wrong if you concentrated on laughs for laughs' sake," he told Harmetz. "I don't think there's a cheap trick in the movie." At toy company meetings Josh is relaxed and playful. One driven executive, Paul (John Heard), finds that immensely annoying. Another high-powered, chain-smoking colleague named Susan (Elizabeth Perkins) eventually is charmed by Josh's ingenuousness and taken by his calm in the face of tense situations. He's grown-up, she says.

The two have an affair of sorts. A thirteen-year-old has sexual urges, which the film acknowledges gracefully and off camera. Josh's success at work earns him a loft the size of a basketball court, which he fills with big toys, games, and machines. On Susan's first visit, he invites her to bounce on his trampoline, which she does with a gradually ebbing sense of distaste until she is delightedly bounding as high as Josh. She hints that she might like to spend the night. "You mean sleep over?" Josh asks. She says that's what she meant. Josh claims the upper bunk. Lying alone in the lower bunk, Susan again is charmed.

The sex comes later, after they have danced at a carnival (Josh's favorite dating spot). By now Susan is in love with him, but we see change ahead. When he suddenly sprouted into his thirties, Josh was horrified and tried to find Zoltar so that he could get another wish and return to age thirteen. But Zoltar had vanished. Now, Zoltar reappears in a corner of the carnival lot. We sense that it's time for a parting with all the thirty-somethings. Despite his innocence, Josh has become seduced by success. That alienates Billy, which disturbs Josh, and for this and other reasons he locates Zoltar.

Susan rushes to the carnival, but Josh has made his wish. She understands that he has to return to childhood, and it's just as well for the both of them. "Identity-switching adventures tend to leave their characters fortified and invigorated, undaunted by lives they previously found taxing and ready to tackle the tasks before them with improved perspective and new enthusiasm," Maslin wrote. That may not exactly describe these two, but they realize they face the inevitable. Josh says Susan could make a wish and become thirteen herself. She says no thanks, she had enough the first time.

Parents might watch the movie first to see if they have problems with the sexual element. There is also one strong profanity (the strongest, in fact). In all other respects the film is fine from about the age of eight, or whatever is comfortable.

12. THE BLACK STALLION

Kelly Reno, Mickey Rooney, Teri Garr, Clarence Muse, Hoyt Axton

DIRECTED BY CARROLL BALLARD
1979. 118 minutes. G

Carroll Ballard has made relatively few movies, but three of them—*Fly Away Home* and *Never Cry Wolf* are the other two—are included in this book. Ballard is skilled with animals, which is a rarity among directors, and he also has a quiet, measured way of telling a story. The best parts of this film involve no dialogue, just the gradual building of a relationship between a boy and a horse on a deserted island. Later on, the movie, adapted from Walter Farley's novel, isn't quite so special when it moves back to civilization and becomes an exciting

The Black Stallion
(Used by permission of MGM Home Entertainment)

if predictable horse-racing story that might be described as a sequel to *National Velvet.*

The critic Pauline Kael, not known for easy superlatives, called *National Velvet* "one of the most likable films of all time" (see page 204). Ballard's *Black Stallion,* she wrote, "may be the greatest children's movie ever made." In 2002 the Library of Congress added it to a national registry of films deemed "culturally, historically, or esthetically important." Others aren't so enamored, as we'll see later. Try it and see what you think.

We begin on a ship off the coast of North Africa in 1949, and it takes but a few shots of the heaving sea to establish Caleb Deschanel's superb cinematography. In a saloon belowdecks a card game is in progress and in a holding pen the stallion called "the black" strains at his tethers. That night Alec Ramsey (Kelly Reno), about twelve, is told a story by his father (Hoyt Axton) about a young boy who will be given a wild horse if he can ride him.

One sudden and cataclysmic storm later (huddle up with small

---

viewers) Alec and the black are the sole survivors on the island. What will develop between a frightened and bereft young boy, still in his pajamas, and a huge, very skittery animal totally fed up with lunatic humans? Still with ropes around his neck, the horse gets tangled in the rocks, and it is all Alec can do to get close enough to cut him loose with the pocket knife his father had won at cards on the ship. Boy and horse are alone together on a long, wide stretch of beach bordered by rock outcroppings. The horse races magnificently up and down the sand. Alec crawls into nooks to sleep and take shelter from thunderstorms.

At this point the film has the feel of a survival movie. We admire sea and sunsets, but we wonder what there is for Alec to eat. He munches on seaweed and seems unconcerned. He offers the horse some greens, and in a prolonged scene the trainers must have worked on at length, they haltingly establish contact. Trusting the boy, the horse romps with him on the beach. Then they swim together and, with one step naturally following another, the boy floats onto the horse's back. There is a wonderful sense of Alec achieving what he has been after all along. Now we'll see if he's the boy in the story his father told him. He and the black burst from the water and go for a gallop. Alec occasionally falls off, but he jumps right back on.

Ballard used four big Arabian stallions in the film and shot the beach scene in Sardinia. In the film, days are dreamy and unhurried. Ballard's visual imagination, Kael wrote in *The New Yorker,* "makes you feel like a pagan—as if you were touching when you're only looking. His great scenes have a sensuous trancelike quality." The "distilled atmosphere makes it possible for a simple boy-and-animal story to be transformed into something mythological."

Once rescued, Alec and the black still go riding, but now it's under the tutelage of Henry Dailey, played by Mickey Rooney. In *National Velvet* Rooney plays a troubled former jockey who trains the horse for the big race. Thirty-five years later it's more or less the same story. Dailey got tired of horse racing and moved on to farming, leaving behind a tack room full of trophies and plaques and old bridles. Then one predawn at a racetrack he puts a stopwatch on the black with Alec in the saddle. While there are problems to sort out—for example, Alec's mother's refusal to let him ride in a race—we know what lies ahead.

In the barn Dailey saddles a hay bale and passes on some interesting tips to the young jockey. Despite their mutual affection, the black is still a wild one and Alec's hands are bloodied by the reins after a sprint around the track. Dailey tells him to stay still in the saddle and let the black do the moving up and down. The trainer has other tips for Alec: to see what's happening behind, don't turn around but look back under his armpits; be careful to stay seated coming out of the starting gate because horses can run out from under jockeys.

Teri Garr is fine as Alec's mother. She has lost her husband in a shipwreck and won't risk her son on a racetrack. Destiny overrules her, of course. By now the film is proceeding in expectable fashion, but with a stylized pace and look that make us feel that it's enacting a kind of American ritual.

The film can't do everything according to Farley's book. "Something huge was missing in the movie," one young commentator wrote on the Web. "It may have been lack of loyalty to Walter Farley's novel, which is an above-average tale for both young and old. Maybe it was the horrible acting. Or perhaps the lack of any plot and character development due to overused nature scenes and film score."

Go figure. Best we retreat to Kael. "One of the rare movies that achieves a magical atmosphere," she wrote. "Seeing it is like being carried on a magic carpet; you don't want to come down."

The shipwreck will frighten and upset small children, and some of the scenes with the black, a pretty wild critter, are a little intense. The right age is up to parents, but perhaps eight is fine. There is no sex or profanity.

13. BOUND FOR GLORY

David Carradine, Ronny Cox, Melinda Dillon, Randy Quaid, Gail Strickland

DIRECTED BY HAL ASHBY

1976. 147 minutes. PG

For kids, a great special effect is a fine way to kick off a film. Here we have a beauty in the form of a tidal wave, not of water but of dust. It's 1936 in Pampa, Texas, and a terrifying-looking wall of topsoil, whipped hundreds of feet aloft by seventy-five-mile-per-hour winds, bears down on a little town that was already about to dry up and blow away in the drought-stricken dust bowl that stretched all across the great plains.

Hal Ashby's film uses clouds of brown cotton to create the effect. When the great storm passes over Pampa, headlights come on in the yellowish dusk and from that moment to the final credits no one gets the sand out of their boots or the sweat and grime off their faces or out of their dresses and overalls. This is Steinbeck's America, and down the middle of it, from Texas to California and back again, strides the lanky poet and balladeer Woody Guthrie, played to a gritty, understated fare-thee-well by David Carradine.

Bound for Glory, a title borrowed from the Guthrie song and autobiography, is a story of Depression-era America told through the eyes of a legendary figure. Children know little of the time, and probably have never heard of the man, but this is a case where a movie instructs while it entertains.

It begins with the plight of the Texas dust-bowl farmer. Married and with children, Woody tries to keep body and soul together in Pampa by working odd jobs and singing and plucking his guitar for anybody who will listen. The man has a gift. Though there is something of the mischievous ragamuffin in him, he possesses a mysterious natural essence that draws people to him. Without half trying, Guthrie gives succor and strength. At one point in the film he is asked to comfort a farm wife so distraught over the death of a child she can't eat or function—"a cat who's climbed far out onto a branch of sorrow and can't find her way back," as Vincent Canby described it in the *New York Times*.

It is not a role he seeks, but, almost Jesus-like, Guthrie walks through the crowd and gently tends to the woman. Such a man has a destiny, of course, and Woody leaves his family behind to hop freight trains to California. There is a distance about him, too, a not altogether warm and unself-involved sense of himself as a man who belongs to the people.

All along the line, we meet threadbare, struggling men, women, and children in the parched, starving gut of America. It's not a view today's children are used to, but it should come as an engrossing revelation in this intensely American movie. Even if it doesn't, there is plenty of adventure and song to hold young viewers. In the fruit groves of California, Woody helps battle the growers' goons and organize the workers. His songs earn recognition, but he turns down a lucrative radio contract when corporate sponsors insist he abstain from politics and protest.

"This land is your land," as the lyric goes. Woody returns to his family and leaves them again, eternally the minstrel riding the rails and singing the story of the 1930s and '40s. Ashby, who died in 1988, had a feeling for quirky characters, as we see in films like *Harold and Maude, Shampoo,* and *Being There.* Woody is more paragon than quirk, but he is an original, and, as depicted by Carradine, he should hold young viewers.

So should the look of the film. Haskell Wexler won the Academy Award for his cinematography (*Bound for Glory* was nominated for best picture but lost to *Rocky*). The freight trains are true costars of this movie, endlessly clicking and clacking through a sun-blasted landscape. Wonderfully set up by the production designer Michael D. Haller, the trains often were shot from a low angle, with their wheels creating a feel of constant motion against the broiling azure sky. Always there is the heat and dust, the extreme stress in anxious faces in the boxcars and in the bedraggled labor camps clogged with the jalopies of the dispossessed, dripping furniture and meager belongings from every hook and knob.

Wexler's camera captures an American scene with a haunting, aching poignancy. Kids can rest assured it happened that way—and in your land, their land, an era lives.

There are some good skull-cracking brawls as management thugs sweep the workers' camps on their runs of intimidation. As is made apparent on occasion, Woody is a sexy guy, but there is no sex or references to it that should trouble parents. Similarly, they talk colorfully but pretty cleanly for folks in such hardship. Age ten to twelve is appropriate, and maybe younger if they're mature kids.

14. BREAKING AWAY

Dennis Christopher, Dennis Quaid, Daniel Stern, Jackie Earle Haley, Paul Dooley, Barbara Barrie

DIRECTED BY PETER YATES

1979. 100 minutes. PG

Kids are often fascinated by movies about slightly older people still recognizably in their youth. Here is one that parents can relate to as well, which adds up to a family picture everybody will enjoy and not just endure for the sake of togetherness. The ingredients are familiar; it's the sensibility that lifts this film well beyond the usual.

The setting, Bloomington, Indiana, is all-American. The climactic payoff—the lunging, last-second triumph of the long shot in a sporting contest—has been staged countless times. The underdogs here are eighteen-year-old working-class high school graduates resentful of the privileged college kids across town at Indiana University. More open-minded than the others, Dave (Dennis Christopher) aspires to race bicycles as fast as a touring team of Italians who are coming to Bloomington for an exhibition. Dave's father (Paul Dooley) used to cut granite in the quarry but has graduated to selling used cars. Mom (Barbara Barrie) is fondly understanding of father and son, not to mention her own narrow confines in Bloomington.

Dave is obsessed with all things Italian. "*Buongiorno,* Papa," he cries as his father winces. Dad is also not thrilled at the sight of his son shaving his legs, the better to achieve speed on his bike. At table the boy wants to steer his folks from the frying pan into the "*ini's*": linguini, fettucine, even zucchini. On the road he screams arias as he pedals. One day he passes a Cinzano truck at seventy miles per hour. Cinzano, it turns out, is sponsoring the team of touring Italians. Dave outraces them, too, but much to his horror they cheat.

Bloomington is a bike-racing hotbed. The college team will compete against Dave and his fellow townies, called the Cutters after the quarry trade, in the race at the end of the film. Dave's teammates and pals (Dennis Quaid, Daniel Stern, and Jackie Earle Haley) could care less about bike racing. For them the focus is on their own prospects, which seem bleak when stacked against those of the constantly replenished crop of college kids passing through on their way to seemingly prosperous, liberated futures.

There is nothing particularly new in any of this. What distinguishes it are the performances and the perspective. Christopher is superb as a kid fighting the odds and disillusionment. So are Dooley as his exasperated, loving, and ultimately supportive father, and Barrie as the knowing mother with a big soul who holds them together. Quaid and Stern are very good as the group firebrand and witty geek, respectively, and it's fun to see them early in their careers. But it's the filmmakers who are mainly responsible for the movie's success.

Breaking Away, somewhat curiously, is high Americanism with a foreign twist. Yates, a British director, has a variety of credits. A former race car driver, he directed *Bullitt,* with Steve McQueen, and other action films like *The Deep*. He received two Oscar nominations for completely different kinds of pictures: *Breaking Away* and *The Dresser* (1983), his adaptation of Ronald Harwood's play about an aging performer (Albert Finney) and the aide (Tom Courtenay) who keeps him going. For *Breaking Away*, Yates teamed with the screenwriter Steve Tesich, who won an Oscar for the film and is most responsible for its effectiveness.

As a small boy in Yugoslavia during the '40s, Tesich longed for the America he saw in the movies, especially westerns. He came to this country at age thirteen to join a father he had never met, and the stresses and divergences of father-son viewpoints often show in his work. Later he went to Indiana University on a wrestling scholarship. He also raced bikes. "I need to know the environment and the people who inhabit it," he said in the *New York Times* in 1980. "If I have to do research on some topic, I know it's not for me."

In the film Dad wonders about his son: "He's never tired. He's never depressed." What are they to do with him? "We could always strangle him while he sleeps," Mom says sweetly. Tesich gives the family, and indeed everything in the film, a feeling of restraint and relaxed credibility. In 1980 he said the film's success was due to the fact that we've all had some kind of experience as outsiders, like the townies, and, like Dave, we've all reached points when it was time to move on.

"And then there was something about that little town and the family life," he said in the *Times*. "*Breaking Away* was full of things that a lot of people assumed were part of the past—the family unit, respect for the unity, family love. But you don't have to go back to the Depression and the Waltons to find it; it still goes on."

Ages ten and up, and maybe younger depending on the child, will love the characters, especially Dave and his friends, and the racing. There is no violence to speak of, but a boy jokingly appears to lock himself in a refrigerator underwater, which could frighten young viewers. Sex is often referred to among young males, and it is apparent that one couple indulges. But sex isn't a problem. Nor is there profanity.

15. BRINGING UP BABY

Cary Grant, Katharine Hepburn, Charlie Ruggles, May Robson, Barry Fitzgerald

DIRECTED BY HOWARD HAWKS
1938. 102 minutes. Black and white. No rating

For a few years during the late Depression, American filmmaking turned to a short-lived genre called the screwball comedy. The country needed entertainment to help steady itself. That meant a lot more than laughing during a time of wealth for few and struggle for most. We needed help in assuring ourselves that economic imbalance—part of the American way, after all—was still all right somehow and the extremes of the Depression were temporary. On-screen, there was something comforting in seeing the rich as vulnerable, yet fairly ridiculous subjects of satire. Despite their money and influence, they could still act like idiots and mess up as badly or worse than anybody else. What's more, they could get down into the ruck and roil with the rest of us. In some cases they could even swap situations with us and see how they liked that.

The result was a peculiar hybrid that could be called elegant slapstick. Everything about screwball was a contradiction, which helps make it a great genre for kids. Here were our finest directors and biggest stars—Frank Capra, Howard Hawks, Preston Sturges, Clark Gable, Carole Lombard, Katharine Hepburn, Cary Grant—turning out films of the utmost sophistication. Yet on-screen these supposed grown-up characters, some of them ever so suave, did goofy things a six-year-old would howl at.

Screwball began essentially with Capra's *It Happened One Night* in 1934 (see page 130) and, having served its era, ended with *Bringing Up Baby*, though Sturges's *Sullivan's Travels* in 1941 (see page 269) could be considered late screwball. *Bringing Up Baby* is most often cited as the classic screwball. How goofy is this story? When David

Huxley (Grant), a stuffy, bumbling paleontologist, locates a tiny "clavicle" for a gigantic brontosaurus skeleton he is assembling at the museum, the rare body part is stolen by a yappy little dog named George. The dog belongs to an affable, stuffy major, who, along with the absentminded paleontologist, presents a type the film can have some fun with. The major is a friend of a very rich dowager (every good screwball needs one) whose daffy, scatterbrained niece, Susan Vance (Hepburn), owns a peaceful pet leopard named Baby.

Susan, a breezy powerhouse of a young woman and a knockout to boot, meets the anxious, reticent David during a wacky game of golf (screwball often gravitates to country clubs and the like), falls for him, and spends the film in pursuit of marriage. David is already engaged to his prim, ambitious assistant, who says she wants no children. The brontosaurus will be their child. In the course of things, the dog buries the clavicle; the placid leopard has a short-tempered counterpart, escaped from a carnival; the two big cats get mixed. Everything gets mixed. Out at the dowager's Connecticut country estate, the local lawman starts locking people up. There's a huge scene at the local jailhouse, with both leopards putting in an appearance. In one very nice touch, a pompous psychiatrist figures everything and everybody exactly wrong. Finally, at the museum, the brontosaurus collapses with Susan swinging from scaffolding and clinging to David.

Kids from about seven will understand every bit of it. The comedy is physical, the developments easy to follow. David, the ditherer, is afraid of the determined Susan, who sashays through every obstacle as if it's just another minor annoyance. *Bringing Up Baby* flopped at the box office, and one reason was Hepburn. The product of a rigorous upbringing in a prominent, accomplished family, she radiated an outspoken sureness and superiority that annoyed producers and audiences. "Now, George, you have to concentrate," she tells the dog at one point. "David has to find his bone." No one can say that like Katharine Hepburn.

Kids will love her and Grant, too. Hawks had improvisatory instincts as a director, allowing actors to experiment with personality. In dozens of films, Grant projected various personalities, each with its shading of strength and vulnerability. Here his character succumbs to a strong woman and remains a fumbler and bumbler to the end, which is how screwball would have it. If Hepburn's condescension seems a little chilly in places, she means nothing serious by it. (One might note the warm, eager soul she portrays in *The African Queen;* see page 6.) In Hawks's film, Hepburn is mesmerizing to look at and listen to, a star at thirty-one more or less impervious to who thought what of her. And she died revered, which helps elevate *Bringing Up Baby* in the ranking of great American films.

The pleasure of *Bringing Up Baby* lies in the wonderfully subtle view it has of silly situations. The movie, which began as a short story by Hager Wilde, belongs to Hawks. Orson Welles called him the most talented of American directors. Hawks made all kinds of films in his career, from westerns (*Red River* and *Rio Bravo*) to gangster and private eye movies (*Scarface, The Big Sleep*) to musicals (*Gentlemen Prefer Blondes*) to science fiction (*The Thing*).

Like Sturges, Hawks had a feel for things American. In his book *Who the Devil Made It: Conversations with Legendary Film Directors,* Peter Bogdanovich quotes the French director Jacques Rivette: "If Hawks incarnates the classic American cinema, if he has brought nobility to every genre, then it is because, in each case, he has found that particular genre's essential quality and grandeur, and blended his personal themes with those the American tradition had already enriched and made profound."

This is one of those movies kids and their parents will enjoy equally. No restrictions or qualifiers whatever, except to say that age three or four may be a little young, though not by much. Some kids may carp about the black and white, but once into the film they will forget that factor in a hurry.

16. THE BUDDY HOLLY STORY

Gary Busey, Charles Martin Smith, Don Stroud, Maria Richwine, Conrad Janis

DIRECTED BY STEVE RASH
1978. 113 minutes. PG

Backstage at the Apollo Theater, Buddy Holly (Gary Busey) and the Crickets (Don Stroud and Charles Martin Smith) have a surprise for the theater's booking agent, Sol Gitler (Dick O'Neil). The famed theater in Harlem books only black artists, and Gitler, who is white, hardly reacts when a black stagehand announces that the new act has arrived. Nothing personal, Gitler tells the man, but all black people look alike. The stagehand agrees that the people in this act do indeed look alike. Only when Buddy and the Crickets are standing before him does Gitler look up.

"You don't mean to stand there and tell me you're white!" he yells.

White performers just don't go on in front of a black audience at the Apollo. Holly would be different. Only months earlier he, the drummer Jesse Charles (Stroud), and the bass man Ray Bob Simmons (Smith) were performing on a radio show broadcast from a roller rink in Holly's native Lubbock, Texas. It was 1956 and a young white performer was supposed to be twanging "Mockin' Bird Hill" and not rocking all over the stage with "That'll Be the Day," which was to become Buddy's first major hit.

On the heels of Elvis Presley, Holly served up what some called western bop or rockabilly. To white folks Buddy's style suggested Little Richard and Fats Domino—"jungle music." Outrage poured into the station and from local pulpits. At the roller rink, though, teenagers were out of their skates and dancing in their socks. And so it is at the Apollo. Against his better judgment Gitler lets Buddy, Jesse, and Ray Bob onstage, and they blow the roof off with "That'll

Be the Day" and have the crowd up and dancing with "It's So Easy (To Fall in Love)."

In real life Buddy won over the Apollo, all right, but it took him a couple of performances. The lyric "That'll be the day" was borrowed from John Wayne, who kept muttering the phrase in the classic western *The Searchers*. Holly had just turned twenty-one when the song reached the top of the charts in 1957. At age twenty-two he was killed in a plane crash (more on this later). Bob Dylan, Eric Clapton, the Rolling Stones, Elton John, and Bruce Springsteen acknowledge Holly's influence. Such a sudden death after such a brief career only accentuates his seminal style and the impact it had on others.

On the DVD Busey and the director Steve Rash tell a story, dramatized in the movie, about the time a cricket got into a garage where Buddy, Jesse, and Ray Bob were recording a demo. Because it's bad luck to kill a cricket indoors, they let it stay and chirp along. Thus the Crickets were born, and in honor of that occasion a young group in England decided to call themselves the Beatles.

It fell to Busey to bring Holly to life. Jon Voight won the Oscar that year in *Coming Home,* but Busey was nominated (along with Robert De Niro, Laurence Olivier, and Warren Beatty), and it is hard to imagine anyone falling more naturally into a role. For children (and everybody else), Busey makes this film. A Texan like Holly, he has been in dozens of movies of every kind, from the biker flick *Angels Hard as They Come* in 1971 to *Slap Shot 2: Breaking the Ice* in 2002. But Busey is also a talented musician, and as the drummer Teddy Jack Eddy performed with Leon Russell and Willie Nelson. And he can sing.

In Rash's film Busey floats and struts and yowls in "Maybe Baby" and the celebrated "Peggy Sue," which begins as "Cindy Lou" when Buddy composes the song in honor of a soon-to-be former girlfriend in the backseat of a car on his way to a gig. At times Busey's furious energy can make the hair stand up on the back of your neck. Tall, lanky, and loose, he prowls the concert stages brandishing his guitar and playing to crowds with an infectious ease.

On the DVD Busey, now fifty-nine, still yelps along with the songs, sounding as good and Holly-like as he did when he made the film in the '70s. He was thirty-three then, not twenty-one, but he pumps enough youth into the role and adds calm maturity to a passionately adventurous figure. From his roller-rink days on, the screen Holly has a nice way of seeing matters clearly and insisting on what he believes is best for him. When a Texas producer says he doesn't make "Negro records," Holly goes home to Lubbock rather than perform in the white mainstream. In New York, the head of Coral Records (nicely played by Conrad Janis) tells Holly that songwriters perform their material but never produce it. Not any longer, Holly tells him.

Holly is an honest, clean-cut boy who asserts himself with a smile full of large white teeth. He wears conspicuously heavy-rimmed glasses, so he decides to do it right and wear the heaviest-rimmed spectacles he can find. He approached everything that way, making the most of what befell him. Children will like the music, the young man, and the pretty young woman, Maria (Maria Richwine), he marries. They will not like the notice posted at the close of the film. The bus has broken down as usual. On the screen we read "Buddy Holly died later that night along with J. P. 'The Big Bopper' Richardson and Ritchie Valens in the crash of a private airplane just outside of Clearlake."

Valens, another rising star, is remembered in the film *La Bamba* (also good entertainment for kids). He and Holly, of course, are celebrated in Don McLean's song "American Pie." It was the day the music died, as the song puts it. "And the rest is rock 'n' roll," Rash's film adds.

Age ten and up is fine for this film, which contains a fair amount of standard profanity and sexual references. Be sure to tell the kids a little about Buddy Holly beforehand and warn them that he died young. On no account should his death be suddenly sprung on them at the end.

17. BUTCH CASSIDY AND THE SUNDANCE KID

Paul Newman, Robert Redford, Katharine Ross

DIRECTED BY GEORGE ROY HILL

1969. 112 minutes. PG

For kids, *Butch Cassidy and the Sundance Kid* is a nice change of pace from classic showdown westerns like *Shane* (see page 241) and *High Noon* (see page 124). In Butch (born Robert Leroy Parker) and Sundance (Harry Longbaugh) we have a couple of lively kid-friendly characters drawn from real life and caught at a time of change in America.

By the early 1900s Butch and Sundance's brand of holding up trains on horseback was about done for. On the DVD, George Roy Hill says that basically his film was about people losing their jobs in the face of technological advancement. Or as Butch and Sundance famously put it as they watch the approach of those indefatigable agents of modernity called the super posse, "Who are those guys?" Actually the super posse climb on their horses one leg at a time like Butch and Sundance, but these boys—the top-hatted Indian tracker Lord Baltimore, the storied Pinkerton man Joe Lefors, and four others—far transcend any collection of mere mortals. They are society itself, come to gather train robbers by the scruff of the neck.

Seemingly the super posse or their mounts need no rest. They can't be thrown off the scent; Lord Baltimore tracks his quarry across solid rock. At one point Butch rails that it would be cheaper for the railroad to pay him and Sundance *not* to rob trains than subsidize the super posse. It's a clever thought in a film full of wit and sagacity. But there is no recourse for men whose time has passed. On-screen as in life, Butch and Sundance and their companion, Etta Place (Katharine Ross), escape to Bolivia, but there too they are finished. In an earlier conversation back in the States, their favorite marshal gets it across to them that their outlaw days are ending. It's a measure of these two that a marshal is among their friends. As reflected in Burt Bachrach's song "Raindrops Keep Fallin' on My Head," they are decent people who take their downfall in surprisingly high spirits.

Butch and Sundance were too much fun for some critics. Most assuredly they are fun enough for viewers age ten and up, who will regard them more as funny, playfully mischievous caper-film types than as bad people. Hill, who died in 2002, was an accomplished stage and television director before he turned to film. His movies, some of them big box office successes, genre-hopped from an adaptation of Lillian Hellman's play *Toys in the Attic* to *The Sting* (also with Paul Newman and Robert Redford) and *Slaughterhouse Five*, adapted from the Kurt Vonnegut book. On the *Butch Cassidy* DVD, Hill says he likes outlaw films because they create conflict and have characters who went across the grain.

This time, though, he worried about his approach. "Were we celebrating aberrant characters?" he asks on the DVD. Should they play this as a comedy, which was a natural temptation, or do it straight with a light touch? In life Butch Cassidy was reportedly a relaxed, moderately jovial fellow who despite a relatively easygoing disposition was able to control the Hole-in-the-Wall Gang, one of the Wild West's last band of very bad guys. Sundance, on the other hand, was by all accounts a volatile drunk and killer. Cassidy apparently was the one person he got along with.

You'd never guess that from Redford's witty, low-keyed characterization. How do you cast a pair like Butch and Sundance? When Steve McQueen saw William Goldman's script, he showed it to Newman. McQueen saw himself as Butch and Newman as Sundance. They considered buying the film, but others beat them to it. McQueen was offered Sundance, but he backed out.

In the early planning, Sundance seemed to be the focal point. One title was *The Sundance Kid and Butch Cassidy,* a jarring eye- and earful and, since Butch ran the show in real life, a historical flip-flop. On the disc Newman says he presumed he would be Sundance until he was made Cassidy. He and Redford made an interesting combination of veteran and relative newcomer. At the height of his career (some said somewhat past the height), Newman had made *Cat on a Hot Tin Roof, The Hustler, Hud,* and *Cool Hand Luke.* Primarily a stage and television actor at that point, Redford made an impression in the Broadway production of Neil Simon's *Barefoot in the Park* and played opposite Jane Fonda in the 1967 film. Hill liked his laid-back quality.

At 20th Century Fox, however, there was the usual resistance to an unknown. Warren Beatty was considered and many others. "Finally they ran out of actors," Redford says on the disc. Hill sent Newman in to push for Redford. Goldman says that on the set "Newman's people" were worried that Redford was stealing the movie. But, he adds, Newman appreciated working with good actors and gave the newcomer his head.

Goldman's screenplay won the Oscar. He calls himself a novelist who does screenplays: *All the President's Men* (Oscar for adapted screenplay), *Marathon Man* (adapted from his own novel), *The Princess Bride* (see page 218), *A Bridge Too Far*. One challenge he faced in this film was to keep Butch and Sundance jaunty and humorous without sliding into comedy. The characterizations work well for children. As he apparently did in life, Butch avoids violence whenever he can, and Hill and Goldman restrain Sundance as well. Ironically, before the final shoot-out the one gun battle they get into—and it's a dandy with bodies flying—is in the performance of an honest job they have taken as security guards in Bolivia.

Hill was worried the scene would turn audiences against Butch, but it didn't. Another nice factor for kids is their companion Etta, a sensitive, loving young woman loyal to both men until she finally leaves them in Bolivia and returns home. Goldman says that in life she was probably a prostitute, but in most historical accounts she is a schoolteacher. Ross makes her a smart, gentle influence.

Sepia prints throughout the film evoke life in the 1890s and early 1900s as the three flee across the country and then to South America. In a memorable finish, Butch and Sundance fall to a fusillade of fire from Bolivian army troops. Hill stops the action short in a sepia freeze-frame. On the DVD, he says he couldn't bear the thought of a prolonged bloody end for such likable figures.

The film is a little rough and violent for small children. Those slightly older will be treated to an unusual, rewarding, and highly entertaining western.

18. CASABLANCA

Humphrey Bogart, Ingrid Bergman, Paul Henreid, Claude Rains, Sidney Greenstreet, Peter Lorre, Conrad Veidt

DIRECTED BY MICHAEL CURTIZ
1942. 102 minutes. Black and white. No rating

Kids of eleven and twelve aren't too young for a brush with a classic. Since they'll be coming across this movie (more specifically, references to this movie) for the rest of their lives, it's a nice film for parents to share with them at the start. In the bargain, they'll get a pretty passable war drama with plenty of intrigue and a little pathos. It's not *Star Wars 2,* but, according to a poll taken by the American Film Institute, it is America's second-best movie (after *Citizen Kane*). And if they haven't seen *The African Queen* (see page 6), it may well be their first Bogie.

A witty script is brilliantly performed by the best in the business— Paul Henreid, Claude Rains, Ingrid Bergman, Sidney Greenstreet, Peter Lorre, Conrad Veidt. The story, adapted from an obscure play, is perhaps the movies' most famous: the love affair between the saloon keeper Rick Blaine (Bogie) and Ilsa Lund (Bergman), the wife of a French Resistance leader (Henreid); the wartime cloak-and-dagger between Nazis and Allies in Vichy Morocco; the fight for love and glory, as the song goes. Like many great films, *Casablanca* has the range and appeal to reach down from on high to scoop up kids whether they fully appreciate all that is happening or not.

The most important thing to take away is a sense of Rick's morality. In the end, he denies himself the woman he loves in the interest of a greater good. "That there are values worth making sacrifices for, that's what this is about," says Howard Koch, who wrote the movie with Julius Epstein and Julius's twin brother, Philip, in a commentary on the DVD.

Kids can appreciate the message, but will they have fun? It's hard not to get involved with this movie once it gets rolling. Be sure to give them some background beforehand. Much of the fun of *Casablanca* is how it was made. Kids like fire drills and it can be truthfully said that the makers of this movie weren't sure what would happen from one day to the next. Expectations were modest from the start. "It was never supposed to be anything special," the screenwriter Julius Epstein told Stephen Humphrey Bogart, the actor's son, in Stephen's memoir, *Bogart: In Search of My Father.*

Bogie was making his forty-fifth movie. "In those days the studios owned the theaters and each studio made a picture a week," Epstein said. "*Casablanca* was just one more picture. It was corny and it was sentimental, and your father made a lot of better films that don't get as much attention. But somehow magic happened and it became a classic."

Tell the kids that *Casablanca* has been called the best bad movie ever made. That's being glib, of course. In her book *Round Up the Usual Suspects: The Making of "Casablanca"—Bogart, Bergman and World War II,* Aljean Harmetz mentions the high degree of professionalism. "The old Hollywood studios did have a golden era when art and commerce and hard work fitted comfortably together," she wrote. Given today's Hollywood, that's more miracle than magic, but it certainly applies to *Casablanca.*

Such a success seemed unlikely. Before filming Bergman and Bogart had lunch to discuss the project. "They thought the dialogue was ridiculous and the situations were unbelievable," said the actress Geraldine Fitzgerald, who was present. The writers fixed that up, and they had to work fast. In what was essentially an assembly-line production, it seemed that no one had completely figured out where the picture was headed.

"We were making changes in the script every day during shooting," Julius Epstein says in Stephen Bogart's book. "Your father didn't like that. He was a professional, always prepared, and he didn't like sloppiness. But that's what it was. We were handing in dialogue hours, even minutes, before it was to be shot." Bergman was confused. In her book, *My Story,* she wrote, "Every morning we said, 'Well, who are we, what are we doing here?' And Michael Curtiz, the director, would say, 'We're not quite sure, but let's get through this scene today and we'll let you know tomorrow.' "

In the film Ilsa's problem is choosing between Rick and her husband, the Resistance leader Victor Laszlo. According to Harmetz, the filmmakers chose Laszlo early on and not at the end of shooting as legend has it. Question is, did they inform the stars? "As soon as we know, we'll let you know," Epstein reportedly told Bergman. Stephen Bogart wrote that his father was on edge. Bogie was a leading man and leading men always got the woman. That there would be any doubt here stirred up insecurities. Bogart obviously was attractive to women, but he often played characters who weren't womanizers. How would the public react to Ilsa abandoning Henreid, himself a leading man, for a forty-four-year-old balding fellow not exactly known for romantic inclinations?

Though the writers knew the denouement, they were unsure exactly how to finish the movie. Harmetz says the ending was rewritten a dozen times. Julius Epstein said the answer came as he and his brother were riding in a car in Los Angeles. With the details in place, the movie is free to conclude in classic fashion. "If *Casablanca* had ended with Bogart going off with Bergman, the romantic ending wouldn't have happened," Koch says on the DVD. "There wouldn't be any legend today."

The film never really took off until after Bogart's death in 1957. "Whatever my father did worked," Stephen Bogart wrote. "*Casablanca* turned Bogie into a sex symbol." There was good chemistry between him and Bergman, but they weren't close. "I kissed him, but I never knew him," she wrote.

Rick shoots a Nazi officer, but it is quite antiseptic. There is absolutely no sex. It was 1942 and the code of decency ruled. "Impure love must not be presented as attractive and beautiful," it read, and the producers took that so seriously Rick's apartment doesn't even have a bed. And the same goes for profanity. By age eleven most children will get the gist of this picture, if not its every nuance. And most will enjoy it.

19. CAT BALLOU

Jane Fonda, Lee Marvin, Michael Callan, Dwayne Hickman, Reginald Denny, Nat King Cole, Stubby Kaye

DIRECTED BY ELLIOT SILVERSTEIN
1965. 96 minutes. No rating

Several genres come together beautifully in Elliot Silverstein's film, which you could basically call a funny western with a musical streak. Lee Marvin won the Oscar as best actor for his dual role as two gunfighters. One is the nasty Jack Strawn, who lacks a nose (bitten off during a fight) and wears a metal replacement. The other, and by far the more famous, is the ever-inebriated, fall-down hilarious Kid Shelleen, who would put away Strawn in an instant if he ever sobered up long enough to slap leather.

Yes, there's a lot of imbibing for a family film. Shelleen raises many bottle bottoms to the sky before sobering up, briefly, toward the end of the film. But this is a spoof and clearly in fun, without being stupid or crude about the situation. Marvin has a gift for broad, physical comedy, and here he and the kid reel wildly through a highly entertaining western saga that will have kids in thrall from start to finish.

A good-hearted romp sends up all the clichés while skipping around saloon and range as if it were at a hoedown. In fact, the characters come together early on at a square dance that could be from a musical. At the core of the story, adapted from Roy Chanslor's novel, is Catherine (Jane Fonda), called Cat, the sweet, gingham-fresh daughter of the beleaguered rancher (Reginald Denny) who is about to lose his spread to the voracious railroad. Upright and a fighter, Cat will become twice the legend Strawn and Shelleen ever were as she battles the comically evil rail baron, Sir Harry Percival. For romance there is a sweetly goofy fugitive, Clay Boone (Michael Callan), who runs from bloodshed and probably wouldn't be considered likely to attract a gal like Cat these days but got away with it in 1965. Among the corrupt sheriffs, sanctimonious parsons, and other western types is Jackson Two-Bears (Tom Nardini), an Indian youth with a wry take on the plight of his people.

Cat becomes such a paragon of resolve, especially after her daddy is shot by Strawn, she even earns a Greek chorus of sorts, with Stubby Kaye and Nat King Cole strolling about singing "The Ballad of Cat Ballou" and embellishing the action in key places. Nine years earlier there were plans to make a musical of Chanslor's book, starring Burt Lancaster and Tony Curtis. A comedy eventually made more sense, but the sight of young Fonda, five years into a major and controversial career, skipping through a big dance number lifts the spirits.

The drunken Shelleen, on the other hand, is thrown out of the boot of a stagecoach as it pulls up in front of the expectant Cat and friends. Needing her own hired gun to combat the noseless Strawn, Cat has sent a $50 retainer to Shelleen, who puts it to predictable use. Arriving virtually senseless, he not only has no gun but can't hit anything with a borrowed one until his system is jump-started with an infusion of the snake that bit him. Marvin was already a star, of course, having played a deadly serious gunfighter in *The Man Who Shot Liberty Valance*.

Silverstein says that he first noticed Marvin's look and manner in *The Wild One* (1954). He is a super comic, with a gravelly voice and hard eyes that become as amusing as they are menacing. Shelleen's braggadocio manner sets himself up perfectly for the pratfalls that follow. One of his first proclamations on arrival, after it has been established that he can indeed still talk and function, is to lament the fact that the West is changing and there is no longer a place for the likes of him. In fact, he growls, last time he passed through Tombstone they had put a roller-skating rink over the O.K. Corral.

Silverstein was primarily a television director. He says that Marvin was fine to work with, though at first he was playing the role more for laughs among the cast and crew. To capture an audience, the performance had to move beyond gags to a richer, broader comedic approach, with some pathos perhaps. But Fonda is the center of the film. Plenty sassy and also sensible, Cat provides a balance, a sense of strength and perseverance and idealism we can use more of in a good kids' movie.

As sprightly as the square dance is, it does end up in a brawl. Cat's dad is gunned down. But this is bloodless stuff, much of it comic. Boone tries his best to end up in bed with Cat and succeeds a couple of times, but very chastely. The movie isn't suitable for the smallest ones, say under seven, but from then on it's a hoot. There is no profanity.

20. CHARIOTS OF FIRE

Ben Cross, Ian Charleson, Ian Holm, John Gielgud, Lindsay Anderson, Cheryl Campbell, Alice Krige, Nigel Havers, Nicholas Farrell, Nigel Davenport, David Yelland

DIRECTED BY HUGH HUDSON
1981. 123 minutes. PG

The producer David Puttnam got the idea for the film from a book, *The Official History of the Olympics,* which he found lying around a house he had rented in Hollywood. In it were stories of two runners who won gold medals for themselves and England in the 1924 Olympics in Paris. Winning for yourself, though not for entirely selfish reasons, is the force driving Hugh Hudson's movie, and from that notion springs the title, borrowed from a poem called "And Did Those Feet" by William Blake, written about 1804, which became a British anthem during World War I. One verse goes:

> *Bring me my bow of burning gold;*
> *Bring me my arrows of desire;*
> *Bring me my spear: O clouds unfurl*
> *Bring me my chariot of fire*

Blake called for imagination and individuality to break free of social and economic constraints. In Hudson's film we have two young runners trying to hang on to the best vestiges of themselves as God and the English move in to exploit their athletic prowess for Christian and national glorification. Eric Liddell (Ian Charleson) and Harold Abrahams (Ben Cross) are sprinters who will compete for England in the 1924 Olympics at the end of the movie. Though they are aware of each other's reputation, they come in contact infrequently and race against each other only once at a national meet. The movie follows each separately as he trains and runs preliminary races, privately tests his motivations for competing, and stands up for his values against powerful elders who would compromise them.

The blond, gentle Liddell is a Christian missionary on furlough from China. At home in Scotland his reputation as an athlete stirs Highlands fields and churchyards. When he says he runs because God made him fast, it's not a boast. "When I run, I feel His pleasure," he says. His sister (Cheryl Campbell) feels that his running detracts from his religious work, but the men from his mission like the idea of "a muscular Christian to make folks sit up and take notice." So Eric's talent now gives him two masters, country and the Lord. "Run in God's name and let the world stand back in wonder!" he is told.

Abrahams is a Jew with very different demands upon him. A brilliant, furiously intense Cambridge student, he feels he must use his speed afoot to defend and champion his Jewishness among a bigoted elite. When asked why he runs, he replies, "I'm more of an addict. It's a compulsion, a weapon."

Hudson's film won the Oscar as best picture, and it is a gorgeously photographed period piece. If you wonder what happens to sports in all this atmosphere and idealism, rest assured that kids will get plenty of competition to go with beauty and issues to consider. With limbs flying akimbo and faces contorted with effort, these runners are a far cry from the sleek professional machines who go for the gold today. Liddell, Abrahams, and company look quaint in their white T-shirts and boxer shorts. Off the track they are dapper in tweeds and formal evening wear in rich settings.

Amateurism and gentlemanly airs prevailed in the '20s. Abrahams gets himself into trouble with the Cambridge hierarchy when he hires a professional coach named Mussabini (Ian Holm) to train him for the Paris games. To perfect Abrahams's stride, Mussabini has him prancing like a show horse, which looks a little silly today. When they blast around the curves and into home stretches, the runners are fun to watch.

Liddell trains in the Highlands. Abrahams watches him compete. "He runs like a wild animal, he unnerves me," he tells Mussabini. But Abrahams is tough, assured, and totally possessed. In their first and only head-to-head encounter at 200 meters, Liddell pulls ahead and wins. Abrahams is so crushed that he sits alone in the stands long afterward. We all know hard losers, but this goes beyond that. For Abrahams winning is life, and the thought goes through our minds that he might end it if faced with defeat. He flails around for a way out.

"If I can't win, I won't run," he tells his girlfriend, a D'Oyly Carte singer named Sybill (Alice Krige).

"If you don't run, you can't win," she replies.

Abrahams is an interesting proposition for kids. The son of a highly successful Lithuanian Jew and brother of a doctor, he arrives at Cambridge with plenty of ethnic attitude. That prompts anti-Semitic cracks from frolicsome students and shudders of alarmed disdain in the vaulted halls of the "gargoyles," as the critic Pauline Kael calls them, who run the university. "Arrogant, defensive to the point of pugnacity," says the master of Caius College (Lindsay Anderson), describing Abrahams. "As they invariably are," replies the master of Trinity (John Gielgud), referring to Jews.

Abrahams, in fact, is multitalented, affable, admired by his fellows. But he can't get around his conviction that Jewishness closes access to influence and power. Running is a means of vindication. "I will run them off their feet," he says.

Kids who are taught that winning isn't everything will just have to swing along with Abrahams—or not. He's not everybody's cup of tea, but we can't help but like him because under his angry desperation is a vulnerability and intelligence that helps him finally to come to grips with his obsession. This leads him to question himself, but his ultimate strength comes through for him under fire.

In perhaps the film's best scene, Abrahams is summoned to dinner and confronted by the masters of Caius and Trinity. There he is lectured on all the virtues of athletics that the university has held dear for centuries—the courage engendered, leadership, loyalty, comradeship, and mutual responsibility. Which brings them to Abrahams. He is told that his use of a personal professional coach not only violates amateurism, it suggests a pursuit of individual glory not conducive to esprit de corps. On top of this, the coach is Italian. Only half-Italian, Abrahams tells them. The other half is Arab.

What shouldn't be lost on kids here is that everything the masters say has an element of truth but is being twisted to fit their biases. "Yours are the archaic values of the prep school playground. You deceive no one but yourselves," Abrahams tells the two masters as he leaves.

"Well, there goes your Semite, Hugh," says the master of Trinity. "A different God. A different mountaintop."

Liddell's God won't let him run on Sunday, which presents a problem in Paris when his best event is scheduled on the Sabbath. The Prince of Wales (David Yelland) suggests that he should put country before God (an ironic request from a man who will later abdicate the throne for a woman), but Liddell stands fast in his belief. Fortunately there are other events and days of the week. As Kael puts it, "The picture is a piece of technological lyricism held together by the glue of simple-minded sentiment; basically its appeal is in watching a couple of guys win their races."

And kids from about age eight will like that, though the philosophizing may be a bit much for some young ones (not to mention a few adults). There is no sex or profanity.

Chariots of Fire

21. CHICKEN RUN

**With the voices of Julia Sawalha,
Benjamin Whitrow, Mel Gibson, Miranda
Richardson, Tony Haygarth, Phil Daniels**

DIRECTED BY PETER LORD AND NICK PARK

2000. 86 minutes. G

Think about this the next time you're around a chicken coop. How would you like to be stuck in a henhouse? "You might think, 'Oh, well, they're just chickens,'" says Nick Park. "But then you realize chickens are people like everyone else." Here several dozen of the most entertaining chickens you'll ever come across toil in the gloomy confines of Tweedy Farm, run by the maniacally production-minded Mrs. Tweedy. They're English, these chickens, doomed to lay and lay forever (if they know what's good for them) in a barnyard that resembles a stalag, or German World War II prison camp. Barbed wire surrounds the compound and one of the henhouses is numbered 17, a salute to a first-rate prisoner of war movie (suitable for older kids).

The littlest ones can dive into *Chicken Run,* though the mood is darker and the repartee wittier than in most animated features. Parents can explain the film's unique form of animation, which also strays far from the standard, whether drawn like *Snow White* or computer-generated like *Monsters, Inc.* Park and Peter Lord, his partner at Ardman Animations, use figures made of clay. The process is called stop-motion claymation and it is unbelievably labor-intensive.

Prior to *Chicken Run,* Americans knew Park by his Wallace and Gromit series (*The Wrong Trousers, A Close Shave, A Grand Day Out*), featuring an absentminded inventor and his dog. Kids will love these films, too, and the three of them, running about thirty minutes each, are available on a single DVD. Like Francis Ford Coppola, Park has the distinction of beating himself out for an Oscar. In 1990, his five-minute *Creature Comforts,* about animals trapped in a zoo, beat *A Grand Day Out* for best short. The other two Wallace and Gromit films won Oscars in 1993 and in 1995.

In other words, Park and Lord know how to manipulate clay figures, whose every move and expression is manually changed every single frame. Here they keep it up for an action-filled eighty-six minutes. At Tweedy's farm, the only holiday is a stretch of solitary confinement in a coal bin. Everybody dreams about escape. Efforts to dig their way out with an incredibly detailed spoon or drill a tunnel with an egg beater are fruitless. "We haven't tried not trying to escape; that might work," one hen suggests.

The one can-do chicken is a scrapper and natural leader named Ginger, who envisions flying out of the place. As we know, chickens don't fly. A catapult is in order, perhaps, or a slingshot. Then along comes Rocky, a flying rooster. Roosters don't fly either, but there he is passing overhead when he gets caught in a weathervane and crash-lands in the hens' feed trough. Rocky is an American. Until this point the only male around the coop has been a starchy old Brit rooster named Fowler, a former RAF man who rules the roost, or tries to, with a blustery spit and polish.

Fowler is a good egg, but no one regards him seriously. Rocky takes the barnyard by storm. On the DVD, Park says they made Rocky a Yank in keeping with World War II days when American GIs made substantial headway with English women. A Yank needs an American accent, of course, and for the voice of Rocky, Park and Lord landed Mel Gibson, who struts his vocal stuff. Like all great animated films, *Chicken Run* has memorable voices, particularly Julia Sawalha's as the spunky, inspiring Ginger, Miranda Richardson's as the threatening Mrs. Tweedy, and Benjamin Whitrow's as the crusty Fowler.

Most of the vocal track was recorded in England. Gibson, a Wallace and Gromit admirer, was in Los Angeles and worked separately from the others, which was difficult for him. The roguish "flying" Rocky, it evolves, was in fact shot out of a cannon at a circus, but that doesn't dissuade him from claiming he can teach the chickens to fly. This makes him a hot dude in the henhouse, but later he has a lot of answering to do when the others discover that he can't get off the ground himself.

Park says he was drawn to Gibson's performance as a lovable rogue in *Maverick*. On the DVD Gibson says he had a hard time with Rocky's short exclamations, but he throws himself into the voice and its many inflections as if he were William Wallace in *Braveheart*. Park and Lord attribute much of the movie's success to Gibson's hard work. "I'm sure he needed this for his career," Park says facetiously.

It is impossible to overstate the complexity of stop-motion claymation. *Chicken Run* began with seven thousand pounds of plasticine. Each molded figure has a tiny jointed metal skeleton. After the slightest movement, including changes in facial expression, the filming stops while the animator moves the figure to the next position. "Animation is the secret world that happens between frames," Park says. Forty animators took two years to create 120,000 frames. On the disc someone figures that each animator turned out 24 frames, or about two-and-a-half seconds of film a day.

The result is striking detail and expression. Lord says that claymation is more interested in energy than smoothness. The faces are the most distinctive in all of animation. "It's all in the eyes and eyebrows. That's where the acting is," he says.

"We lay day in and day out, and when we don't lay enough, they kill us," says one hen. Indeed, when one of them is found with no eggs in the nest, she is led off for a Tweedy dinner. An execution scene takes place in shadow. Park says it was designed over and over to lessen the effect, and when the ax falls it is with a quiet chop that is heard and not seen. But Chicken Run *doesn't shrink from reality. When egg production doesn't keep pace with Mrs. Tweedy's profit objectives, she plans to feed all the birds to a huge potpie maker, which graphically chops vegetables and other ingredients. No chickens end up in the thing, but the prospect could be upsetting to little ones. Otherwise, while this isn't the sunniest cartoon fare, it is adventurous viewing for kids from about the age of six up.*

22. CLOSE ENCOUNTERS
OF THE THIRD KIND

Richard Dreyfuss, Teri Garr, Melinda Dillon, Cary Guffey, Bob Balaban, François Truffaut

DIRECTED BY STEVEN SPIELBERG
1977. 134 minutes. PG

An encounter of the first kind involves reports of aliens. In the second kind of encounter there is physical evidence—burned holes in the ground, telephone lines down, animals missing, stalling car engines, and the like. In a close encounter of the third kind you meet the alien face to face. At the climax of Spielberg's film two varieties emerge from the giant spacecraft set down on a Wyoming plateau. Some are tall, sticklike Giacometti-style figures strongly backlighted to obscure the wires supporting their spindly limbs. Others are short and blobbish.

Neither strain of alien is shown clearly or in much detail, which retains their mystery. A certain amount of obfuscation also helps reduce menace. What these aliens look like isn't the point anyway. Spielberg wants to stress that we are not alone in the galaxy, and we have nothing to fear from others out there.

Kids get a superb action adventure, and there are good lessons about being open to the unknown. Spielberg addresses all aspects of the film in an interview on the DVD. He is a very good talker. By his twenties, he says, he had accepted the idea of extraterrestrial life, long before UFOs became an "alternative religion," as he calls it. The seed was planted in his boyhood when his father woke him in the middle of the night and drove him to a field where they and a crowd of others lay on their backs watching a meteor shower.

In the film a wildly excited electrical line worker named Roy Neary (Richard Dreyfuss) is stopped, transfixed, in his pickup truck while a spacecraft in a glaring white light blows out transformers, makes signs and mailboxes jiggle, and leaves him with a sunburn. From then on Neary patrols the night with equally obsessed fellow witnesses hoping for further encounters. One saucer gazer is Jillian Guiller (Melinda Dillon), whose toddler son (Cary Guffey) has such an affinity for the visitors that he is drawn into their control and goes off with them for a while in their gigantic mother ship.

Cast for the role at age three, Guffey had never seen a movie, let alone appeared in one. Before the shoot his parents took him to see *Bambi*. Spielberg describes him as a listening, thoughtful child, an ideal specimen for aliens who have been borrowing humans and keeping them for decades, and, as happens at the end of the film, returning them unharmed and not a day older.

Scarily obsessed, Neary rips up the shrubbery and carts loads of dirt into his living room in a crazed effort to re-create an unidentified tower of rock that has sprung into his consciousness. Dreyfuss is famous for over-the-top performances. He and Spielberg had just finished *Jaws,* with Dreyfuss as a beleaguered scientist, and he lobbied hard to play Neary. The director didn't see him as right for the part. At first Spielberg went after Steve McQueen, who told him he couldn't take the role because he couldn't cry on-screen.

Spielberg considered Dustin Hoffman, Gene Hackman, and Al Pacino, but they all turned him down. Meanwhile, Dreyfuss went right on campaigning for the role. He was a family man so playing one would be perfect for him, he said. Spielberg was still unpersuaded. Then Dreyfuss finally struck a nerve. "You need a child," he said. Spielberg says he cast him instantly.

Kids watching the film will know exactly what Dreyfuss meant. Neary becomes a wild child in his rush to connect with the aliens. He and other believers stream across the country to Devil's Tower in Wyoming, where the government has set up a landing site for a secret rendezvous with the space visitors. It is here, too, that we encounter another major Spielberg casting coup in the person of the French director François Truffaut, who plays the director of an international team of scientists and officials. To meet the cautiously friendly aliens Spielberg wanted an official with humanity. Truffaut, he says, had a kind, charitable face.

Used to the intimate feel of French film, Truffaut was amused at the huge scale of *Close Encounters*. Guffey, now a young man, remembers how natural the Frenchman was with kids. So was Spielberg, whose films often have a nice way with children (*E.T, Hook, Empire of the Sun, A.I.*). "Spielberg communicates with kids," Guffey says. "On the set he always explained things so I wouldn't get scared."

Kids watching the movie will get a kick out of the five-note signal earthlings send by way of greeting to the mother ship filling the sky over Devil's Tower. Spielberg agonized over getting it just right and hundreds of signals were tried. Seven notes would have sounded too much like a song. The director wanted more of a doorbell.

For all the film's appeal, there are some scary and disturbing moments, but it would be a shame to rule out such an entertaining and thought-provoking film. At home Neary changes from loving father into a virtual maniac who smashes up the house and frightens the wits out of his own kids, prompting his wife to pack herself and them off to her mother's house. And there is another alarming situation that could upset some young kids. To discourage civilians from approaching the landing site it has prepared for the alien ship, the government fakes a toxic-gas scare, even going to the extent of littering the roadside with the bodies of "dead" cattle. When the threat is described as nerve gas, panicky townspeople vie for gas masks and places in departing trucks. Young children could be upset by the Nearys' breakup and the situation in Wyoming, but a little explanation should ease any fears. Depending on your child, age nine is a good time to start.

23. THE DAY THE EARTH STOOD STILL

Michael Rennie, Patricia Neal, Sam Jaffe, Billy Gray

DIRECTED BY ROBERT WISE

1951. 92 minutes. Black and white. No rating

The alien called Klaatu (Michael Rennie) looks at the mangled little gizmo in his hand. He had intended it as a gift for the American president. The device would have revealed something about life on other planets, not that anyone in Washington seems too receptive. Ringed by troops on the mall, Klaatu is shot on the spot as he tries to introduce himself. He'll recover, but a mission that took five months traveling 250 million miles is off to a bad start.

To be fair, a degree of jumpiness might be expected from guardians of public safety at the sight of an alien waving a strange instrument as he emerges from his ship in the middle of the nation's capital. Space visitors often spell trouble on the big screen, popping up in assaults from Pennsylvania to India in M. Night Shyamalan's *Signs* (2002), for example, or obliterating the White House in Roland Emmerich's *Independence Day* (1996). Unless, of course, the visits are comic or satiric, as in Tim Burton's *Mars Attacks!*, which spoofs alien-invasion flicks of the 1950s.

Very much a '50s creation, Robert Wise's film isn't of the invasion genre, nor is there the slightest thing silly about it. *The Day the Earth Stood Still* is an original, not quite seminal—since there is little else quite like it—but certainly a classic. In spirit the film jumps almost three decades to Steven Spielberg's *Close Encounters of the Third Kind* (1977), which promotes the Spielbergian contention that an alien incursion needn't be threatening. In that film (see page 66) a peaceful visit from another world is elaborately coordinated with the government. Klaatu, by contrast, pops in unannounced in a flying saucer that circles the Washington Monument like a white Frisbee before settling on the mall.

Crowds scatter in panic but soon regroup, hundreds deep, behind barriers thrown up by police and the army around the ship. Serving as the CNN and Fox News anchors of their day, the radio newsmen H. V. Kaltenborn and Drew Pearson fill in the folks at home who are gathered on porches and in kitchens. For a long while the ship just sits closed and silent, but eventually a ramp slides from its innards and Klaatu emerges. Movie space visitors come in myriad otherworldly configurations, but this one is a slender, distinguished-looking human. His manner is civil but stern. He seems to be on some sort of diplomatic mission, but has no chance to say what that might be before he is shot. At this point a more standard denizen of an alien movie appears in the form of a menacing eight-foot-tall robot, who melts down the troops' weapons with his laser beam.

In an interview Wise said that, like Spielberg, he's a UFO believer and wanted to convey the idea that Klaatu's arrival needn't lead to strife. But calm is hard to promote with the likes of Gabriel Heater ranting on the radio about "wild animals," menace from other worlds, and retaliation.

On the DVD the director Nicholas Meyer, who sits in on a commentary with Wise, says that he watched the fifty-two-year-old film with a contemporary eight-year-old. She sat mesmerized from start to finish, he says. That the movie is in black and white, sometimes anathema to young viewers, never occurred to her. The characters and story took her over. The few primitive effects don't seem to matter because the movie focuses on the human drama.

The saucer's Frisbee-like landing is slightly ridiculous, accompanied eerily by electronic theremin music, but once on the ground the exterior of the ship becomes little more than a generic spherical structure. Inside the craft more detail is required, but the film avoids too much realism by creating an Art Deco motif with lighting and nondefined panels activated by a wave of the hand. (In 2002 Tom Cruise does much the same thing in Spielberg's *Minority Report*.)

Instead the film focuses on its characters and its thrillerish aspects. An attractive, intelligent widow, Helen (Patricia Neal), and her young son, Bobby (Billy Gray), come to the aid of Klaatu, who is hounded and vastly misunderstood by everybody else he comes across. Bobby's affinity for Klaatu lays the groundwork for movie kids' good relations with aliens that run through Spielberg's *E.T. The Extra-Terrestrial* (1982) and *A.I.* (2001). Rennie, an unknown at the time, cuts an urbane figure, unfailingly civil and rather fascinating to watch as a '50s figure taking on his problems not as an alien but as a gentleman around the boardinghouse where Klaatu takes up residence.

The studio wanted Claude Rains for the role, but Wise preferred Rennie because an unknown wouldn't distract audiences from the story. For kids it might be something of a revelation to watch '50s characters interacting with civility and without so much as one profanity. But the stakes are just as dire as they are in *Independence Day*. Offered a meeting with the president, Klaatu refuses. He has brought a message for all the world's peoples, not just one country. If the world allows violent uses of atomic energy to escape the planet, the robots will destroy it.

While the film encourages peaceful conflict resolution, it leaves the door ajar for violence if earthlings don't cooperate. Klaatu demands a global conclave. The secretary of state tells him that's impossible, given the climate of the Cold War and the Soviet-American stalemate. Klaatu says he isn't interested in Earth's petty squabbles. But despite his dictatorial take-it-or-leave-it edict, we like Klaatu, ever calm and polite. Such a meeting between man and alien finally takes place, not unlike Spielberg's finale in *Close Encounters*. In that film the culminating encounter is an enormous affair. Here it's fun to watch such portentous issues unfold in such a simple fashion, almost like a local town event.

Wise's film is based on a story by Harry Bates and imaginatively adapted by Edmund L. North. On the DVD, Wise, now eighty-nine, says he was surprised that Darryl Zanuck, the head of 20th Century Fox and the film's producer, agreed to go ahead with a film on such a politically charged subject, especially at the dawn of the McCarthy era. But Zanuck, he says, thought a film promoting the peaceful uses of atomic energy was important.

Wise, an enormously proficient technician and no-nonsense moviemaker, says that it was vital to avoid sci-fi vagaries and unrealities. Analysts notice a religiosity in the film, an obvious reference to the coming of Christ. Wise says that he was completely unaware of any such meaning and that it had to do with Rennie's stately appearance.

Bobby shows Klaatu around Washington. At the Lincoln Memorial the alien says that what they need is a Lincolnesque figure, or failing that an internationally recognized sage who can rally a meeting of influential types who might sway world opinion. Bobby suggests an Einstein-like figure named Professor Barnhardt, played by Sam Jaffe. So they march over to his house and ring his doorbell. Imagine trying that these days.

Kids from about the age of seven will understand the film and be enthralled by it. Klaatu is shot not once but twice, but there is no other violence. And the proceedings are certainly proper, with no sex or profanity.

24. DICK TRACY

Warren Beatty, Glenne Headly, Charlie Korsmo, Al Pacino, Mandy Patinkin, Paul Sorvino, Dustin Hoffman

DIRECTED BY WARREN BEATTY
1990. 105 minutes. PG

"How's the food?" asks the boy called Kid (Charlie Korsmo).

"Good," replies Dick Tracy (Warren Beatty). "How's the food there?"

"Good," answers Kid.

At this point Tracy is in prison and Kid in an orphanage, but the humor stays plentiful and tasty all through Beatty's film. Movies based on comic strips can come out a little overdone for very young audiences, too dark, perhaps, or too violent or cultish. *Batman* and its sequels, *X-Men,* and even the stupendously popular *Spider-Man* all have harsh edges.

"*Dick Tracy* is a great uninterrupted grin," Vincent Canby wrote in the *New York Times*. "It goes from ear to ear, from the pre-title opening sequence to the ending in which Tracy may or may not commit himself to his patient companion, Tess Trueheart (Glenne Headly). It's a movie that finds funniness in the most unexpected places and characters."

Chester Gould's strip with the jut-jawed detective first appeared in the *Detroit Enquirer* in 1931. "As a draftsman, Gould was not much above journeyman level," the art critic John Russell wrote in the *Times*. "His dialogue was workmanlike at best. As a narrator, he never put on airs. But with these fair-to-middling capacities, he fashioned something that worked year in, year out, like a freight locomotive that always came in on time." All who made the movie said the strip was their bible, but like all films based on the comics, this one savors its own stylizations. The film won an Oscar for the prosthetics that distort gangsters like Pruneface, Flattop, The Brow, The Rodent, Shoulders, and Itchy. It also won for art direction, with painterly sets that turn a cityscape into splendidly evocative, nostalgic backdrops.

Vibrant, wildly mismatched colors are thrown together in contrasts so jarring they seem to belong together. Milena Canonero, the costume designer, followed the strip but didn't exclude other influences, such as German post-expressionism. "They used colors in unorthodox, aggressive ways, and the faces they painted were grotesque," she said in the *Times*. As an artist, Gould was plain and direct, and in that spirit Richard Sylbert, the acclaimed set designer, avoided the fancy. "The key to *Dick Tracy* is that the production design is not there to overwhelm anything," he said in the *Times*. "It's absolutely stripped, and what happens is you see a world that's so simplified, it becomes sophisticated."

There is much Depression-era violence. When Tracy dukes it out with a tough guy in a shack on the waterfront, the entire building sways to and fro. During numerous shoot-outs and gangland massacres enough bullets spray from submachine guns to supply a marine battalion. One burst of gunfire is so prolonged that an entire automobile is riddled with bullet holes. In other movies that could be horrifying, but in this one it becomes both a joke and a minor work of art.

Young children won't understand the nuances, but there is no gore and enough comic flavor to carry them over these patches and move the film into the realm of family viewing. Of course, there are Madonna's torrid advances as Breathless Mahoney, the mobsters' moll and Club Ritz chanteuse who falls for Tracy. Later in this book, we'll meet Madonna playing center field in Penny Marshall's *A League of Their Own* (see page 149). Kids love Madonna's honesty, plainspokenness, and the way she sticks up for herself and others. When Tracy tells her he's going to take her downtown and sweat it out of her under the lights, she says she sweats better in the dark. That's certainly suggestive enough, but sex, like the stylized violence, stops short of disqualifying the movie for kids above the age of eight or so.

The plot doesn't interfere with style. Tracy battles the mob headed by the explosively manic little hunchback Big Boy Caprice, played with crazed, rubbery abandon by Al Pacino. In the film's best scene, the furiously frustrated Big Boy turns hoofer himself trying to whip Club Ritz's clumsy chorines into a decent act. Tess worries that Tracy's hard-wired devotion to crime prevention will cost them their relationship but tries to stay supportive just the same. Abandoned and starving when Tracy finds him, Kid constantly cadges donuts and tags around after the detective by hopping rides on back bumpers.

Then we have Beatty as Tracy. In the film he is always in a snappy yellow fedora and flowing yellow overcoat, always spotless no matter the thrills and spills (Burberry made ten of the coats so Beatty always stayed fresh). Gould put his man in a plain trench coat, buttoned up tight. "That buttoned-up look was important to the popularity of the original Tracy," Russell wrote in the *Times*. "Readers loved the idea that the bigtime gangsters of the early 1930s could be broken wide open and busted in the depth of the Depression by a big, strong clean man who didn't drink, didn't smoke, kept clear of women, and never waffled. These were desperate times, and they wanted to believe that the straight arrow could still hit the bull's-eye."

Tracy's reason for existence, Russell noted, was to further justice. Beyond that, he had no feelings, or nerves, dreams, inner life or outer life. Could such a colorless fellow reside in the famously rakish Beatty, or could Beatty be contained in Tracy? Russell said that in a way the Andy Warhol Tracy paintings of the '60s opened up the character. Beatty gives him a slightly befuddled air, but everything about this Tracy is stylish and charming. And he's warm and funny, but plenty tough when he has to be.

"He is Beatty doing his very best to be Dick Tracy, but we do not see in him the blank that readers of the strips were free to fill in as they wished," Russell wrote. Tess is patient with Tracy, though she knows his compulsion to chase the next alarm crackling over his wrist radio will never be quenched. She may never get him to propose marriage formally, but at least this Tracy pauses long enough to toss her a ring.

Take good note of the violence and sexuality discussed above. Some parents will be put off by the shoot-outs and Breathless Mahoney's pursuit of Tracy. Most, it is hoped, will decide they don't taint a splendid piece of entertainment.

25. DR. STRANGELOVE OR: HOW I LEARNED TO STOP WORRYING AND LOVE THE BOMB

Peter Sellers, George C. Scott, Sterling Hayden, Keenan Wynn, Tracy Reed, Slim Pickens

DIRECTED BY STANLEY KUBRICK

1964. 93 minutes. Black and white. No rating

Children's movie guides assign different appropriate ages to Kubrick's film. Some say age twelve at the youngest; others hold that *Strangelove* is suitable for all ages. Released before the Motion Picture Association of America's rating system took effect, *Dr. Strangelove* now carries a PG on the DVD case, but judgment is subjective. The film has psychosexual aspects, and it does treat the grim subject of nuclear holocaust. But it also is a fast-moving comedy full of antic characters and silly business. Kubrick may end the film with Armageddon, but he originally planned an all-out food fight. On the DVD there are stills of generals and diplomats so covered with custard pie they are hardly recognizable.

Kubrick decided that went too far, even for a film that has a cowboy B-52 pilot (Slim Pickens) riding a bomb out the bomb-bay doors while whooping and waving his Stetson as if he were astride a bronco. *Strangelove* as comedy took even Kubrick by surprise. Approaching the subject of nuclear holocaust with his typical obsessiveness, he read fifty books and decided to make a serious adaptation of the novel *Red Alert* by Peter George. But as he developed the film, he kept running into absurdities that seemed out of place in a straightforward treatment—such as phoning a deli for some take-out at the height of crisis.

A black comedy would be a more effective way to convey the antiwar message. Kubrick hired Terry Southern, a novelist and screenwriter with hip existentialist credentials, to help him with the script. Together they heightened the absurdities. When the Russian ambassador (Peter Bull) arrives at the war room in Washington to confront the American president Merkin Muffley (Peter Sellers), he first stops to peruse an elaborate buffet.

Before watching the film, parents should talk with children (ages eleven and twelve might be appropriate) about the world situation in 1963 when the movie was made and how it compares with today's troubles. Then we had the Cold War and fresh memories of the Cuban missile crisis, the beginnings of the Vietnam quagmire and so forth, but every era has parallels. In the film Group Captain Lionel Mandrake (Sellers) needs a dime to phone the president, but Col. Bat Guano (Keenan Wynn) is reluctant to shoot his way into a soda machine. During the Grenada invasion in the '80s a pay phone was used to coordinate American forces.

In *Strangelove,* of course, Brig. Gen. Jack D. Ripper (Sterling Hayden) determines that the president and the military establishment have authorized him to send bombers on an unstoppable attack of the Soviet Union. Muffley, a fey little chief executive who handles the pressure with a mix of consternation and a politician's unfailing instinct for self-justification, phones the Soviet president. "Now then, Dimitri, you know how we've always talked about the possibility of something going wrong with the bomb," Muffley says. Befuddled by drink, Dimitri doesn't remember exactly. "The *bomb*, Dimitri," Muffley says. An American base commander "went and did a silly thing," he continues.

Children will appreciate Sellers, who had worked for Kubrick in *Lolita* (1962). Sellers had his comedic start in films like *I'm All Right, Jack* and Richard Lester's short *The Running, Jumping and Standing Still Film*. He has three roles in *Strangelove* and might have taken on a fourth, the B-52 commander, Maj. T.J. "King" Kong (Kubrick was none too subtle with his names), but decided that he couldn't manage four parts, especially one with a Texan accent. Sellers is very fine as Captain Mandrake, a desperately and hilariously stressed-out British officer who finds himself trapped with the crazed General Ripper at besieged Burpleson Air Force Base. He also plays Dr. Strangelove, a black-gloved, wheelchair-bound takeoff on the kind of Nazi physicist the Americans and Soviets competed for after World War II.

Sellers died in 1980 and Kubrick in 1999. On the DVD others who were on the *Strangelove* set recall how Sellers improvised and how he and Kubrick essentially jazz-riffed their way through much of the dialogue. Both were nominated for Oscars, as was the film, but all lost to, respectively, Rex Harrison, the director George Cukor, and *My Fair Lady* (see page 200).

Two other outsized performances will appeal to children. Hayden is perfect as General Ripper, and George C. Scott will live forever as the blustery, buffoonish Gen. Buck C. Turgidson, chairman of the Joint Chiefs of Staff. At one point Turgidson gets into a scuffle with the Soviet ambassador. "Gentlemen, you can't fight in here. This is the war room," President Muffley tells them.

Children will follow most of the humor, which can be slyly juvenile. Kubrick's own sense of humor frayed when Sidney Lumet's *Fail Safe,* a deadly serious drama on the same subject, was scheduled to open at the same time as *Dr. Strangelove.* A lawsuit delayed the Lumet film, but Kubrick's movie, scheduled to open on November 23, 1963, was held up itself by the assassination of John F. Kennedy, a somber non-beginning for what the American Film Institute now ranks as the third-best comedy of all time.

Appropriate ages are discussed above. The film is renowned for its sexual references, but most of them will escape children or be interpreted differently. For example, Major Kong's ride on the bomb has phallic implications, but he's also a cowboy performing a nutty stunt. Reed appears in a bikini as Miss Foreign Affairs, a Playboy *centerfold, and Buck Turgidson's secretary and mistress, but aside from innuendo nothing transpires. There is no profanity.*

26. DUCK SOUP

Groucho, Harpo, Chico, and Zeppo Marx, Margaret Dumont, Edgar Kennedy, Louis Calhern

DIRECTED BY LEO MCCAREY
1933. 70 minutes. Black and white. No rating

Not everybody appreciates *Duck Soup* or the Marx Brothers. "There's hardly any plot to speak of, but I did get the impression that this was supposed to be a very early form of political comedy," writes an unidentified young commentator on the Internet site Teen Movie Critic. "All the so-called 'actors' simply 'act' like imbeciles, which doesn't strike me as a very difficult thing to do." (She might exclude Zeppo, the straight Marx who wore a suit and tie in this film and then retired from the movies.)

Other critics compare the brothers' craziness to the absurdist leanings of Salvador Dalí, Samuel Beckett, and Eugene Ionesco, who, according to the critic and author William Wolf, once said the three greatest influences on him were Groucho, Chico, and Harpo. While any view of the Marx Brothers is probably as valid as any other, this teenager makes a mistake by trying to attach the film to a genre and calling the brothers actors. Don't even try to make sense of the title. The critic Tim Dirks wrote that it comes from a recipe of Groucho's: try it and you will forever duck soup.

On-screen *Duck Soup* is anarchy. Children between six and eleven, say, are likely to take it as slapstick, which coincides with the brothers' links to vaudeville through their mother Minnie, who was from a vaudeville family, and their early stage work in the 1920s. Groucho's puns (we should take up the tax/better take up the carpet) and double entendres will often fly past kids, leaving the impression of a pretty loony guy and a very rude one, too, which is kind of fun, considering the pompous idiots he has to deal with as leader of the country of Freedonia. Harpo's big physical gags with horns, shears, and other props concealed in his voluminous clothing will please, as will Chico with his Tyrolean hat, Italian accent, and sassy attitude.

Plot is certainly loose-form, but fortunately for young viewers, identifiable things do happen. Rufus T. Firefly (Groucho) is put in charge of the country and, through deliberate neglect and outrageous behavior, marches it straight into war with neighboring Sylvania. All of it is completely stupid, as it's supposed to be, and much of the inferences about war and politics can be shared with children.

For instance, how does a crude little man like Firefly get to be head of an entire country in the first place? All the movie tells us is that an heiress named Mrs. Teasdale (Margaret Dumont, who frequently played the matronly foil for Groucho) has decided she won't give another $20 million to Freedonia (forever broke despite its retinue of formally clad officials) unless it appoints Firefly as leader. And she means supreme leader, no matter how crazy or stupid. Teasdale is stupid herself, of course, a kind of numb one-woman body politic veering off on a lunatic tangent. Why she centers on Firefly is never explained. Teasdale allows that he reminds her of her late, revered husband, but how is anyone's guess.

It's a question that has some current application. What did we do, or not do, to deserve the people who lead us? In fact, where exactly is Firefly? An elaborate welcoming ceremony with blaring trumpet flourishes and maidens strewing flower petals produces no one.

Finally Firefly materializes as one of the greeters on the edge of the crowd. He wonders what's going on. Mrs. Teasdale extends the welcome of every citizen of Freedonia and the film indulges in the first of its non sequiturs. Firefly tells her to forget that and pick a card. She asks what she should do with it and he tells her to keep it. He has fifty-one left.

It took at least four writers to supply the machine-mouthed Groucho with enough gags like this to last a movie. Many of them are flat-out dumb (albeit sounding all right coming from Groucho), but they help stoke an atmosphere of nonsensical chaos. Freedonia, which looks like a little mountain kingdom out of an operetta, is bordered by Sylvania, which happens to look just like Freedonia. In fact, Sylvania is Freedonia in one scene, perhaps as a budgetary consideration. Unlike Freedonia, Sylvania is represented by a suave diplomat (Louis Calhern) who would like to take over Freedonia by marrying Teasdale. War becomes inevitable, so much so that when Firefly decides that peace makes more sense he has to talk himself out of that notion and back into a fighting mood.

Firefly's determined nonsensicalness turns off some viewers. The brothers themselves had that effect. The film's director, Leo McCarey, won an Oscar for the screwball comedy *The Awful Truth* (1937), starring Cary Grant and Irene Dunne, and worked with the likes of W. C. Fields, Mae West, and Harold Lloyd. In his book *Who the Devil Made It: Conversations with Legendary Film Directors,* the filmmaker Peter Bogdanovich asked McCarey how he liked working with the brothers on *Duck Soup.* McCarey replied that he didn't. "They were too irresponsible," he said. "The amazing thing about that movie was that I succeeded in not going crazy. They were completely mad."

Nazism was on the rise in 1933 and the Depression rolled on. In the film the war between Freedonia and Sylvania is an amalgam of the Civil War and World War I and is fought with glib insouciance. Some viewers resented remarks about soldiers being suckers and cracks about treating gas attacks with bicarbonate of soda. The film flopped when it was released, but was revived by college students in the 1960s and now is generally regarded as a brilliant piece of satire. The critic Roger Ebert wrote that we tend to like films, shows, and people who appear to get away with something: *Some Like It Hot, The Producers,* Monty Python, *South Park,* Howard Stern.

"There is a kind of admiration for material that dares something against the rules and yet is obvious," Ebert wrote in *Roger Ebert: The Great Movies.*

But Firefly might go too far with Chicolini (Chico):

FIREFLY: "Now go out there on that battlefield and lead those men to victory."

CHICOLINI: "I wouldn't go out there unless I was in one of those big iron things that go up and down like this. What do you call those things?"

FIREFLY: "Tanks."

CHICOLINI: "You're welcome."

Not all children will like this film, but there is enough physical comedy and craziness to appeal to most. There is some slapstick violence of a mild nature, but no profanity. As for sex, a bit of mild innuendo passes between Firefly and the torchy Vera Marcal (Raquel Torres), who is dispatched to distract him while the ambassador woos Teasdale, but this is nothing to worry about.

27. EDWARD SCISSORHANDS

Johnny Depp, Winona Ryder, Dianne Wiest, Alan Arkin, Anthony Michael Hall, Vincent Price, Robert Oliveri

DIRECTED BY TIM BURTON
1990. 100 minutes. PG-13

Inching nervously into the towering entry hall of a fearsome and seemingly deserted hilltop castle, the bespectacled Peg Boggs (Dianne

Wiest) puts on her cheeriest suburban smile. "Avon calling," she cries out into the eerie void. It remains one of the movies' better hellos. Upstairs, far upstairs, she will come across a strange, shy boy of about eighteen in black leather with a scarred, chalk-white face and several sizes of scissors for hands. At least the movie's title refers to them as scissors. The longer blades hanging from each arm are shears, and the longest, from the looks of the splendid topiary in the gardens below, are used to trim hedges.

The thunderstruck Peg supposes she'll just be leaving now and sorry to disturb. Edward (Johnny Depp) advances a step toward her and tells her that he's "not finished," which alarms her all the more. Of course, he's referring to the fact that he has no hands. As we learn later, he is the creation of The Inventor (Vincent Price), who equipped Edward with shears for fingers and died just as he was presenting him with a pair of hands with human digits.

How did such characters as Edward and The Inventor wind up in such a great old pile of a place looming in such proximity to Peg's candy-cane suburbia? Kids should realize that we are in a Tim Burton fairy tale. As in *James and the Giant Peach* (see page 134), the Roald Dahl story Burton helped adapt for the screen, the view is darker, more cynical, and more sophisticated than Disney. The castle is huge beyond any sense of reality, as if it belongs in a dream. In contrast to the groomed gardens, it's wonderfully fall-down decrepit. Kids will relate to Edward's loneliness and pain. As we see later, he has no idea how to get food into his mouth, so we don't know how he has fed himself. (If hands weren't available, maybe a knife and fork would have been more practical than scissors.)

Clutching her Avon case, Peg may be an agent of banality, but suddenly she becomes a fairy godmother. Edward often cuts himself accidentally, as Depp occasionally did while wearing the scissors to prepare for the movie. "A good astringent to help prevent infection," says Peg, swabbing him with lotion from her case.

Depp was considered a brooding type, but this is the role that established his sensitivity. Peg is charmed by Edward. Nothing will do but to take him home with her, to which he certainly doesn't object. Heading down the hill into suburbia, he rides in her car with a look of quiet delight. In search of a nondescript place, Burton went to

Florida and rented fifty houses in a subdivision east of Tampa. He describes conditions as harsh. The heat was oppressive, and the bugs drove the cast and crew crazy. The locals were invited to participate as extras, but they got tired, bored, and as exhausted by the conditions as the movie people, so they left. Burton painted their houses various pastel colors, which adds to the dreamlike quality and the incongruity of the great Transylvanian castle that looms above them.

Burton says he drew someone with scissors for hands when he was a teenager living in Burbank, California, and the image stuck. The year before this film he had made *Batman,* one of the biggest money-makers of all time. Before that there was *Beetlejuice* (see page 30). Warner, the *Batman* studio, passed on *Edward Scissorhands,* but 20th Century Fox jumped at it. "Like a lot of things—*Pinocchio, E.T.*—it's both very new and very familiar," said Fox chairman Joe Roth, as quoted in *Tim Burton* by Jim Smith and J. Clive Matthews. "It takes something that is very odd and lets it show what's right about us and what's wrong about us."

What's right is the Boggs family. Following Peg's lead, the rest of the Boggses do their best to treat Edward with an open mind. Wiest, terrific in any kind of role, had played mother figures in such films as *Footloose, The Lost Boys, Bright Lights, Big City,* and *Parenthood,* and would do so again in *Little Man Tate* (see page 161). Burton calls her the film's steadying hand. Alan Arkin stays cool as Bill Boggs, a father who takes it as it comes. The closest in age to Edward, Kim Boggs (Winona Ryder), falls in love with him as a high school senior and as an old woman who relates the Scissorhands story to her grandchild.

Puns abound about scissor hands as metaphor. Edward is simply cut off, left alone forever on the outside. He talks and understands what is said to him, but no one can know what he feels. "It's in the inability to communicate, the inability to touch, being at odds with yourself. How you are perceived as opposed to what you are," Burton says in *Tim Burton.*

And how is he perceived in the suburbs? Here life is managed by a gaggle of women who at the first sign of anything the least bit odd—which in a place this sterile could be anything at all out of the ordinary—burn up the telephone lines and gather on street corners. On the DVD, Burton says that in Burbank when he was growing up, people never emerged or communicated unless it was to pounce on a piece of neighborly misfortune. In this film, he dresses the gaggle garishly and has them act accordingly. To a one, the women he cast—particularly Kathy Baker as Joyce, the ringleader—are superb at making the normal weird and vice versa.

For a while they love Edward, who cuts complex paper dolls at school show-and-tells, sculpts bushes into fancy figures, gives dogs and ladies stylized haircuts, slashes away at big blocks of ice at Christmas, and has everybody cooing when he says how wonderful everything is in a televised interview. For Edward, though, it can't last. Trouble arises from one misadventure, and misperceptions escalate. As quickly as it embraced him, the town turns on him. Then another incident, again misperceived, fans the situation and sets up a showdown with Kim's brutal boyfriend, Jim (Anthony Michael Hall).

Burton's fairy tale ends violently in the castle when Edward in self-defense gives Jim a blade to the midsection. Criticized for springing such a confrontation so suddenly in a movie without serious violence before this, Burton said that fairy tales are symbolic and the violence is abstract. You be the judge. On the DVD he praises Fox for resisting Hollywood's usual insistence on a happy ending. "I was always grateful I didn't have to go through that struggle," he says.

The book has numerous movies for littlest ones, and here's one for eleven- and twelve-year-olds, though a "mature" ten might sneak in. Kids will love Edward, Kim, and the Boggs family, and they will understand Edward's plight. If they don't understand all the nuances of the suburban scene, they will find the neighbors amusing. Later on when the climate turns ugly, some scenes could be threatening. The fight at the castle is certainly violent, but it is brief and nothing most young viewers haven't seen before. There is no sex and moderate profanity.

28. EMMA

Gwyneth Paltrow, Jeremy Northam, Ewan McGregor, Toni Collette, Alan Cumming, Edward Woodall, Greta Scacchi, Polly Walker, Sophie Thompson

DIRECTED BY DOUGLAS MCGRATH
1996. 120 minutes. PG

Since Emma (Gwyneth Paltrow) is so involved with arranging marriages for other people, why isn't she strategizing one for herself? "I have no inducements to marrying," she says airily. "I lack neither fortune or position and never could I be so important in a man's eyes as I am in my father's." From nineteenth-century English gentry, she is twenty-two and lives at home with her elderly parent. Emma loves her father, who provides a convenient cover. Certainly there is no hurry to commit herself. "It is only poverty that makes celibacy so contemptible," she declares. "A single woman of good fortune is always respectable."

Many children will see through that bit of posturing. All her guises and declarations don't help Jane Austen's matchmaker. Paltrow calls Emma a true solipsist, unable to see beyond her own experience. That finishes her as a romantic handicapper, as does her reliance on class distinction, almost to the exclusion of any other reason people should be together. Austen's book asks something more from Emma than does Douglas McGrath's adaptation. "One of the most important lessons Emma must learn in the novel is the error of her own false sense of class superiority," Carol M. Dole wrote in *Jane Austen in Hollywood*, a collection of essays. Essentially a romantic comedy, McGrath's film doesn't go that far. Emma realizes she has seriously misled people, for which she is genuinely sorry, but one doesn't sense too much of a stand-down from her insular views.

When they're a little older, kids will love *Clueless* (1995), Amy

Heckerling's R-rated take on *Emma*, with Alicia Silverstone as a Beverly Hills High School matchmaker named Cher. Austen's stories— *Sense and Sensibility, Pride and Prejudice, Persuasion, Mansfield Park, Northanger Abbey*—have been made into more than a dozen films and television productions. Many are very fine, but this *Emma*, McGrath's first feature, is a good way into Austen for children from about the age of eight.

McGrath wrote for *Saturday Night Live* and cowrote the Oscar-nominated screenplay for *Bullets Over Broadway* (1994) with Woody Allen. "I thought Jane Austen would be a good collaborator because she writes . . . superb dialogue, she creates memorable characters, she has an extremely clever skill for plotting," he told Todd Purdum in the *New York Times*. "And she's dead, which means, you know, there's none of that tiresome arguing over who gets the bigger bun at coffee time."

Like numerous filmmakers before him, McGrath has good fun with our obsessions with English class. Much in Austen, Dole wrote, "meshes perfectly with contradictory American attitudes, which combine the rhetoric of equality with the practice of social stratification based on education, income, race, and ethnicity." Adults find all this delicious, or perhaps repulsive, but for children the film introduces a cultural and historical otherworld. Some kids wonder how these people have time to be so totally preoccupied with such foolishness. Does no one work?

Movies have always loved such social manipulation. McGrath wanted the film to have the breezy feeling of a Hollywood romantic comedy of the '30s and '40s. *Emma* never turns into screwball, but there is a taste of it. Paltrow glides through the film "with an elegance and patrician wit that brings the young Katharine Hepburn to mind," the critic Janet Maslin wrote in the *Times*. "And as with Hepburn, that very refinement turns sly, bestowing a serenely polite veneer upon her character's sneaky meddlsome tricks."

Kids will get caught up in the entanglements. At the center is Harriet (Toni Collette), an eager young woman who is both well-off and illegitimate, making her a tricky proposition in Emma's scheme of things. Turning her into a kind of test case, Emma plugs poor Harriet into various potential matches. Emma supposes that Harriet is above the farmer Mr. Martin (whom Harriet eventually marries) but suitable for the clergyman Mr. Elton (Alan Cumming). Elton, of course, has designs on Emma, a presumptuous overstepping in her estimation. And who to pair with Frank Churchill (Ewan McGregor)? Harriet maybe, since Elton, rebuffed by Emma, has run off to Bath and married more according to his own pompous assessment of himself. But Churchill, supposedly attracted to Emma, goes off and gets engaged to Miss Fairfax (Polly Walker)—without Emma's knowledge, let alone approval.

As for Emma, she isn't as impervious as she thought, but she has become so turned about she doesn't know how she feels. Churchill, or so she guesses, has given her reason to suppose he's in love with her, so until his defection with Miss Fairfax, she supposes she's in love with him. As Emma will eventually discover, of course, she is really in love with her rich, high-born friend and brother-in-law Mr. Knightly (Jeremy Northam), who may be sixteen years older but is the most substantial of the lot, male or female.

Knightly looks askance at Emma's plotting and points out, for example, that Martin is a perfectly respectable mate for Harriet. He also catches Emma up in an interesting social gaffe that leaps jarringly out of nowhere in the film. At a picnic gathering of Emma's circle, a word game is proposed. Clever, witty sayings will be rewarded; three dull ones amount to disqualification. When the simple, well-meaning Miss Bates (Sophie Thompson) offers to play, Emma says Bates had better not because she will be limited to only three dull sayings.

Everybody is appalled by Emma's rudeness, which is sudden and quite odd. Knightly is so put off by her bad behavior he goes traveling for a while, a typical withdrawal for a gentleman of that period in times of duress. But for all her affectation, Emma is greatly upset when she sees that she has hurt someone. After she sheds a few tears, Knightly returns, the incident is forgotten, and we are set for a glorious finale with everybody snug in their cocoons.

These are movie stars, remember, not figures from the page. The film was designed to make Paltrow's career. "Paltrow cannot avoid her reputation as the golden girl," Nora Nachumi wrote in *Jane Austen in Hollywood*. After all, at the time she had just landed

Brad Pitt, so Knightly may seem to be easy pickings. "Moreover," Nachumi continued, "as a star, Paltrow's apparent perfection works against the notion that Emma must get off her pedestal and rejoin the human race. Despite her faults, this Emma ends the movie where she begins it, firmly fixed upon Mount Olympus."

The film is fine for all who can keep up with the twists and turns. There is no sex or profanity.

29. E.T. THE EXTRA-TERRESTRIAL

Henry Thomas, Drew Barrymore, Robert MacNaughton, Dee Wallace Stone, Peter Coyote

DIRECTED BY STEVEN SPIELBERG
1982. 115 minutes. PG

Five years after *Close Encounters of the Third Kind,* Steven Spielberg was back with the same message: aliens, be they creatures or ideas, needn't be the menaces we insist on making them. Young viewers will understand this. It's also no surprise that kids take the lead in both Spielberg space films because children approach aliens with an open mind.

In *Encounters* (see page 66), a toddler goes off with them like a miniature Dorothy. *E.T.,* Vincent Canby observed in the *New York Times,* flips *The Wizard of Oz* upside down. Dorothy lands here in the form of a stumpy, leathery-skinned little space fellow left behind when his mother ship has to blast off in a hurry to avoid advancing humans. Kansas is outer space; Oz is the California subdivision where E.T. takes refuge in a backyard toolshed.

The story was Spielberg's idea and can be told in a sentence: E.T. must reestablish contact with his kind and arrange a rescue. Kids expedite the arrangements on Earth after a ten-year-old named Elliott (Henry Thomas) discovers the alien in his yard. The two exchange screams of terror, but unlike many of the adults in the story, Elliott has the presence of mind to accept what he sees before him and approach it with a gentle curiosity. Soon his teenage brother, Michael (Robert MacNaughton), is in on the secret and finally his little sister, Gertie (Drew Barrymore), who is full of wry observations. Later, friends will pitch in to get the alien back where he belongs.

It's the adults in the movie who are strange. That doesn't include the kids' harried mother (Dee Wallace Stone), who has recently separated from her husband and in her slightly crazed state of perpetual exasperation is a perfectly homey and familiar figure. But many of the other grown-ups, including security and scientific personnel, are vague, shadowy types, backlit, threatening, unidentifiable, unknowable—in other words, exactly how a lot of other movies would characterize the aliens.

The story "comes directly from my childhood fantasies," Spielberg said in an interview in *Premiere* magazine. "Part of it evolves from my childhood and my friends as I knew them growing up, and the other part of it evolves from a yen to bring outer space down to earth for a very personal, seductive meeting of the minds."

In 2002, on its twentieth anniversary, Spielberg reissued the film with a couple of new scenes added and some digital adjustments. A new generation of critics is also on hand. "*E.T.* is at once a great movie about children and a great movie for children," A. O. Scott wrote this year in the *Times*.

The relentless pursuit of E.T. is already on as the movie begins. In the new version, Spielberg uses computer-generated imagery to remove the guns from the hands of police officers and replace them with walkie-talkies. He had wanted to do that for some time. "I regret that a gun was used as a threat to stop children on bicycles," he said in a 1995 interview. "I really regret having any guns in the movie."

But guns aren't the issue. The enforcement people are strangers on their own planet. One exception is Keys (Peter Coyote), the doctor who heads the medical team frantically trying to revive E.T. after he becomes diseased with earth's pollution. Only the kids are aware that the alien isn't dead at all, after which it's up and away on that grand bike ride with E.T. evading the cops, into the sky and across the sun to the place in the redwoods where the mother ship will land for the pickup.

In lesser hands than Spielberg's the film might drown in sentimentality, which is indeed the fate of most of the crass extravaganzas foisted on kids today. True, at the very end Spielberg lets John Williams's score get loud, leading to "an all-out assault on the emotions that depends, it seems, more on the rising volume of this music than on the events portrayed," Canby wrote in the *Times*.

Otherwise, Spielberg runs a very tight production. The mark of a truly great filmmaker is all over this movie. One reason the fantasy works well is that it is so well set in reality. No one presents the crash and clutter of suburban family living like Spielberg. Dad's off with the new girlfriend in Mexico, and Mom's so rushed and stressed she can barely slam the groceries in the fridge, jam a thermometer in her kid's mouth (he's faking so he can stay home to get better acquainted with the alien), and back the car out of the driveway without wiping out the trash barrels. In the house, shelves collapse, oceans of milk go flying, and mountains of every piece of junk anyone has ever bought for their kids are in a constant state of avalanche. No wonder Elliott is level-headed and cool under fire.

This may be the greatest children's movie ever made. There is some scuffling, and the occasional obscenity gets loose. Very small kids could be scared when E.T. is pursued through a cornfield. They might also be upset by the skulking security types, and they could well be disturbed by E.T.'s apparent demise in the care of the fumbling earthly medical establishment. In the main, though, the film holds up perfectly, an American institution and an absolute must for everybody from about the age of six up.

30. FIDDLER ON THE ROOF

Topol, Norma Crane, Leonard Frey, Molly Picon, Paul Mann, Rosalind Harris, Michele Marsh, Paul Michael Glaser, Neva Small

DIRECTED BY NORMAN JEWISON

1971. 181 minutes. G

Topol, the thirty-five-year-old Israeli actor who plays Tevye in Jewison's film, was young to be the film's father of three marriageable daughters, so before each day's shooting gray hairs were plucked from Jewison's head and glued onto Topol's eyebrows. However regularly that was done, the transplant adds a small detail to a large canvas.

Kids and parents will share a famous story told as captivatingly and movingly as any in a movie musical. "The film is about the breaking down of traditions in a family," Jewison says. That's certainly a familiar theme, and to it add the glories and sorrows of parenting and inevitable separation. The film also explores poverty and the art of thriving materially and spiritually on as little as possible. God in his so-called mercy ("Don't do me anymore favors," the beleaguered Tevye implores Him) is also inveighed as religious oppression takes away one way of life and opens opportunity for another.

The critic Pauline Kael describes *Fiddler* as one of the root stories of American life. It begins in a Russian shtetl at the turn of the twentieth century and ends with Tevye and his family driven from their village and on their migration to America. *Fiddler* is drawn from the short stories of Sholom Aleichem, the so-called Jewish Mark Twain. On Broadway, it was directed and choreographed by Jerome Robbins. The music and lyrics for stage and film, as memorable as any, are by Jerry Bock and Sheldon Harnick.

Jewison began his film at dawn in honor of the song "Sunrise, Sunset," which is sung later at his daughter's wedding. The fiddler on the roof, framed against the morning sky as he energetically saws away, was inspired by the figure from the Chagall painting *The Musician*. On the DVD, the director explains that in most Jewish shtetls south of Kiev there was a clarinetist, a bass player, and a drum. Like everything else, music was a tradition. Ironically, Jewison, whose name means son of a Jew, is a gentile and had to school himself hard and long in the ways of Jewish tradition.

In the film tradition is shattered when Tevye's three oldest daughters marry husbands of their own choosing and not Tevye's. All three disappoint their father, but they do so respectfully, lovingly, and firmly with strong support from their spouses-to-be. Tevye doesn't make the best judge of marital material anyway. In the case of his oldest daughter (Rosalind Harris), he prefers a prospective son-in-law who is older than he is. True, the fellow is prosperous, which can't be said about his daughter's choice, a penniless tailor (Leonard Frey, who received an Oscar nomination for best supporting actor).

Faced with the inevitable, Tevye consents to the tailor, and he reluctantly also goes along with his next youngest daughter (Michele Marsh), who falls in love with a political radical (Paul Michael Glaser) finally banished to Siberia. Earlier she had told Tevye that the pair wasn't asking his permission, but they would like his blessing. Late in the film she goes to join her husband after a wonderfully executed and truly heartbreaking farewell with her father at a wintry and desolate rail stop.

But the youngest of the three daughters, Chava (Neva Small), goes too far and marries a gentile. Tevye all but disowns her, but there is a flicker of reconciliation as he and the remainder of the family start their long trek to America while Chava and her husband trudge off in another direction. Again there is a powerful feeling of separation.

This is a big, magnificent-looking film, full of richly detailed village life. Jewison describes his cinematographer, Oswald Morris, as an eccentric Englishman who insisted on shooting the entire movie with a silk stocking stretched over the lens to mellow and enrich the scene. Jewison allowed that, though the vast skies sometimes look a little brown. At home the film looks best on DVD and a big screen.

Jewison made *Fiddler* in Yugoslavia. His actors were mostly Eastern European Jews chosen for their heritage and looks. On Broadway, Zero Mostel was renowned as Tevye, but Jewison felt that his stage style was too comedic for the film. On-screen, Tevye needed to be a more realistic figure, darker and larger, more expansive and into the rural peasant life.

And so it was with the music. Onstage, of course, songs stand as little dramas in and of themselves, usually in a spotlight and sometimes culminating in a blackout. In a film, no one stops and there is no dimming of the lights. Jewison wove the numbers into the action. "We wanted it staged so that everybody kept moving with the musical numbers, so that it was a dramatic story that broke into song." So while Tevye tells us "I Wish I Were a Rich Man," he practically does a full morning's work.

Children will begin to enjoy the film around the age of eight. Older kids should love it. Remember, though, that it is hugely long and contains an intermission. So take a break, maybe several breaks. Realize too that there is some violence when goons in the employ of the village commissar attack the wedding of Tevye's oldest daughter and pretty much wreck the place. Later mounted Cossacks attack a political rally in Moscow, but the violence is brief and not that graphic. Still, these scenes could upset some young viewers. There is no sex or profanity.

31. FIELD OF DREAMS

Kevin Costner, Amy Madigan, James Earl Jones, Ray Liotta, Burt Lancaster, Gaby Hoffmann, Timothy Busfield

DIRECTED BY PHIL ALDEN ROBINSON

1989. 107 minutes. PG

If Phil Alden Robinson's film proves one thing, it's that sentiment doesn't have to be sappy. That may come as news to kids and their parents stuck with the sticky and manipulative glop that passes for honest feeling in most mainstream movies today. True, unbridled schmaltz appeals to many viewers, otherwise Hollywood wouldn't indulge in it so blatantly and repeatedly. It's also true that some kids might not be bothered by overblown emotion as much as their parents (or maybe that's the other way around). Nevertheless, it can be argued that too much schmaltz can make a tiresome exercise of an otherwise entertaining experience.

Field of Dreams walks the narrow edge. The year is 1978. When Ray Kinsella (Kevin Costner), a Berkeley-educated farmer in Iowa City, hears a voice from the beyond tell him, "If you build it, they will come," he turns a cornfield into a ball yard designed to entice Shoeless Joe Jackson and his mates from the scandal-ridden 1919 Chicago White Sox back from the beyond to frisk around the diamond once again.

Dreams are involved, and individualism, and just about every value this country holds holy. "Field of corn," says a director of another popular baseball picture. Spiritually, though, the film itself strays into the corn (as in cornball) only infrequently. "The fact that I don't believe in voices or ESP or reincarnation enabled me to tell the story in a way that touches a lot of people who don't believe in the cosmic," Robinson says in a director's commentary on the DVD.

A lot of critics would go along with that. "A work so smartly written, so beautifully filmed, so perfectly acted, that it does the almost impossible trick of turning sentimentality into true emotion," Caryn James wrote in the *New York Times*.

Robinson adapted his film from the acclaimed novel by W. P. Kinsella, no relation to Ray, whose surname is a nod of appreciation to the writer. Bill Kinsella tried the idea on at the Iowa Writers Workshop. He had heard some stories from his father about Shoeless Joe, the best known of the players who threw the 1919 World Series. Kinsella started his book as a short story about Jackson and kept going from there.

On the DVD, Bill Kinsella says, "To write in the fantastical, you have to have an extraordinary grip on reality. You can be in the here and now and appreciate the what-if quality." Perhaps. In the film and on the page, Shoeless Joe was a hero of Ray Kinsella's father, and the son uses the field and Jackson's "resurrection" to reconnect with that father, whom he still blames for dying young. Ray Kinsella's restless energy and pushy intelligence wear well on Costner, and Kinsella has a spirited, supportive wife (Amy Madigan), a '70s Berkeley soul mate to back him up when Ray's dreams and stubbornness get him into financial straits.

Costner describes the film as a kind of *It's a Wonderful Life* for the '80s. As with many ideas that don't make marketing sense (see *To Kill a Mockingbird,* page 281), the studios were initially hostile to the idea. The film was too esoteric. Larry Gordon, one of the film's producers, says that even he went back and forth on the idea. When he helped pitch the film, he said it was his favorite project. Then he became president of 20th Century Fox, and as a studio head he felt obliged to turn it down. Reminded that it had been his favorite project, he then agreed to it, telling Robinson that it was good he had the right script and talent because they were going to take a lot of knocks. "Everybody wants to say no in this business," Gordon says. "It's much safer."

Then Gordon left Fox, and *Field of Dreams* was again adrift. Finally, Universal agreed to make the picture. An Iowa farm couple provided the property, which Robinson pretty much reconstructed inside and out. Shoeless Joe and others emerge from and retreat back to the netherworld through a field of high corn. Getting it to an adequate height proved a major problem. There was a drought and the field had to be irrigated. Brown grass had to be continually painted green.

The movie is about dreams, ideals, death, and what it means. By age ten most children will be caught up in a film that provides nothing in the way of big-game action but still is a gripping experience. The performances are wonderful. In real life Shoeless Joe was a simple southern boy without a lot to say for himself. "I wanted an edge of danger about him," says Robinson, who cast Ray Liotta in the role because he projected strength and mystery. Burt Lancaster is a thoughtful, charming Archibald "Moonlight" Graham, a player from the Jackson era who got into one big-league game before becoming a small-town doctor of distinction in Minnesota.

Ray goes to find Graham in the company of Terence Mann (James Earl Jones), a famous and cantankerously reclusive writer from the

'60s who serves as a bridge between Kinsella's private vision and the beliefs and ideals of a larger world. In the novel Mann represents the famously reclusive J. D. Salinger, who strenuously objected to the use of his name and threatened to sue if appropriated for the film.

The shoot began in May 1988. Costner had just made *Bull Durham,* and it was feared that he had just so much baseball movie in him. While he still brought freshness to the subject, Costner did have to leave for another project by August 15. Robinson describes himself as a seriously nervous type who was in a continual state of panic and at times close to fleeing the set. Daily rushes revealed little about how well the movie was doing, which is frequently the way with dramas, as opposed to action films or comedies with more immediately apparent visual payoffs.

On the surface, the days came and went. Very little happens over long stretches on a movie set. Bill Kinsella showed up to watch but quickly got bored and left. It was very hot. "The flies in Iowa. Man, they're serious," Jones says on the disc. "It's the manure, you know."

This is a beautifully visual film, but there is a lot of talk and much to get hold of for children under, say, nine. You know your kids, so you decide. There is no sex and little profanity.

32. FLY AWAY HOME

Anna Paquin, Jeff Daniels, Dana Delany, Terry Kinney

DIRECTED BY CARROLL BALLARD
1996. 107 minutes. PG

Lindbergh didn't have a better welcome. As a crowd of hundreds in a North Carolina wildlife refuge anxiously peruse the skies, a tiny ultralight craft with a thirteen-year-old girl at the controls materializes out of the blue, glides in, and smoothly sets down on a dirt path. Landing with her are a dozen geese. All have flown in tight formation from Ontario, Canada.

The acclaimed documentary *Winged Migration* lets us fly with birds, but here the adventure is fiction. Many filmmakers will tell you that three things they could do without on the set are animals, children, and unruly weather. Ballard, though, is a magician with animals on-screen, as is amply evident in *The Black Stallion* (1979) and *Never Cry Wolf* (1983), both included in this book (see pages 36 and 206). This time he decided on geese after watching a segment on the *20/20* television news magazine about a Canadian sculptor and inventor named Bill Lishman, who in real life escorted the birds by plane on their way south.

In the film Lishman becomes Thomas Alden (Jeff Daniels). The ultralight pilot is Alden's thirteen-year-old daughter, Amy, played by Anna Paquin, who three years earlier won an Oscar as best supporting actress in *The Piano*. So when it came to children Ballard wasn't exactly saddled with a neophyte. As for the weather, it stays pretty much gorgeous. Amy, a New Zealander (as is Anna Paquin), goes to live in Canada with her father after her mother is killed in a car crash. No child will be able to resist this film, but young ones may have a tough time coping with her mother's death, which isn't shown graphically but is played obliquely in a dark, rainy setting behind the opening credits.

We next see Amy in a hospital bed with her head bandaged and her face cut and swollen. Her father delivers the news, but he doesn't have to. She knows. Once again a children's movie kills off a mother so that the child can venture forth on her own. Here, of course, the loss of a mother will play out thematically with parental loss in the natural world. Still, it's a load for the little ones in an otherwise thrilling adventure.

The wildlife makes this picture. To fill lonely hours in Ontario, Amy raises a dozen orphaned goslings who pop out of eggs she rescues from a nest destroyed by a bulldozer. A game warden tries to clip their wings but gets swatted with a cooking pan and thrown out of the Alden house. But if they are to fly in the right direction, it is mandatory that they learn the winter migratory route taken by wild geese. Without elders to guide them off the ground, that won't happen.

The idea occurs that Amy might lead the way. Through a process called imprinting, the stumpy-winged little yellow fluff balls come to regard her as a surrogate mother and race around after her wherever she goes. When migration time comes about six months later, Alden decides to see if they will follow his daughter into the air.

He and his daughter are Hollywood inventions, but the real-life Lishman, a mercurial character from the woodlands, had spent years trying to help a variety of birds with migratory problems brought on by destruction of traditional landing areas and other environmental encroachments. The DVD has a good documentary about Lishman. He was an inveterate builder of ultralight aircraft, tiny gossamer-winged, open-seated erector-set affairs powered by what looks like little more than a lawn mower engine. One day he found himself flying in the midst of thousands of ducks headed south. As is documented on the DVD, Lishman not only aided ducks and geese, but tried to help cranes and swans. But the bigger birds weren't as aggressive or physically adaptable as geese, who took off from land and would run beside the ultralight as it left the ground.

The route to North Carolina is carefully charted, much the way Lishman did it in real life. The flight, at thirty-two miles per hour, proceeds in legs across Lake Ontario and then southward with several overnight stops. Amy flies the lead ultralight with the geese strung out beside her. Her father follows in another ultralight.

During training sessions Tom Alden urges his daughter to drive the birds hard. Wild geese are used to covering a thousand miles and are a lot tougher than domesticated birds. In life, Lishman had trouble keeping his geese together and accountable, especially after landing. On-screen Ballard's geese stay right on the mark. It is a spectacular piece of filmmaking, free and soaring and pumping with energy. At one point a fog breaks and the whole procession whizzes among the skyscrapers of downtown Toronto.

Suddenly, Hollywood just has to take a hand with some late dramatics. Tom's plane develops a problem and down he goes. (Other than a wrenched shoulder, he's fine.) Now the movie has set up Amy to carry on alone with her geese. Maybe that's as it should be, even though Dad had the idea in the first place.

The "mother thing" is over with at the start of the film, but it's strong and it resonates later. By then most kids will be caught up in Ballard's green world, the wonders of Tom Alden's workshop, the very lifelike sensations of being aloft during flight, and, of course, the geese, plucky strivers all. Any age is a good age for this film, depending on how parents feel about the opener.

33. GANDHI

Ben Kingsley, Candice Bergen, Edward Fox, John Gielgud, Trevor Howard, Geraldine James, Roshan Seth, Rohini Hattangady, Martin Sheen

DIRECTED BY RICHARD ATTENBOROUGH
1982. 188 minutes. PG

Early in Richard Attenborough's film, Gandhi (Ben Kingsley) arrives by train amid a teeming mob waiting to greet him. The British rule India, and Gandhi, recently returned from South Africa, has only begun to become a political force, but already he has generated a mystique that precedes him. The crowd appears to have materialized from nowhere. "He is coming," someone says. "Who the hell is he?" another asks.

Gandhi may be one of the most famous figures of the twentieth century, but that doesn't mean kids, or their parents, can identify him. One short answer might be that as spiritual leader of millions of Indians struggling toward independence, achieved in 1947, he personified methods of nonviolent disobedience that became the model for the civil rights movement in this country in the 1960s.

In South Africa, where Gandhi agitated for human rights before returning to India in 1915, he describes himself as a representative of an ancient civilization with rights as inviolable as any other. "Why shouldn't we walk as other men?" he asks racist authorities. Before Indian independence, he tells the people they must defy the British "not with the violence that will enflame them, but with the firmness that will open their eyes."

Nonviolent resistance, called *satyagraha,* recalls the pacifism of Martin Luther King Jr., but the film also has connections to September 11 and fanaticism and strife from Afghanistan to Kashmir and Iraq. After India's independence, Gandhi and Jawaharlal Nehru, the prime minister and Gandhi's longtime friend and political ally, struggled to stem violence between Hindus and Muslims. Gandhi himself fell victim and was assassinated by a fanatic in 1948. If nothing else, the film points to a huge and complicated world for American kids and their parents to contemplate.

Kingsley, a British stage actor in his second film, provides the mesmerizingly powerful physical and emotional presence that every big film needs to grip audiences. Half-Indian, his facial features strongly resemble Gandhi's, and his high purpose and immaculate theatrical training help build a convincing persona.

This is not a movie to fall in love with. It is riveting in many places, a little stiff in others. It certainly is huge and colorful—and long. In theaters there was an intermission. Attenborough wouldn't be thrilled at this recommendation, but at home you can break up the movie any way you like. "It has huge, rather emotionless scenes of spectacle that are the background for more or less obligatory historical confrontations in governors' palaces and, best of all, for intimate, small-scale vignettes from Gandhi's life," Vincent Canby wrote in the *New York Times*.

Attenborough, who was knighted in 1976, is the director of *Chaplin, A Bridge Too Far,* and *Young Winston,* among other films, but he may be better known as an actor in films like *Jurassic Park* (see page 137), in which he plays an authoritative type who oversteps himself. It took him eighteen years to sell Hollywood on a film about "a little brown guy in a sheet," as studio people regarded the Mahatma, or "Great Soul," as he was called by his followers.

A caption at the start of the film reads: "No man's life can be encompassed in one telling. There is no way to give each year its allotted weight, to include each event, each person, who helped to shape a lifetime. What can be done is to be faithful in spirit to the record and to try to find one's way to the heart of the man."

The film sticks to historical events presented in textbook fashion, which may be the easiest way to handle this story and certainly a valuable one for kids following the developments. Crowds are immense. Even smaller moments seem outsized. The conflict is epic and extreme, such as the massacre at Amritsar when British troops shot down hundreds of demonstrators. "The problem, though, is that all films about saintly men tend to look alike," Canby wrote in the *Times*. "That's one of the limitations of what is called the 'grammar' of conventional filmmaking. We are shown saintliness not in terms of ideas but in terms of far more easily dramatized scenes of confrontation and physical courage."

Still there is much to be learned. The film is criticized for ignoring Gandhi's bad relations with his children, his tempting of himself with young women, and his obsessions with diet and his bowels, among other peculiarities. "Unquestionably, he was cranky," Mr. Attenborough told Barbara Crossette in the *Times*. "He had idiosyncrasies . . . but they were relatively minor parts of his life."

Nehru gave the movie his blessing. When the filming started in India, Attenborough told Crossette, "Nehru willingly said to me: 'Look, he had all the frailties, all the shortcomings. Give us that. That's the measure, the greatness of the man.'" Gandhi certainly had a dry sense of humor. Close to death during one of his fasts, he suggests to an overweight colleague that perhaps he should join him.

As indicated, this isn't a film for small children on any level. The massacre at Amritsar is graphic and prolonged with ranks of troops shooting down men, women, and children. Protesters are clubbed down, and during religious rioting women and children are dragged off to their deaths. There is no sex or profanity.

34. GHOSTBUSTERS

Bill Murray, Dan Aykroyd, Harold Ramis, Sigourney Weaver, Rick Moranis, Annie Potts, Ernie Hudson

DIRECTED BY IVAN REITMAN

1984. 107 minutes. PG

For all its appeal at the box office ($300 million being a fortune in 1984 and halfway serious money today), Ivan Reitman's film was said to be off-putting to little kids. "Hell dogs" chasing Rick Moranis through New York streets; brawny green arms bursting out of Sigourney Weaver's sofa; a big bass baritone erupting from Weaver's mouth; lightning-rent skies announcing Zuul, the gatekeeper. Very young viewers might still dive for cover, but a quiet advisory from parents beforehand should forestall outright panic. Other than these instances, about the scariest stuff this movie dishes out is a green blob resembling Casper and a giant marshmallow man. (Okay, so he does damage a few buildings.)

Of course, the ghostbusters themselves are terrified, at least at first. Students of the paranormal, Dr. Peter Venkman (Bill Murray), Dr. Raymond Stantz (Dan Aykroyd), and Dr. Egon Spengler (Harold Ramis) are summoned to the New York Public Library where books have been floating around all by themselves and index cards have been flying out of their cases by the thousands (needing to be picked up after each take). There they encounter a spectral old woman reading and minding her own business until their prying annoys her and she becomes a snarling skull.

Fleeing to their lair at Columbia University, the three decide to go into the ghostbusting business, or, as their card puts it, "Professional Paranormal Investigations and Eliminations." By now reports of ghosts are being filed all over town and business is booming. The boys drive a van, wear brown jumpsuits, carry enormous mechanical

Ghostbusters
(Used by permission of Columbia Tristar Home Entertainment)

backpacks with long spray nozzles, and ask questions like, "Does the building have a history of psychic disturbance?"

Yes, they resemble exterminators. "Someone saw a roach on twelve," Dr. Venkman tells a man at a hotel where the crew has been summoned to purge spirits from a banquet hall. Outside the contaminated area Dr. Stantz encounters a disembodied green blob gorging itself at a food cart, and he and his partners swing into action. Don't tell the Environmental Protection Agency, but those backpacks are really unlicensed nuclear accelerators that emit long, loopy streams of electrostatic discharge. If ghosts are hit at all, they merely yowl with annoyance. Surrounding areas are blasted into smoldering ruins.

In a commentary on the DVD, Reitman says he knew they had a hit when *Ghostbuster* T-shirts began appearing during the second week of release. Schoolteachers reported that small youngsters wanted proton guns.

Aykroyd originally introduced the idea for the movie years earlier as a forty-page treatment with a central role for John Belushi, who died in 1982. The proposal involved fifty ghosts, which would have cost zillions. Ramis was brought in to pare down and massage the idea, and everybody repaired to Aykroyd's place on Martha's Vineyard to write the script. That took a month and resulted in a $30 million budget.

Ramis, also a writer and director, plays a nerd with a high brainiac haircut. Aykroyd is the heart, intense and caring. Murray, as is usually the case in his roles, is the mouth. Judging from the DVD, he was a handful on the set but remained amenable to the movie. "He liked doing it . . . I think," Ramis says.

As writers, actors, and directors, the key players had worked together before on the television shows *Second City TV* and *Saturday Night Live* and such films as *Caddyshack, Meatballs, Stripes, National Lampoon's Animal House,* and *Trading Places.* Weaver, though, came from a higher rung theatrically and her presence as a beautiful and cultured musician turned torrid demon was critical. She had done *Alien* and *The Year of Living Dangerously* and wanted a comedy. Here, Reitman said, "she elevated the tone of the casting" and brought a sense of reality. He thought of her as the grounded center of a Marx Brothers movie.

The special effects are a mix of the physical and optical with some digital blending. The film hired a consultant from Cal Tech to describe possible conditions in haunted areas. He mentioned changes in electromagnetic fields, odors, and kinetic disorders of all kinds. In the library the floating books are on wires and the index cards are sent flying by blasts of air through copper tubing. Reitman said that on the one hand he regrets not being able to do the apparitions with more up-to-date effects, but on the other he liked the cartoon effect. Ghosts that alarmed little ones in '84 will probably make them giggle now, but keep a precautionary eye out nevertheless. The so-called hell dog that comes roaring through a posh lobby and out onto Fifth Avenue seems pretty hilarious these days, but you never know.

With its tension and rhythm, New York is certainly a star. Gargoyles and wonderfully complicated rooftops are everywhere in the film. Reitman credited his production designer, John DeCuir (*Hello Dolly, Cleopatra, South Pacific*), with a keen eye for city panoramas. At the climax of the film, the marshmallow runs amok and the cardinal shows up in the mayor's office. "We're headed for a disaster of biblical proportions," his honor is told. Where else but New York?

During the shoot traffic was stopped all over town. One day near the set the cerebral Aykroyd spotted the writer Isaac Asimov, one of his heroes, trying to make his way along a sidewalk clogged with equipment and movie people. With great deference, the actor introduced himself, but, he said, Asimov only complained about the hubbub.

Beware of the spooky-scary stuff as described. Also ghost disposal by nuclear accelerator can be quite violent even if clearly comic. Little ones not attuned to the humor could well be alarmed. Realize, too, that Weaver turns steamy, and sexual acts are intimated if not performed. As the rating says, parental guidance is suggested.

35. THE GOLD RUSH

Charlie Chaplin, Georgia Hale, Mack Swain, Tom Murray

DIRECTED BY CHARLIE CHAPLIN
1925. 96 minutes. Black and white. No rating

"Pure visual comedy has been dead for forty years in the cinema," Walter Kerr wrote in his book *The Silent Clowns*, published in 1980. We may think we encounter it, but we don't. Screen comics—a Robin Williams, say, or a Jim Carrey—provide us snatches, but, Kerr wrote, "visual comedy in the hands of its greatest practitioners, Chaplin and Keaton, was closer to the poetry of dreams than to humor." That's true, but half the fun of watching *The Gold Rush* and other Chaplin films is getting aboard his satiric sense and sharing his connection with everyday bedevilments.

Without parents having to make too fine a point of it, most kids will recognize comic genius when they see it. In this case they will hear it, too. In 1942 Chaplin revised the film and added his own dramatic narration in place of the title cards kids typically balk at when presented a silent film. On the DVD we listen to him reporting on his own masterfully constructed mock drama. We are in the Klondike in the midst of a perpetual blizzard, in itself hilarious in a satiric sense. Times are tough and so are the characters. "Somewhere in that nowhere the law was looking for Black Larsen," Chaplin tells us, his voice full of feigned menace. Chaplin, of course, can't get rid of him.

Larsen is a big man, and so is Big Jim McKay, the mountainous, fur-clad prospector who strikes it rich. Caught in the middle of these behemoths, not to mention a huge natural and historical setting, Chaplin is "the little fellow," as he refers to himself with dry relish. "The silent screen produced just two comic epics: Chaplin's *The Gold Rush* in 1925 and Keaton's *The General* in 1926," Kerr wrote. "A comedian's qualities are not at all what an epic wants. An epic wants an event of great scale and significance, one rooted in a historical moment, a moment so representative that it takes on mythological status. And it wants a hero at its center who certainly need not be perfect but whose high aspirations are matched by his capabilities. . . . Epic quality vanishes under the assault of the clown."

Or so had been the case on the stage, but by the mid-'20s, Kerr wrote, the advent of the documentary lent Chaplin and Keaton "an authenticity inside which they could continue to be funny." News photography helped Keaton take on the Civil War in *The General*. Chaplin became interested in Alaska and the gold rush in pre-Depression days when the country had gone money mad. At the start of *The Gold Rush* a long column of men struggles upward through the drifts toward Chilkoot Pass. Next we see the little fellow matter-of-factly traipsing along an icy, impossibly narrow trail over an abyss in those famously oversize street shoes. A bear follows him for a bit but detours into a cave.

Kerr and others note Chaplin's strong inclination toward intimate interior spaces, which are tough to come by in Alaska. "He wanted to be with us at close quarters so that we should miss nothing, however infinitesimal the detail might now be," Kerr wrote. Alaska being nothing but the great outside, how would he get himself back indoors? The answer was two cabins and a dance hall. A great storm, wonderful in its exaggerated intensity, prompts the little fellow to take shelter in a shack earlier appropriated by, as luck would have it, the elusive Black Larsen. But shelter is a relative term here. We know it has to be at least five below zero in the cabin, and when the door flies open, as it does repeatedly, the wind screams through the place and lays the little fellow almost parallel to the floorboards as he struggles to keep his feet before being blasted out through another door back into the storm.

Like Keaton in *Steamboat Bill, Jr.* (see page 265), Chaplin loved battling great winds. Crawling and clawing his way back inside, he finally closes the door and regains his feet. "Get out!" shouts Black Larsen, as if the little fellow can do anything but. We can theorize all we want about the gold rush as mythological symbol and artistic underpinning, but this is simply breathtaking physical comedy. All the scene needs is Big Jim McKay, the size of a grizzly in his shiny black fur coat. McKay and Larsen battle for the lone shotgun and the only chicken bone, which must feed all three.

In addition to Alaska and the gold rush, Chaplin had read about the Donner party, a group of starving snowbound emigrants who may have resorted to cannibalism on their way to California in the 1840s. That may not immediately suggest humor, but "in the creation of comedy," Chaplin writes in his autobiography, "it is paradoxical that tragedy stimulates the sense of ridicule; because ridicule, I suppose, is an attitude of defiance: we must laugh in the face of our helplessness against the forces of nature—or go insane."

Anyway, in an advanced state of hunger the little fellow boils one of his shoes to falling-off-the-bone tenderness, with the lace serving as a long piece of linguini. But shoe leather doesn't suffice for Big Jim, a chronic whiner, and soon he starts hallucinating that his cabin mate has turned into a plump chicken. With a shotgun handy, the chicken is one step from the pot, but every time McKay goes to shoot, the chicken becomes the little fellow. McKay is ready to shoot nevertheless. In desperate self-defense, the little fellow shoots a bear (offscreen) and instantly sets the table.

More comic than epic, the routine is one of the most famous in silent film. Later another cabin provides food and warmth enough for the little fellow to practice the poetry of dreams Kerr wrote about. Here and in the town saloon he stokes his romantic fantasy involving the dance hall girl Georgia (Georgia Hale). Then it's back to the first cabin for a spellbinding comic crescendo as the structure teeters on the edge of a cliff before plunging into a chasm.

The little fellow rescues Big Jim at the last second and is rewarded when McKay, a just man for all his self-centered histrionics, gives him a half share of the gold strike. How many people would be so generous? The two are now rich, which puts the little fellow more or less in the position of having to follow through and "get the girl" to create a responsibly happy ending suitable to an epic. Chaplin swore he'd never let that happen again.

Black Larsen guns down two lawmen in cold blood. Other violence is clearly in the comic vein.

36. THE GREAT ESCAPE

Steve McQueen, Richard Attenborough, James Donald, Charles Bronson, James Coburn, Hannes Messemer, David McCallum, Donald Pleasence, James Garner

DIRECTED BY JOHN STURGES
1963. 172 minutes. No rating

At first look, John Sturges's film may be a little too pretty. On a brilliant, breezy summer day, a German military convoy rolls through sumptuous green fields. As we'll see in a moment, the trucks are loaded with the most die-hard American and British escape artists who ever broke out of a concentration camp. Having rounded them all up once and for all, the Germans will plant them in a new super-camp, Stalag Luft III. But are we headed for incarceration or a day at the lake?

"There vill be no ezcape from zees camp," the commandant, Colonel von Luger (Hannes Messemer), tells the British Group Captain Rupert Ramsey (James Donald). Who would want to escape such a scene—which is the whole idea, of course. Set in neat rows, the barracks-style lodgings are so fresh and clean you can almost smell the lumber.

Great prison-camp movies like Billy Wilder's *Stalag 17* (released in 1953 and a worthwhile film for older children) give off a cold, drab feel. This one, adapted from a novel by Paul Brickhill and filmed in the hills near Munich, has a whiff of travel brochure. Reflected in black-and-white photographs from the era, the story is a true one that took place in the muddy, real-life confines of a German stalag in Sagan, Poland.

The duty of Allied officers caught behind enemy lines is to break out and divert the large number of enemy troops needed to find them. Stalag Luft III has been built to contain prisoners who are particularly determined to escape. Dossiers of some of the new arrivals show fifteen attempts or more. No sooner are they let out of the trucks than several of them are trying to sneak off disguised as members of a Russian work detail.

In a spick-and-span meeting hall Squadron Leader Roger Bartlett (Richard Attenborough) briskly outlines plans for a mass escape. In *Schindler's List* (for those age fourteen at the youngest), Bartlett might not have got away with such an open gathering. But this is a prison-camp movie for the whole family, starting at about age eight (with one strong note of warning to come). Colonel von Luger is stiff and determined, but a humane fellow. Ranking prisoners have their own rooms with built-in bookshelves. Gardening, sports, and visits to the camp library are encouraged in hopes of keeping the prisoners on the premises.

Especially troublesome individuals like the boyish American Captain Virgil Hilts (Steve McQueen) do relatively untaxing stretches in solitary confinement, a concrete room without furnishings but clean and new like the barracks. The gestapo are hard-core "Heil, Hitler" types, but they aren't around much, and the guards, while stern, are lenient enough to allow the escape effort to take shape.

The plan is to dig not one but three tunnels—code-named Tom, Dick, and Harry—thirty feet down (to avoid sound detectors) and across into the trees. If Tom is discovered, the operation will move on to Dick or Harry. Bartlett envisions 250 escapees rolling underground on a mini-set of miner's tracks before emerging to fan out and wreak havoc in Germany. An operation of this size needs tools, building materials, clothing, documents, cash, communications devices, myriad little items. Here it all materializes as easily as if it had come from a store or office: stacks of lumber needed to shore up the tunnels, bolts of fabric to turn prisoners into well-dressed members of the civilian community, forged identification papers better than the originals.

The Germans discover Tom, so the prisoners push on with Harry. One challenge is how to hide mountains of sandy soil from the excavation. In charge of "dispersal," Lieutenant Commander Eric Ashley-Pitt (David McCallum) devises little soil sacks that prisoners conceal in their trousers and empty while standing in flower beds. The Germans did recommend gardening, after all.

At that rate, soil disposal could last until Vietnam and beyond, but John Sturges's movie wisely doesn't worry about such details. This is a grand broad-brush adventure, full of heroes and derring-do set to an appropriately edge-of-your-seat score by Elmer Bernstein. Nevertheless, as is often true with major and minor classics (and many films in this book), Sturges had trouble selling the project to Hollywood. Studios worried about certain plot developments and lack of love story.

By then Sturges, who died in 1992, had made *Bad Day at Black Rock* (1956), with Spencer Tracy, *Gunfight at the O.K. Corral* (1957), and *The Old Man and the Sea* (1958), again with Tracy. Then came his western *The Magnificent Seven* (1960), which was produced independently and became a huge hit (see page 182). "After that I think if I wanted to direct the telephone book they would have at least given me a hearing," he says in an interview on the DVD.

That film and *The Great Escape* proved him a fine ensemble director. McQueen, James Coburn, and Charles Bronson were in both movies. Several cast members had been prisoners of war themselves. The British actor Donald Pleasence was held by the Germans; Messemer, a German, by the Russians; Hans Reiser, another German, by the Americans. The novelist James Clavell, who wrote the screenplay with W. R. Burnett, was in a Japanese concentration camp.

Though *Escape* is a true story, the characters are composites. Each has a specialty. Pleasence plays the forger. Bronson wasn't a prisoner of war, but he was a former coal miner so he portrays the chief tunneler. James Garner, in real life a decorated veteran of the Korean War, is the "scrounger," adept at coming up with pickaxes and foodstuffs.

Most of these characters do break free, if not for long. Outside the camp, they try to dodge recapture in beautifully picturesque German towns and countryside. A scene on a train is especially vivid. Death awaits many prisoners. In one scene that puts the movie out of bounds for small children, the gestapo massacres fifty of them. We aren't shown the details, but a brief burst of machine-gun fire makes it perfectly apparent what has happened.

Sturges had a reputation for being well organized, but on this film there were eleven versions of the script. Improvisations were common. McQueen, a prima donna on his way to a big career, walked off the set after six weeks of shooting. In keeping with the McQueen image, his character, Hilts, was a raffish loner who did all his breaking out on his own and looked askance at a group effort. Invited to join the great escape, he at first declines. "Steve wanted to be a hero without doing anything heroic," Garner says on the DVD.

McQueen agreed to do the film because as Hilts he got to steal a motorcycle and zoom around the fields. An ardent biker, McQueen also played German motorcyclists in pursuit of Hilts, so sometimes McQueen is chasing McQueen. Garner says that after the walk-out he sat McQueen down and asked him what the problem was. McQueen replied that he wanted to be a hero. "We told him he was one," Garner says.

Some children's guides make no special note of the group execution. Others flag off young children. Parents will have to decide, but by age ten most kids will handle the event. Otherwise, if this isn't exactly a family film in the most precious sense, it is one the family will enjoy watching together.

37. GREAT EXPECTATIONS

**John Mills, Anthony Wager, Jean Simmons,
Valerie Hobson, Finlay Currie, Martita Hunt,
Alec Guinness, Bernard Miles, Francis L. Sullivan**

DIRECTED BY DAVID LEAN

1946. 118 minutes. Black and white. No rating

For children three generations ago the opening of David Lean's film ranked as about the scariest thing ever on the big screen. On a bleak, blustery day along an embankment on the Thames estuary the young Pip (Anthony Wager) bends into the wind as he makes his way to a misty church graveyard to lay a scraggly bouquet by the grave of his parents. Above him bare branches whip back and forth in the gale and around the tombstones odd noises put Pip on the alert. But nothing prepares him or us for a sudden shock. In our faces is the escaped prisoner Magwitch (Finlay Currie). Sudden doesn't describe it.

Years ago, Magwitch's instant materialization brought a shriek from audiences. Wes Craven gets screams from teenagers today with his bloody surprises, but in the '40s Lean's artful and nonviolent bushwhacking was especially effective with children. The scene may not land quite the same punch these days, but it still hits with shivery, delicious impact. It's nice that a frightening moment invites rather than flags off younger kids. Lean's adaptation of Charles Dickens's novel is for the young as much as anybody. "The film is emotional, exciting, full of action; sequences are planned in terms of heightened dramatic contrasts and sudden, scary tensions," wrote the critic Pauline Kael.

Lean, who died in 1991, is best known for such epics as *Lawrence of Arabia, The Bridge on the River Kwai,* and *Doctor Zhivago.* One of the greatest filmmakers, he is described as an imperious man who put work above all. On a personal level, according to biographers, that might be reflected in his six marriages, in a couple of cases to

---

women he seems to have paid scant attention to. Professionally he's remembered as a perfectionist and a complete master of technique. That said, there is no lack of passion and humanity in his films.

As with other great directors (Preston Sturges, Howard Hawks, George Stevens) Lean's vision seems to scoop up all ages. Any of the three films above could be recommended to older children. One, *Lawrence of Arabia,* is included in this book (see page 146). *Great Expectations* came early in his career and is one of his two masterful Dickens adaptations. (The other, *Oliver Twist,* is also highly recommended for children.) There is a wonderful vibrancy in his treatment. Story and characters speak to children, especially the young Pip, Dickens's boy of the Victorian working classes who is summoned to Miss Havisham's decaying pile of a mansion to play with Havisham's haughty ward, Estella (Jean Simmons).

What are children to make of Havisham (Martita Hunt), the jilted, crazy dowager straight out of *Alice in Wonderland*? It's not nice of Havisham to entice Pip to fall in love with Estella for the sole purpose of having her reject him as Havisham was rejected when her groom walked out many years earlier. Still, we remain somewhat fond of Havisham. The older Pip (John Mills) stays attractively vulnerable and kid-friendly as he trains uncomfortably to climb the London social ladder after suddenly and inexplicably becoming well-to-do. The mystery of Pip's unknown benefactor will engage children. So will Pip's cheery upper-crust friend Pocket, a childhood boxing opponent who teaches Pip how to get along in the big city. Parents should point out that Pocket is portrayed by the young Alec Guinness, who most children will encounter as Obi-Wan Kenobi in *Star Wars*.

For all his ferocity, kids will even sense something decent in Magwitch. In the churchyard he threatens to cut Pip's throat, but we know he won't. Later, of course, we meet the man in an entirely different light. After many years and a change in circumstances, his menace has turned to nobility and warmth, a very nice turn of events for children. At the start, though, the escaped prisoner is a big man with an eye patch who pulls the terrified Pip up into his large face before bending him backward in stages as he delivers orders to bring food and a file to sever his chains. As Dickens writes, "He came close to my tombstone, took me by both arms and tilted me as far back as he could hold me; so that his eyes looked most powerfully down into mine, and mine looked most helplessly up into his."

Reams of analysis have been written on Lean's adaptation of the book. Much of it speaks either of visual liberation from Dickens's thickets of detail or of Lean trying not to make too much of an ass of himself in the presence of literary genius. In truth, Lean wasn't too concerned about Dickens. He hadn't read the book before deciding to make the movie. One gets the impression of one master appropriating another for use in a different medium without too much worry about bungling the crossover. "Lean's style, with its command of editing and its integration of elements of mise-en-scène, ensures the film's own coherence," wrote Brian McFarlane, an Australian commentator. "It avoids the merely 'literary' by making time and space work harder than is necessary or even possible in a novel. Visually and aurally it creates its own style—a blend of the discreet and the Gothic—that is something more than a reverent straining for equivalences."

Another critic calls the film more "resemblance" than adaptation. But Lean certainly worked to preserve the Dickensian spirit, which is apparent from his picaresque minor characters with their ruffled fronts and tufts of hair sticking straight out. "Again and again Lean organizes screen space so as to ensure our sympathetic alignment with Pip," Mr. McFarlane wrote. "One of the most striking symptoms of this is in the repeated shots in which Pip is seen dwarfed by large, looming, sometimes menacing adult presences."

Lean shot his film in Rochester, south of the Thames, an area familiar to Dickens. He wanted a dynamic look with contrasts and long black shadows. "What we wanted to create all the time was the world as it seemed to Pip when his imagination was distorted with fear," Lean told the biographer David Brownlow. "That after all was what Dickens himself did." Fortunately, the movie never gets grim about it.

The young Pip and his trials will intrigue most young children from roughly the age of eight. Later on his humility and loyalty to relatives from his impoverished childhood are good for kids to see. Passages in London when Pip and Estella reconnect as adults might drag a bit, though probably not for kids ten and older. The last thirty minutes of the film should have plenty of interest for everybody. There is some violence, with soldiers keeping order and a Newgate mass hanging depicted though not directly shown. There is no sex or profanity.

38. GROUNDHOG DAY

Bill Murray, Andie MacDowell, Chris Elliott, Stephen Tobolowsky

DIRECTED BY HAROLD RAMIS

1993. 101 minutes. PG

"You're not a god—this is twelve years of Catholic school talking," Rita (Andie MacDowell) says to Phil Connors (Bill Murray). Phil might be excused for thinking he has taken on divine powers. Nothing that happens to him—including running head-on into a speeding train—has any lasting consequence. The next day everything is fine.

In this film the next day is always the same day, or, if you prefer, the day before. Phil is living the same day over and over, so he always knows what will happen in advance, which allows him to alter events on any particular day. The next day starts from scratch—forever Groundhog Day. "Buddhists love this film," says the director Harold Ramis. "It's a yoga movie." Why the day repeats is totally unexplained, but it really doesn't matter. The movie kind of grins and shrugs.

Kids get a funny film they can grasp on a basic level, with lots of fast repartee from Murray, an attractive foil in MacDowell, and a bit of action on the mildly violent side. Having absorbed all that, they can hop more easily onto the message. Not to get heavy, but the movie is a fable, and we don't mean Aesop's or a dose of gooey Hollywood moralizing. *Groundhog Day* has some lessons to share, and kids can absorb it naturally and entertainingly.

On the DVD, Ramis says he was first attracted to Daniel Rubin's script because it began right in the middle of the story with the days repeating and Connors reacting. But that would have left the viewer in the dust without a proper introduction to the situation, a fatal mistake for any film. So Ramis and Rubin backed up and set the stage. A snide and thoroughly burned-out Pittsburgh weatherman, Connors goes to Punxsutawney, Pennsylvania, every year to report whether "the large rat," as Phil calls him, will see his shadow in the nationally celebrated observance. This year he stays in a bed-and-breakfast the night before the ceremony and wakes up at 5:59 A.M. to the strains of Sonny and Cher's "I Got You, Babe" on the radio. In the town square he reconnoiters with Rita, the show's lovely, warmhearted producer, and a long-suffering cameraman (Chris Elliott).

The groundhog's emergence from its cage is presided over by enthusiastic top-hatted town officials. After his usual snotty commentary, Phil fully intends to lead his little crew back to the big city. But a blizzard, totally unpredicted by weatherman Phil, intercedes and they are stranded in Punxsutawney until the next morning.

Or so it would appear. When Phil awakes, Sonny and Cher's "I Got You, Babe," is playing on the radio, exactly like the previous morning. When he looks outside, he sees that there is no blizzard. It's Groundhog Day all over again, as it will be for many, many days to come. Phil is the only one aware that the day is repeating. Rita and the others stay frozen, props, as it were, in the same daily scenario. Rubin the screenwriter wanted it to go on for a thousand years, but Ramis the director indicates that probably wasn't called for. However long it goes on, one suspects the repetition is intended to teach the arrogant Connors a thing or two. Ramis calls it a cosmological lesson.

Murray's own personality fueled Connors's disposition. Ramis had written and directed films like *National Lampoon's Animal House, Meatballs, Caddyshack,* and *Ghostbusters* (see page 102), some of them with Murray. *Groundhog Day* was their sixth collaboration. "Bill has a nastiness. There's a self-centeredness and vanity," Ramis says on the DVD. He adds that there's also a warm, more magnanimous side to Murray.

Both Murrays show up in Phil Connors. At the start there is the Connors who tells an old high school classmate he has just encountered, "I would love to stay and talk to you. But I'm not going to." In fairness, the fellow is pretty obnoxious, but Phil feels he can be rude to anybody at any time, and he has a tongue like a razor. Eventually he realizes the futility of such behavior and adopts a new approach.

The primary reason is Rita, and by extension MacDowell herself. Ramis and Rubin say that Murray wasn't always the most pleasant person to deal with on the set, but he acted differently when he was around MacDowell. The filmmakers don't go so far as to say that Murray was smitten by MacDowell, but he was better behaved around her. Murray doesn't contribute to the disc, but MacDowell goes on at some length about what a talent he is. Rubin calls them Beauty and the Beast.

On-screen Connors falls for Rita, which requires a behavioral makeover. Phil can behave any way he likes because he knows that the next day, always Groundhog Day, starts from scratch for the others, so no one will remember. He mines Rita for her likes and dislikes and uses the information the next day to gradually worm his way into her heart. That's not the noblest behavior, but it is something of an improvement, and it rubs off on Phil's other activities around town.

In the beginning he uses his foreknowledge to play tricks. For example, one day he can rob an armored truck in the secure knowledge that on the next day it won't have happened. (Kids will love every minute.) Later on the mellower, love-stricken Phil, knowing exactly what everybody does exactly when every day, can be on hand to intercede in helpful ways. Every day he is there to help the same women change a flat tire, and every day he is in the right place at the right time to catch a little boy falling out of a tree. At the groundhog celebration he quotes Chekhov. Do we have a town hero in the making here?

Ramis made his movie in Woodstock, Illinois, which at first upset the people in Punxsutawney. But Woodstock had the perfect town square for a movie-style groundhog observance. Ramis says that Punxsutawney residents eventually understood that the real thing wasn't good enough for Hollywood and supported the film. One convenience of making a film set on the same day over and over is that scenes that repeat with whatever variation can be shot at once in sequence. One difficulty is the weather. Every day has to look exactly the same, so it helps to pick the right one.

Sex is involved in a couple of places. Phil and a woman he tries to seduce grapple briefly on a bed, but they are clothed. Later he and Rita lie benignly beside each other, covers pulled to their chins. There is also some violence when Phil decides to kidnap the groundhog and engages the police in some action-movie mayhem. But it is in a comic vein and hard to take seriously. There is some rough talk, but not much or too strong.

39. A HARD DAY'S NIGHT

John Lennon, Paul McCartney, George Harrison, Ringo Starr, Wilfrid Bramble, Norman Rossington, John Junkin, Victor Spinetti

DIRECTED BY RICHARD LESTER
1964. 85 minutes. Black and white. G

As an essential film, Richard Lester's *A Hard Day's Night* qualifies as one part cultural record and one part cinematic marvel. In a poll taken several years ago in England, only 43 percent of the respondents could name the four Beatles, but in 1964 they were about to take over the world. With their extraordinary music still evident everywhere, no kid should miss a film by a master chronicler of the mod sixties who uses multiple cameras, often handheld, and a scenario that mixes fact with just the right amount of unobtrusive fiction to give it structure and mood.

For kids it's a romp; for parents it's a good family film with plenty to observe and talk about. A precocious American, Lester moved to England at age twenty-two and started directing in the then new and raw area of British commercial television. One day he received a call from the actor and comedian Peter Sellers, who had just watched a show of Lester's. "He said either it was the worst thing he had ever seen or you're on to something," Lester says in an interview on the DVD special edition. In 1959, a Sellers-Lester comedy short called *The Running, Jumping and Standing Still Film,* with Sellers at one point dressed as a charwoman and scrubbing away at a piece of pastureland, was nominated for an Oscar. Later it attracted the Beatles.

United Artists, known for liberal-thinking projects, financed *A Hard Day's Night.* Lester says UA simply told him the amount of money he had to spend and they would see him at the premiere. Above all, he wanted the Beatles to be themselves and feel comfortable. By then the boys were in the early stages of the craze called Beatlemania. They had just returned from the United States where they made multiple appearances on *The Ed Sullivan Show,* performed in Washington and New York, and ran all over town followed by hordes of press, screaming adolescents, and the documentary filmmakers Albert and David Maysles. For his film Lester wanted the same pressure and feeling of constantly being hounded.

Asked to describe a Swedish tour, John Lennon replied "a car in a room, a room in a car, and a cheese sandwich." Lester was after that kind of crush, a sense of everything being smashed together into very tight spaces and time frames. For a fictional plotline the Beatles are scheduled for a live television appearance in a theater with a cramped backstage area teeming surrealistically with opera performers, chorus girls, U-boat commanders, and assorted stage characters all jammed into impossibly tight quarters.

Always outside, separated by barricades and ranks of bobbies, crowds of kids threaten to break through in a great surging swarm. At the start the Beatles are chased through the streets in a wonderfully merry dash by a mob of girls and not a few boys, all of them in shirts and ties, or so it appears. But the scene quickly grows oppressive and the Beatles just have to break out, which leads to furrows on fictional handlers' brows as the Fab Four get to run around a bit on their own before being reeled back into fame's regimen.

The film finally had to let the hordes in for the Beatles studio concert. Extras recruited from drama schools were Beatles fanatics themselves and as berserk with adulation as the crowds in the streets. Barrie Melrose, the second assistant director, recalls that all the crowding and furor backstage caused a lot of small accidents on the set, with people falling and being knocked down. At one point, Melrose says, kids used burglar tools to break through the theater roof and storm downstairs. Bedlam was at such a pitch the film crew couldn't be heard eighteen inches from one another.

The Beatles were somewhat sheltered from all of this, but they would grow accustomed to it. Everybody associated with the film says how easy they were to work with. "They went home, learned their words, came in and read them," says the actor John Junkin, who plays one of the group's fictional managers. George Martin, who wrote the film's music with John Lennon and Paul McCartney and ran Abbey Road Studios where the Beatles recorded, says that at the first meeting one was struck more by their warmly charismatic personalities than their talent. Lester calls them four parts of a marriage, very much alike and very protective of one another.

For the film, Martin says, he made George Harrison the mean one, McCartney the cute one, Lennon the cynic, and Ringo the sort of odd man out who feels unloved. In reality, he adds, Harrison was the most accurate performer. He never tried too much or too little but always hit the center in the same way Ella Fitzgerald did. "Whatever he had to do he did it very well," Lester says. He calls Lennon the most interesting, whip smart and quick-witted. Lennon suffered fools badly, hated pomposity and the authority figures who treated the Beatles like servants. McCartney, on the other hand, tended to the theatrical and on occasion tried to act too much. "Had he been less enamored with the trappings of cinema and theater, he might have been more relaxed," Lester says. Ringo was "up the back," meaning that as a drummer he held the group together. But personally Ringo was bothered that people didn't pay more attention to him and accord him more respect.

Martin says that in the early days at Abbey Road Studios all the Beatles were nervous and respectful. In *A Hard Day's Night*, the dozen or so songs—"Can't Buy Me Love," "All My Loving," "I

Wanna Be Your Man," "She Loves You," "Don't Bother Me"—either had been written for the film or would be. The group wrote so fast that it was a struggle to keep up. Ringo, also the group's linguistic Yogi Berra, had come up with the wording "a hard day's night" and Lennon suggested it as a title. Lester liked it, so Lennon and McCartney wrote up the song that evening, scrawling it on a matchbook.

The Beatles were matter-of-fact about their film work. Lester says the movie showed them that they could stand up and be themselves, cushioned against an outside world that often treated them with condescension. "I think they liked it," he says, though he doesn't sound all that sure. He and the Beatles would make another movie, *Help!*, the next year, but they never discussed their first one again.

The film is good clean fun for all ages. There is no violence or profanity and, other than plenty of runaway hormones, no sex.

40. HARRY POTTER AND THE SORCERER'S STONE

Daniel Radcliffe, Rupert Grint, Emma Watson, Maggie Smith, Robbie Coltrane, Richard Harris, Alan Rickman, Tom Felton, Ian Hart

DIRECTED BY CHRIS COLUMBUS
2001. 152 minutes. PG

Critics generally disliked this movie and for one reason. As Elvis Mitchell wrote in the *New York Times,* "The filmmakers, the producers and the studio seem panicked by anything that might feel like a departure from the book—which already feels film-ready—so *Harry Potter and the Sorcerer's Stone* never takes on a life of its own."

But some kids thought that there wasn't enough of J. K. Rowling's book, the first of five Harry Potter stories published and seven planned. "The movie skipped part of the book, but I thought it was great," a Manhattan sixth-grader said in the *Times* when the movie opened in November 2001. Opinions differ, but it can be said definitely that if Chris Columbus's film failed to assert an independent cinematic viewpoint, neither did it embarrass itself in the presence of a children's literary phenomenon.

What we have here is a good-looking, extremely competent children's movie. The second film of the series, *Harry Potter and the Chamber of Secrets,* also directed by Columbus, doesn't stray from its book either. In fact, the books could well dominate the movies as long as Rowling writes them. She was a constant presence on the *Sorcerer's Stone* set, which, some critics note, couldn't have given Columbus any strong feeling of independence. Rowling seemed to like the director's approach. "He really gets the book," she said.

Kids will have the last say. "I like the books for the mystery, the magic, and all the different classes and characters," another sixth-grader said in the *Times.* "For the movies a lot of it depends on how good the next three books are. If I don't like the books, I may not want to see the movies."

Rowling's Harry Potter and J. R. R. Tolkien's *Lord of the Rings* are sources of cinematic juggernauts that should roll on for years. Columbus's movie certainly pleases kids. Maybe its strongest feature is Hogwarts School of Witchcraft and Wizardry. Towering and regal on a mountain peak, its scores of lights glow from massive interiors, suggestive of ritual and the mysteries of a rarefied world apart.

Winston Churchill came out of a school less magical but not unlike this (a Hogwarts scene was set at the Harrow School, which Churchill attended). *Sorcerer's Stone* is a boarding school movie, a subgenre anchored by the likes of *Goodbye, Mr. Chips* and, more recently, *Dead Poets Society,* as well as films like *Lord of the Flies* and *The Winslow Boy* (see page 299), which carry the boarding school culture off-campus.

English boarding schools also bespeak bloodied backsides and creepy perversions. In its own fantasy world, Hogwarts is both a warm and a dangerous place. As wizards in training, students are in the hands of a well-oiled operation that has been turning out wizards for centuries. All of this becomes clear during student orientation, which has some of the best scenes in the movie. In the gigantic vaulted dining hall, mountains of glorious foodstuffs magically materialize on long tables. (One presumes the cleanup is just as miraculous.) At the head table, Professor Albus Dumbledore (Richard Harris), the magisterial headmaster with knowledge of all deep goings-on (if not control of them), calls on a talking leather hat to assign the newcomers to dormitories with names like Slytherin and Gryffendor. Older students lead the younger ones up and up massive, magically shifting staircases lined with portraits found in great English houses to cozy nooks, common rooms, and dorm beds overlooking a vast and misty countryside.

Hogwarts is a great, craggy living being. In its convoluted, seemingly endless innards lie myriad forbidden areas for Harry (Daniel Radcliffe) and his pals Ron (Rupert Grint) and Hermione (Emma Watson) to stumble upon and explore with a pounding sense of adventure. Kids at schools from time immemorial are warned to stay out of these places. At Hogwarts, they are guarded by an immense three-headed dog, and trespassers could pay with their lives. Rumbling from catacombs in the basement, a mammoth troll puts the entire institution to rout until finally felled by Harry's intrepid trio. Later in that same basement, the heroic little Ron will win a chess game against thirty-foot-high armor-clad pieces that destroy one another as if on a medieval rampage.

Harry is finally left on his own to battle Voldemort, the agent of the dark who killed Harry's parents and slashed the Z-shaped scar on his forehead. Critics found Daniel Radcliffe's portrayal a little on the wan and passive side. Experienced with child actors, Columbus (*Home Alone, Mrs. Doubtfire,* see page 194) hadn't found a suitable Harry after a year of looking. Then David Heyman, the film's producer, spotted Radcliffe with his father at a play in London. "I saw this boy who combined a wonderful sense of curiosity, openness, and generosity with a warmth that wasn't sentimental or too cute," Heyman said in the *Times.* "He seemed accessible, an Everyboy."

That's a lot to surmise in one random theater sighting, but Radcliffe got the part. Some observers point out that like Harry Potter and

Frodo Baggins in *Lord of the Rings,* heroes of epic fantasies lasting many books and movies should be steady, consistent types, not colorful personalities. Besides, young Harry has plenty of strong points, beginning with the fact that he's an orphan. "Which is really good," a seven-year-old says in the *Times,* "because he can sneak out at night with his friends, and also when you don't have parents you get to be the main person."

Scenes with the three-headed dog and the giant chess pieces in the dungeons are very violent, and there are many other scary moments for children under the age of eight. There is no sex or profanity in these precincts (at least in this first installment). All in all, Columbus's film makes fine viewing for everybody from nine up and especially so on the DVD, which includes games and puzzles.

41. HIGH NOON

Gary Cooper, Grace Kelly, Lloyd Bridges, Katy Jurado, Ian MacDonald, Lee Van Cleef

DIRECTED BY FRED ZINNEMANN
1952. 84 minutes. Black and white. No rating

Kids love showdowns and Fred Zinnemann's western is eighty-four minutes of pure showdown. That is not to say it's continual action. The movie erupts later on, but in its steadily building tension, it grips the attention. Children from about age ten can understand and appreciate the predicament facing Marshal Will Kane (Gary Cooper). Parents will enjoy getting reacquainted with this film, too. As with another western, *Shane* (see page 241), that means a good family film.

Forget azure skies and "Howdy, pardner." Three years later Zinnemann would make the exuberant *Oklahoma!,* but here he was after the documentary effect and a stark look in black and white. He was an Austrian, an unusual bedfellow for a western. "I jumped at it because it was a first-class script," he says in a documentary on the DVD narrated by Leonard Maltin. Here was a Viennese at the helm of one the greatest American films ever. "It wasn't too difficult with people like Cooper," he says.

Cooper was a mainstay of the genre. "I like westerns because the good ones are real," Coop said. "You feel real while you're making them. You don't feel actorish."

Kane is beset from every side. In eighty minutes, along dead-straight railroad tracks extending to the horizon, Frank Miller (Ian MacDonald) will be coming to kill him. The marshal sent Miller to prison and now vengeance is in order. For good measure three of Miller's gunmen are waiting at the station to meet the boss and help him get the job done. As for Kane, in the immortal words sung by Tex Ritter, he must face the man who hates him.

A lousy job—marshal. Any man this outnumbered can use some help, but the fearful citizens of the sere little town Kane has defended many times in the past turn their backs on him now. Zinnemann's film is adapted from a magazine story called "The Tin Badge," the kind of badge Kane will toss in the dust when all this is over and he walks out on those who deserted and betrayed him. Leaving with him will be his bride, Amy (Grace Kelly), a Quaker pacifist who earlier staunchly disagreed with Kane's decision to fight Miller and was ready to leave town on the same train Miller arrives on. She stays, though, and is about the only one to aid in Kane's defense.

At the start of the film, Kane has quit his job to honor her pacifist beliefs. Faced with the Miller situation, he and Amy do some powerful soul searching, weighing their love and marriage against differing views that haven't been an issue until now. Their predicament is clear and riveting, and kids will understand the choices: stand and fight on principle or, perhaps equally as courageous, give way in favor of gentler, more spiritual influences.

Kane's marriage is far from his only problem. For much of the movie, which runs almost exactly the same time it takes Miller to arrive at high noon, the marshal roams the town asking, begging, for help. His deputy (Lloyd Bridges) quits because Kane won't recommend him as his successor. Townsfolk gathered to assess the coming storm waffle but agree with the mayor (Thomas Mitchell), who wonders why anyone in Kane's position wouldn't find it a whole lot easier just to leave with Amy and resume life elsewhere.

Kane, of course, knows that Miller would track him down wherever they went, but that's not his primary reason for staying. This is a matter of morality, and kids will get this, too. It should be explained that the film was written by Carl Foreman, who refused to cooperate with the House Un-American Activities Committee and was blacklisted before *High Noon* opened. Many equate the desertion of Kane by the fearful town with the pressures of the McCarthy era.

Cooper, who died in 1961, was suffering from various physical ailments. His Kane looks gaunt and pushed to the limit. Cooper is often depicted as a phlegmatic type whose eloquence began and ended at "yup." In this film, he argues his positions forcefully, but it's the anxiety on his face that tells the story. Freeze any frame on the DVD and his expression is a study in resolve, hurt, or bewilderment. Kane is scared all right. He is only human. At one point he seems close to tears.

Zinnemann says he liked the empty tracks because they represent an unseen approaching evil. Clocks are everywhere in the film. As noon approaches they get bigger and their pendulums move more slowly. At noon they stop. A train whistle is heard. By now Dimitri Tiomkin's famous score has the picture at a fever pitch. Harry Cohn, the studio mogul, called *High Noon* a piece of junk, but, as Maltin notes in the documentary, Cohn saw the film without the music.

The movie had other detractors. "Howard Hawks, for instance, frequently derided *High Noon*," Rick Lyman wrote in 2001 in the *New York Times*. Hawks, who directed many westerns, wondered "what kind of hero Cooper was portraying, scampering all over town begging for help from townspeople just because a few bad guys were headed his way. In fact, Hawks said his own *Rio Bravo* (1959), with John Wayne playing a tough frontier sheriff, was to some extent a reaction to *High Noon*."

The Duke might not want to mess with Kane. In the gunfight Miller and the boys go down like tenpins; Amy even shoots one. In the bargain, kids get a western with some soul and a lot to think about.

Kane and his former deputy brawl in a barn. (In the DVD documentary Bridges reports that his young son Beau was given permission to watch the scene from a hayloft but broke out laughing in the middle, forcing everybody to start over.) The gunfight itself is violent, as what gunfight isn't, but not bloody or graphic. There is no sex or profanity (and no rating system then if there had been). The action doesn't kick in until the end of the film, but the building tension will hold most children. Ten is a good age, but depending on the child a little younger is perfectly possible.

42. THE IRON GIANT

With the voices of Eli Marienthal, Jennifer Aniston, Harry Connick Jr., Vin Diesel, John Mahoney, Christopher McDonald

DIRECTED BY BRAD BIRD
1999. 86 minutes. PG

Brad Bird's animated feature tells the story of Hogarth Hughes, age nine, and a big metal man he finds in the woods. With his mother off at work, Hogarth is home alone enjoying himself immensely doing the one thing she has asked him not to do: watch a scary movie. When the television signal goes awry, he climbs to the roof and finds that the antenna has been broken off—chomped off, might be a better term. Invaders!

Annie, his gentle and doting mother, dismisses such notions. But then in the woods by the seaside village of Rockwell, Maine, Hogarth discovers a giant male figure about fifty feet tall and made entirely of iron. As the story evolves, it appears the fellow arrived from outer space during a wild storm. His appetite is as big as he is and his diet is anything made of metal.

Automobiles qualify and so do television antennas. When Hogarth comes across the giant, he is eating the stanchions at a power station. Felled by arcing bolts of electricity, the big man crashes to earth. Watching in horror, Hogarth starts a mad dash in the opposite direction. Then, despite himself, he stops. "When the kid gets past his fear to stop and help, that's the core of the movie right there," says Brad Bird, director of a most unusual and involving animated film.

We see that same mix of courage and curiosity in other movie kids. Elliott in *E.T.* (see page 88), for example, stands and delivers when faced with an alien in his toolshed. In *Spirited Away* (see page 259), young Chihiro faces up to all she encounters when left to her own devices in a forbidding land. These are children with a presence of mind and sense of responsibility not always found in adults. It is left to them to take up the cause of whatever threat frightens or offends society, often by simply having a more open attitude.

In Hogarth, kids get a smart and enthusiastic contemporary. His new metal friend is a winner, too, perhaps the world's first kindly walking fortress. Bewildered by his surroundings, he is willing to learn and is soon building a vocabulary. The trick is to keep him hidden. A fifty-foot iron fellow is a disquieting prospect, so Hogarth does what he can to keep the metal muncher concealed among the taller pines. "People always wig out and start shooting when they see something big," Hogarth tells him. As supportive as his mother is, "we get the screaming problem again," the boy says.

Luckily Hogarth knows Dean, a sculptor and the area's nonconformist. Dean runs a scrap yard outside of town. What junk he doesn't sell at fairly good prices, he turns into artwork, which hardly sells at all. Early in the movie, before anyone has seen the giant, Hogarth meets Dean in a diner and hears him defend being different. "If we don't stand up for the kooks, who will?" Dean says. Derisive old boys in the diner immediately slap the kook label on Dean. Harry Connick Jr., who is his voice, calls him a '50s hepcat.

Dean reluctantly agrees to let the giant hide out in the scrap yard. "All you can eat," Hogarth tells the big one. Dean warns him not to eat the profits and to stay away from the sculpture.

It surprises some people to learn that the iron man originated with Ted Hughes, England's former poet laureate who died in 1998.

Hughes wrote the story to help comfort his children after the suicide of their mother, the poet Sylvia Plath. Hughes was conveying the thought that life goes on after such a loss. Bird, well known for episodes of *The Simpsons* and *King of the Hill*, expanded that into a reflection on good and bad things technology does to society.

At one point the iron man tries to eat the railroad tracks, which derails an express train. In the crash he is dismembered, but then we begin to see just what technology might mean for surgical reconstruction. Responding to signals from his dented head, scattered body parts retrieve themselves and reattach with a satisfying whir of tightening bolts. With the last tiny screw, its retrieval signal light flashing, the reclamation is complete.

Weapons are concealed in his huge iron frame, but these won't be revealed until the final scenes. Iron man seems to be unaware of them himself. The year is 1957, *Sputnik* is passing by overhead, and in Rockwell the perceived red threat is a crisis for some people and in the back of the minds of everyone else. "It was a time when prewar innocence meets postwar paranoia," Bird says on the DVD. "A good place to drop a giant into."

The government dispatches its man, Kent Mansley, a pipe-puffing xenophobe, who whips up fears and calls in the army. The iron giant rescues two children from a fall in the heart of Rockwell, but any approval or sympathy that might inspire only fans Mansley's determination to be rid of him. Cornered in the woods by tanks and buzzed by jet fighters, the metal man resorts to his own arsenal. Earlier in the movie he witnesses two hunters kill a deer and gets some bite-sized instruction: Guns kill; it's bad to kill; things die, it's a part of life; souls don't die. Unable to match the giant's firepower, Mansley calls for a nuclear attack. But don't worry, the giant intervenes.

Hogarth prevails with the support of Dean and his mother. The film strongly conveys a healthy single-parent relationship, which will be appreciated by a lot of kids. Jennifer Aniston is the voice of Annie. "A lot of kids grow up that way," she says on the DVD. "I grew up that way." Bird's film was highly acclaimed, and he gives Aniston a lot of credit. "No one thinks of her as the all-American mom," he says.

Vin Diesel is the voice of the iron giant. If you doubt the effort name actors put into being voices in animated films, watch Diesel trying to get the right inflections into the giant's basso. "Anyone who knows me knows I like misunderstood characters," he says.

A pitched tank battle is fought at the end, but this and other violence is highly stylized to convey the idea and not the carnage. Hogarth is threatened now and again, and there are fleeting scenes of intimidation that could upset small children. There is no sex and only a mild epithet or two. Kids from about seven up will love this film. Parents will, too.

43. IT HAPPENED ONE NIGHT

Clark Gable, Claudette Colbert, Walter Connolly, Jameson Thomas

DIRECTED BY FRANK CAPRA

1934. 105 minutes. Black and white. No rating

Here we have the first, or nearly the first, example of that mid- to late-'30s breed called the screwball comedy. (For a definition, see *Bringing Up Baby,* page 45.) Capra's film is smashingly entertaining for kids and families, but to hear him tell it in his autobiography, *The Name Above the Title,* no big star would touch the movie as it was first written. "Sure, you've got some good comedy routines," the story editor Myles Connolly told him, "but your leading characters are nonsympathetic, non-interest-grabbing. Take your girl: a spoiled brat, a rich heiress. How many spoiled heiresses do people know? And how many give a damn what happens to them? Take your leading man: a long-haired, flowing-tie Greenwich Village painter. I don't know any vagabond painters, and I doubt if you do. . . . Another zero. And when zero meets zero, you have zero interest."

So what would Connolly recommend?

It Happened One Night
(Used by permission of Columbia Tristar Home Entertainment)

"Your girl," he said. "Don't let her be a brat because she's an *heiress,* but because she's *bored* being an heiress. More sympathetic. And the man. Forget that panty-waist painter. Make him a guy we all know and like. Maybe a tough, crusading reporter—at outs with his pig-headed editor. More sympathetic. And when he meets the spoiled heiress, it's *The Taming of the Shrew.* But the shrew must be worth taming, and the guy who tames her must be one of *us.*"

Put it that way, pal, and you land Clark Gable to play the reporter Peter Warne. Claudette Colbert plays the heiress Ellen Andrews to modulated and down-to-earth perfection. Ellen is so bored and furious at her controlling father (Walter Connolly) that she dives off his yacht in her dressing gown and swims for freedom. With Daddy and his flunkies in hot pursuit, she gets on a bus headed for New York and runs into an inebriated Warne, who has just been fired by the editor of his paper.

The two hit the road. They are lively, open characters who speak plainly and simply enough for a child of eight to understand. What's more, they won't let a family audience down with sexual encounters in a motel where they find themselves bunking together out of necessity, not choice. Warne erects what he calls his "wall of Jericho," a blanket strung on a line between the beds. "Just wondering what makes dames like you so dizzy," he growls at Ellen. Seventy years after the fact, the talk is dated, but these are big, appealing stars, completely timeless. One of the charms of this picture is that a lot of its characters talk like reporters yelling for rewrite, fedora tilted back over the forehead—or like directors and studio chiefs going head-to-head over what cockeyed idea will either fly or crash on the big screen. Capra and his bosses at Columbia Pictures dueled long and loudly. "Just another bus picture," they told him. "Besides, that mile-long title, *It Happened One Night*. How you gonna get it on the marquee?"

Capra adapted the film from a magazine story called "Night Bus," which he spotted in a barbershop in Palm Springs. "Bus" is a short word, as is "night," but Harry Cohn, the head of Columbia and Capra's boss, couldn't abide the notion of a bus movie. And even with a rewritten script, they couldn't get a star. Cohn was griping about this to Louis B. Mayer, his counterpart at MGM. "I got an actor here who's being a bad boy," Mayer told him. "Wants more money. And I'd like to spank him. You can have Clark Gable."

"Louis, s'pose *he* don't like the script?" Cohn replied.

According to Capra, Gable showed up as drunk as Warne to discuss making the movie. "I picked up the script and riffled it," Capra wrote. "Mr. Gable, you and I are supposed to make a picture out of this." Gable responded in language not appropriate for family audiences, but in the end he was more or less obliged to make the film and plunged in wholeheartedly.

Colbert wasn't an easy sell either. She was about to leave on a four-week vacation in Sun Valley when Capra and the screenwriter Robert Riskin went to pitch the film to her. Colbert's poodle bit Capra. "Froggy was in a French tizzy," he wrote. She told them she was packing and leaving in a half hour. What would it take to get her to change her plans? Normally she made $25,000 a picture, she said. Double it and she might consider.

The other stipulation was that she absolutely had to be finished shooting in four weeks. That meant they began filming the next day, which necessitated some of the slick little tricks filmmakers resort to when pressed for time and money. (For the epitome, see *Rocky,* page 228.) For example, in the film Ellen Andrews's suitcase is stolen at a bus stop, eliminating the need for an extensive wardrobe. Ellen wears one outfit almost the whole time, as does Warne.

When they were done, Colbert told friends that it was the worst movie she had ever been in. Actually, it was a smash. "No one has ever fully explained what gives this basically slight romantic comedy its particular—and enormous—charm," Pauline Kael wrote in *The New Yorker.* It was the Depression and audiences wanted screwball.

At the time Capra was more enthusiastic about his film *Lady for a Day,* which was up for a flock of Academy Awards in 1934 but won none. At the Oscar ceremony in 1935, *It Happened One Night* swept every top category: picture, director, actor, actress, adapted screenplay. Each time the presenter said the word "It," the audience roared in unison, "Happened One Night."

As discussed, one of the great comedies works for everybody who is old enough to understand what is happening. Among the gents there is some truculence but no violence. Sex is hinted at but kept at bay. There is no place for obscenity.

44. JAMES AND THE GIANT PEACH

**Paul Terry, Joanna Lumley, Miriam Margolyes,
Pete Postlethwaite, and with the voices
of Simon Callow, Susan Sarandon,
Richard Dreyfuss, David Thewlis**

DIRECTED BY HENRY SELICK
1996. 80 minutes. PG

Renowned for his children's stories, Roald Dahl is about as famous for being a hot potato for moviemakers. The man had a dark side that surfaces in startling developments, warranting cautions about upsetting the little ones. Here, for instance, we have a very fine animated kids' movie, guaranteed to delight one and all from the age of about six, in which not one but both of the title character's parents are immediately killed off. Parenticide, of course, is a common narrative device, but Dahl, it must be admitted, performs the act with special gusto.

As he relates it in the third paragraph of *James and the Giant Peach,* "Then, one day, James's mother and father went to London to do some shopping, and there a terrible thing happened. Both of them suddenly got eaten up (in full daylight, mind you, and on a crowded street) by an enormous angry rhinoceros which had escaped from the London Zoo." Bad enough for them, but at least, Dahl continued, "*their* troubles were all over in a jiffy. They were dead and gone in thirty-five seconds flat."

By contrast, James, age four, loses his seaside home and all of his possessions and is plunged into a living hell in the care of two aunts. "Their names were Aunt Sponge and Aunt Spiker, and I am sorry to say that they were both really horrible people," Dahl wrote.

But was he really that sorry? Dahl, who died at seventy-four in 1990, had a tough time as a kid and wasn't reluctant to sound a warning. His father died when he was four, and at nine he was shipped off to a brutal English boarding school, an experience he describes in *Boy,* the first volume of his memoirs. A tall, witty, arrogant man, he went on to a high-profile and contentious career and life, which makes us wonder at his ability to produce such captivating children's tales as *Charlie and the Chocolate Factory, Matilda, The Witches,* and *James and the Giant Peach,* published in 1961.

Perhaps Dahl fancied himself in the dark tradition of the brothers Grimm, but as is evident in *Peach* and Henry Selick's treatment of it on-screen, Dahl was not that fierce. He certainly liked to conspire with kids against adults. "To be sure, he was eager to offend taste, and did it with a zest that kids appreciate," Ann Hulbert wrote in the *New York Times.* "He knew how to be frightening, and often gave his readers the pleasure of being truly, if briefly, terrified. He took pleasure in being unceremoniously honest about adults' vicious hypocrisies and about children's tyrannical appetites. Along with a gift for embroidering on basic infantile fantasies (from chocolate to witches), he had a sharp satiric eye and ear: it was a one-of-a-kind blend."

For the screen adaptation of *James and the Giant Peach,* Selick was in the employ of Disney, which by the late '90s was beginning to lower itself gingerly into darker waters. Three years earlier he had made *Tim Burton's Nightmare Before Christmas,* and five years later he would direct the underrated and distinctly unsunny *Monkeybone.* Here Selick shows no skittishness whatever in polishing off James's pastel parents in the prescribed thirty-five seconds flat.

At the outset the happy little family rhapsodizes about going to New York together, but that will never be. About twenty minutes of live action highlight James's misery with his aunts whereupon the film suddenly enters a highly stylized animated world inside a huge piece of fruit. The peach is sprung Jack-and-the-beanstalk style not from seed but from tiny crocodile tongues boiled in the skull of a dead witch for twenty days and twenty nights. Escaping inside its orange, juicy interior, James discovers new friends in the form of a professorial grasshopper, a motherly spider, a scrappy centipede, an earnest glowworm, and an anxious earthworm. Together they harness the peach to a squadron of seagulls and fly it across the Atlantic to New York.

Ahead of them lies a strikingly imaginative journey with an excellent mix of animation (drawn and computer-generated) and a few neat tricks. Maybe the best of these comes earlier when the peach rolls crazily toward the sea and flattens a picket fence, which gets impaled all the way around the fruit and serves as a catwalk for the crew as they soar across the ocean.

James is a stalwart little kid, the steady center holding all together through the perilous journey. As adventurous as Disney was, relatively speaking, the film can't bring itself to go all the way with Dahl on some major and minor details. For example, Dahl makes no mention of any family dream about traveling to New York. In the book James is simply desperate to escape the crushing loneliness he endures with his aunts, one of whom is played by Joanna Lumley of *Absolutely Fabulous* fame. The peach in the book arrives over the Big Apple purely by chance. For Dahl, making friends and flying off to a new life is enough purely for its own sake.

The movie can't have this, however. For Disney, for Hollywood, every family movie needs a moral, in this case a "dream" to fulfill. In the book, the aunts are flattened in their automobile by the peach as unceremoniously as the rhino took the parents. In the film, the aunts suddenly reappear in New York, emerging from their battered car, which they apparently rode across the Atlantic. But, hey, so the movies never can leave well enough alone. At least in this case they let the parents rest in peace and allow James to go off and live in the peach pit in Central Park and be eternally in the good company of the city's children. For Dahl, that probably would beat being with the old folks any day.

True, the very young might be upset at the parents' death and James's mistreatment by his aunts. But the deaths are quickly dispensed with and the harridan aunts are more ridiculous than scary (though a four-year-old might not agree with that).

45. JURASSIC PARK

**Sam Neill, Laura Dern, Jeff Goldblum,
Richard Attenborough, Samuel L. Jackson,
Wayne Knight, Joseph Mazzello, Ariana Richards**

DIRECTED BY STEVEN SPIELBERG
1993. 127 minutes. PG-13

This is a weird kind of film to be discussing in a children's movie book. By definition any Spielberg picture about dinosaurs gets elevated in the children's pantheon, but isn't *Jurassic Park* just as much a horror film? Spielberg has a way with kids, as we see in *E.T. The Extra-Terrestrial* (page 88), but he also has a habit of giving them a very rough time on-screen and scaring the devil out of them in movie theaters.

In *Jaws* (1975), a classic but a horrific one, children went to a gory demise. In *Jurassic Park* the grandchildren of a driven theme park developer are terrorized in an overturned vehicle by a Tyrannosaurus rex and later by a pack of sly and vicious velociraptors. The T-rex chomps and swallows humans in a show of pure horror, but the most horrifying thing in the film is the look of terror on the face of the little girl crawling around under the crushed sport utility vehicle as the monster snuffles around to get a good bite. Many kids will have nightmares for a month.

Or as Janet Maslin put it in her review in the *New York Times*, "Parents and guardians take note: Children who think of a Tyrannosaurus rex as a huge hunk of friendly, prehistoric exotica will not want to see a T-rex bite a lawyer in half." Of course, she was writing in 1993 when the dino craze was fairly new and building to a crescendo. Today no kid on the planet would think of a T-rex as friendly, but that in no way lessens the scare factor of this film. Use extreme caution.

"I have no embarrassment in saying that with *Jurassic* I was just trying to make a good sequel to *Jaws*," Spielberg said in a 1994 interview. *Jaws* is no kids movie. Nevertheless, *Jurassic Park* belongs in a book of great films for kids. The dinosaurs are the draw. "In writing *Jurassic Park*, I threw out a lot of detail about the characters," the screenwriter David Koepp said in a 1997 interview. "Whenever they started talking about their personal lives, you couldn't care less. You wanted them to shut up and go stand on a hill where you can see the dinosaurs."

In the film the dinosaurs have been derived from the DNA of a mosquito found in a chunk of amber. More than 65 million years ago the mosquito bit a dinosaur extracting a sample of blood. Now that bug is on the tip of a cane belonging to the developer John Hammond (Richard Attenborough), whose team has sprouted all kinds of the big critters and put them on an island off the coast of Costa Rica. Let the tourism begin. First, though, he needs a little accreditation from the scientific community so he flies in a couple of leading paleontologists, Dr. Alan Grant (Sam Neill) and Dr. Ellie Sattler (Laura Dern), who are romantically involved, and the mathematician Ian Malcolm (Jeff Goldblum).

Malcolm is by far the most entertaining and the most critical of Hammond's project. Viewers of all ages get a good illustrated briefing on the dangers of genetic engineering, especially for essentially frivolous commercial purposes. Malcolm wants to know the consequences of taking creatures made extinct through natural causes and suddenly and artificially reintroducing them in an environment they know nothing about. Everybody is about to find out.

A documentary on the DVD describes what Spielberg wanted with his dinosaurs. Rather than huge, ponderous animals, he wanted a T-rex and velociraptors that were fast and smart, designed more like bird dinosaurs. That makes them more threatening and lethal. Even the big one can run after a jeep at thirty miles per hour, like a huge fanged ostrich. In the film, the park manager notes that the T-rex and others are testing every section of electrified fence that surrounds them to find any weak spots. The creepy thing is that they remember where they have tested and pick up where they left off. During the climactic scene, velociraptors open doors. They're smart ones, for sure.

Man tampering with nature to his regret is a classic horror theme, and Spielberg sets the stage for a couple of sequels, *The Lost World: Jurassic Park,* which he directed, and *Jurassic Park 3,* directed by Joe Johnston, in which the dinosaurs start thinking like humans. Neither sequel is a match for the original. On the DVD Spielberg says that the dinosaurs began as movable miniature figures with elaborate robotic skeletons. Then George Lucas's company, Industrial Light and Magic, demonstrated the superiority of computer-generated imaging and Spielberg decided to use that method exclusively. Scenes were carefully measured to include empty spaces to be filled in later by computerized dinos.

On the island a simple power failure enables the most dangerous beasts to escape their confines. Earlier the inquisitive Malcolm had wondered at the likelihood of something going wrong. Hammond reminded him that Disneyland had its share of glitches. "When Disneyland breaks down, the pirates don't eat the tourists," Malcolm answers.

Age ten seems absolutely the low end, but parents will decide. There is no sex, though Malcolm gets quite flirtatious with Ellie. There is some profanity, but it's minimal and fits the dire circumstances.

46. THE KING AND I

Yul Brynner, Deborah Kerr, Rita Moreno

DIRECTED BY WALTER LANG
1956. 133 minutes. No rating

Yul Brynner is all skull and ego in Walter Lang's film. Almost fifty years later he remains perhaps the most instantly recognizable figure in American movie history. The King of Siam is a strutter and fretter, stopping to throw his hands on his hips and pout and glare and issue his "et cetera, et cetera, et cetera" whenever he feels it beneath him to finish his thought. That is about every other sentence, but beneath the bravado there is deep doubt and insecurity.

When Anna Leonowens (Deborah Kerr) arrives from England in 1860 to teach his multitudinous children (twenty little princes and princesses, sixty-seven if you count all the children of wives currently not in favor), the king is wrestling with encroachments and realities his forebears never had to contend with but which now crowd in on him with troubling insistence. Basically, he can no longer be quite so sure of his infallibility. Certainly he can bluster and bully quavering subjects into beseeching lumps before him, but he is lashing out irrationally to assert himself and keep control.

Old rules of absolute authority are giving way. In the past "what was so was so and what was not was not," as he puts it in a song by Richard Rodgers and Oscar Hammerstein. Now he has doubts about everybody being so sure of themselves. That might even extend to himself, not that he can allow the slightest bit of uncertainty in public. If he's feeling challenged and unsure, he throws a tirade.

Brynner's posturing in the role can seem a little shopworn by now, even if we haven't come across the film for a while. But the king remains a fine figure for young children to consider. On the one hand, he is like the spoiled brat who threatens to stop the game and take his ball home if he doesn't get his way. In the king's case, that could translate into a beheading or a lashing. Anna, the assertive, even-keeled British gentlewoman, is particularly perplexing to him when she defies his will.

Another side of the king is much more accessible and promising. He wants to be a man of science and learning and often can be found sprawled on the gleaming marble floors of his palace ensconced in one of the huge volumes he has hauled down from the towering shelves around him. There are limits here, mind you. When Anna introduces an updated map of the world to his children, he becomes defensive. Siam is but a thumbprint and not the center of the world it is on the palace fantasy map beneath it.

Word has come that the British regard him as a barbarian and might try to remove him from power. He tries to come to grips with modernity, but this is a man who wants everything both ways. He can express admiration for Abraham Lincoln and the emancipation of American slaves, but keeps slaves by the hundreds himself. At a banquet for visiting British dignitaries, he startles the guests by proclaiming that through their disagreements men of science and men of faith arrive at the same conclusion.

At the dinner his newest wife, Tuptim (Rita Moreno), stars in an exquisite Siamese dance performance of "Small House of Uncle Thomas" (or *Uncle Tom's Cabin*), but the king is angered at the play's unfavorable depiction of slaveholders. During the show Tuptim, a slave herself, comes close to imploring him directly to let her go and be with the man she loves. Later he is about to have her whipped, but Anna intercedes.

Children will see a man in constant conflict. He is a loving father, at times a playful one. A woman of the court who is in love with him sees a man who stumbles and falls but always tries. You have to look pretty hard to see that in this king, but perhaps. Anna says that he lets vanity get in the way of his heart. And, of course, his end is tragic.

Brynner performed the role 4,625 times onstage over the decades. Anna is based on the real Anna Leonowens, whose account of her experiences in Siam in the 1860s was adapted for the film *Anna and the King of Siam* (1946), with Rex Harrison and Irene Dunne. That movie attracted Gertrude Lawrence, the Broadway star, who wanted it made into a musical. Some of the Rodgers and Hammerstein songs are among their most famous: "Getting to Know You," "Whistle a Happy Tune," and, to accompany one of the most familiar scenes in a movie musical, "Shall We Dance?"

Brynner won the Oscar in 1956. He starred in other big films, most notably *The Magnificent Seven* (1960, see page 182), but *The King and I* forever consumed and stamped him. At first he wanted to direct the film with Marlon Brando as the king. Five years earlier he had shaved his head, joined the stage show in New Haven, and continued for 1,246 performances on Broadway.

There was speculation about Brynner's origins, and he wasn't reluctant to fan myths about himself. It was rumored that he was a Gypsy. He referred to himself as Mongolian, which was plausible given his look, but it was said that he was born on Sakhalin Island off the coast of Siberia. Others have him born in Vladivostok, the son of a Swiss-Mongolian engineer and a Russian doctor. For a while he was a singer and guitarist and a trapeze aritist with the Cirque D'Hiver in Paris. A heavy cigarette smoker for much of his life, he died in 1985 after participating in a stark and memorable anti-smoking campaign on television. Like the king, he remained a hidden figure. "People don't know my real self and they're not about to find out," he once said.

Small children may be upset by the king's death and a few other intense moments. Otherwise it's a grand experience for children from about age eight.

47. KING KONG

Robert Armstrong, Fay Wray, Bruce Cabot

DIRECTED BY MERIAN C. COOPER
AND ERNEST B. SCHOEDSACK
1933. 100 minutes. Black and white. No rating

Myriad theories dog Merian Cooper's big ape. Communists liked to think it was Karl Marx himself breaking through those gigantic gates on Skull Island. The darkness of Kong's complexion spoke to the plight of black Americans, or so it was thought, and that transferred to class struggle in the midst of the Depression. Some saw the crucifixion in Kong's spread-armed bondage. Freudians, of course, saw the phallic in the Empire State Building and the battle between the Ego and the Id in civilized society's attempt to tame savagery. Others found elements of Beauty (Fay Wray) and the Beast and Tarzan and American notions of the wild man, to be brought from the jungle and refined in our image. Still others invoke *Moby Dick,* with the film's documentary filmmaker and showman Carl Denham (Robert Armstrong) playing Ahab to Kong's white whale.

Denham gathers a film crew, attracts the ape with a beautiful blonde, and drags him off to civilization with famously disastrous consequences. Breaking free from the Broadway theater where he has been put on display, Kong derails some subway cars, scrambles up the Empire State Building, and in turn is himself destroyed. Regardless of theories, we have always tried to humanize Kong or certainly to soften him. The critic Pauline Kael describes him as part monster, part pet, part unrequited lover, and part misunderstood kid. We see a nobility in a creature dragged from its habitat. Kong has no human personality as does Beauty's beast, so young viewers today cannot get to know him in the same familiar way. But they will feel sorry for him, perhaps even fond of him.

He does have a winningly goofy befuddlement, but you can't get too cozy with Kong. Steven Spielberg loved this film as a kid, and the ape and dinosaurs Kong battles on Skull Island are predecessors of the T-rexes and velociraptors barreling around the *Jurassic Park* movies. There is a flavor of horror here. People are shaken from trees and crushed in Kong's giant footprint. Like Spielberg's creatures, Kong pops humans in his mouth like hors d'oeuvres, dribbling them from his lips good and crunched and obviously ready to be finished off by a fifty-foot fall.

In *The Making of King Kong* by Orville Goldner and George E. Turner, Cooper says, "I want Kong to be the fiercest, most brutal, monstrous damned thing that has ever been seen." Warned by his special effects man, Willis O'Brien, that he would lose audience sympathy, Cooper didn't agree. "I'll have women crying over him before I'm through, and the more brutal he is the more they'll cry at the end."

To comply with the production code, the more graphic violence was cut, but it was eventually restored. Children's movie guides today don't seem too put off by the mayhem, but it could be disturbing to kids under ten, or any sensitive person for that matter.

A two-fisted filmmaker and adventurer, Cooper conceived the idea of a fifty-foot ape attacked by planes as he perches atop the world's tallest building. At first he also wanted to stage a good brawl between gorillas and giant lizards on Komodo Island west of Sumatra in the Lesser Sunda Islands of Malaysia. That proved impractical, but the island's soaring crags and drooping jungle stuck in his imagination.

A pilot in World War I, Cooper was shot down and badly injured. He served with American relief in Poland and was imprisoned in a Russian labor camp. For a while he was a newspaper reporter and later jumped on a schooner to sail around the world, write books, and make movies. On the trip he met the cameraman and adventurer Ernest B. Schoedsack, exactly his age and a veteran of many of the same experiences. Together they went to Iran to make *Grass* (1925), a wild and fascinating documentary about the Bakhityari tribe on its perilous annual migration to grazing lands for its flocks. Two years later they were in Siam (now Thailand) to make *Chang,* a hugely successful dramatized documentary about a family's struggle to survive harsh natural conditions and wild elephants and other beasts.

It was here that Schoedsack invented a process called Magnascope and he and Cooper learned to think big with their animal shots. Cooper had been to a lot of wild places but never to Komodo, so he relied on a description by a naturalist friend. In his mind's eye, primitives would succumb to sacrificial instincts in such a place. Skulls would be on pikes.

In the film the gigantic Kong routs the natives and does in much of Denham's landing party before being knocked out by a gas bomb on the beach. Denham is beside himself with excitement. "We'll teach him fear," he cries to what's left of the crew who brought them ashore. "We're millionaires, boys! I'll share it with all of you! We'll be up in lights on Broadway! Kong—eighth wonder of the world!" For a moment there, with Kong passed out peacefully on the sand, we wonder which is the Ego and which the Id.

Like Denham, Cooper talked in exclamations. "How then to capture him?" he says in Goldner and Turner's book. "I had it! Schoedsack and I had gone to remote places to make wild animal pictures. King Kong would be found in such a remote place—a survivor of the early world—and he would be captured through a fragile and beautiful girl. There is only one thing that may undo a brute, provided the brute approximates man, and that is beauty!"

Schoedsack had reservations on that score. "Everyone seems to think that stories, to be vital, must have a love interest," he said. "A picture can't be good unless it's built around a throbbing scene between a male and a female. That's a mistake, as Cooper and I tried to show with *Grass* and *Chang*. We focus our lenses, not on silly close-ups of lovesick females, but on the elemental clashes between nations and their fundamental problems, between man and nature."

As Ann Darrow, Wray is gorgeous, a competent actress who did little else of note in her career but become virtually a part of the English language in this role. In this case, Kong is the lovesick one. At one point he strips away pieces of her clothing, but he seems more bewildered than aroused. Denham recruits her to go on the Kong voyage after she is apprehended stealing an orange from a stand near the Woman's Home Mission. He's a fast talker, but the spiel he hands her in a coffee shop today would have a girl calling security. Then again, these are Depression times, and you took your breaks where you found them.

"Holy mackerel, what a show!" Denham roars as he and his crew view the exotic sacrificial goings-on among the natives prostrating themselves before whatever looms behind those enormous gates. Gigantism is much of the appeal. Actually the beast was an eighteen-inch model, manipulated muscle by muscle by stop-motion photography and served his little victims by rear projection. After that the imagination took over. "His furry outside is made of 30 bearskins," it was written in *Time* magazine. "During his tantrums there were six men in his interior running his 85 motors."

Beware of the more horrific events as described above. This is a loud, often intense film, but kids from about age nine should be fine. Fay Wray loses her clothes at one point, and while this is sexual it really isn't too sexy. There is no profanity.

48. LAWRENCE OF ARABIA

Peter O'Toole, Omar Sharif, Jack Hawkins, Alec Guinness, Anthony Quinn

DIRECTED BY DAVID LEAN
1962. 221 minutes. PG

At the edge of an immense expanse of desert, the British adventurer T. E. Lawrence (Peter O'Toole) asks the tribal chief Sherif Ali Ibn El Kharish (Omar Sharif) where their objective lies. "On the other side of that," Ali replies.

"And how much of *that* is there?" asks the impatient Lawrence.

"I'm not sure," Ali answers.

However much, it's nothing that David Lean's monumental film can't handle. Of all the major epics, this is one of the more interesting ones for kids. It really hasn't dated that much in forty years, especially if watched on DVD on a large screen that does justice to the spectacle and huge vistas. If you haven't tried DVD, this film is a reason to start. Documentaries with the film are informative and fun (learn camel riding). Picture quality on disc, especially the impressions of light and heat, is excellent and so is the sound. The great desert battles provide plenty of action, with some nifty cavalry charges on camel and horse.

Ironically, the darker elements of the film also make it worthwhile for children, albeit not the youngest. Released in theaters well before the Motion Picture Association of America's rating system, *Lawrence* lately has been given a PG for video and television. In places it is quite violent, though not as graphically, or certainly gratuitously, as movies now routinely stamped PG-13, let alone R. This is thinking man's violence.

Assigned to the Middle East during World War I, Lawrence parlayed his affinity for all things Arabic into a leadership role with the desert tribes fighting the Turks. At one point he is obliged to execute

Lawrence of Arabia
(Used by permission of Columbia Tristar Home Entertainment)

a man. "There was something about it I didn't like," he says. "I enjoyed it." Later he is captured and tortured by the Turks, which puts him in a murderous frame of mind before an attack on Damascus. "Take no prisoners," he orders. Succumbing to blood lust, he takes none himself, which troubles him greatly.

All of this is tastefully handled, as evidenced by the rating. While this aspect of the film may not seem particularly ideal for a young audience, the intelligent, rather regal treatment of violence makes *Lawrence* a good jumping-off place for a family discussion about what is, after all, a basic human instinct.

Along with the violence there is much about reality and custom in a part of the world children hear much about these days. In one famous scene Ali first appears to Lawrence as a tiny black speck on a camel approaching in a shimmering mirage. Lawrence is standing with an Arab guide in the windy, blazing heat by a well in the middle of nowhere. The guide has taken a drink from the well. A shot rings out and he falls dead. Ali gradually grows larger as he approaches. A thunderstruck Lawrence asks him why he killed the man. "He is nothing. The well is everything. And it is mine," Ali replies.

Proprietary instincts are strong throughout the film, as are issues of honor, loyalty, and personal responsibility. Primarily, though, this is grand filmmaking of a kind now and again approximated by Steven Spielberg but few if any others. That may not necessarily sell it to kids, but *Lawrence* is a natural for those who let it envelop them. Lean shot much of it in the Jordanian desert, with King Hussein providing aircraft to ferry stars and dignitaries to the remote sets. The temperature rose to 130 degrees. Cameras were cooled off with wet towels and stored in refrigerated trucks. O'Toole spent a month beforehand learning to ride a camel. Sharif says that camel riding is something one must practice for hours, days, months even, until one gets the rhythm.

The sands were basically rock and salt and tough to work on. For the mirage scene lorries were driven round and round at high speed to create a sandstorm as a distant backdrop. Lean decreed that no unnecessary tire track or even footprint would mar the desert. As if in compliance, camels put one foot precisely in front of another, leaving tracks only one foot wide. After carefully raking and grooming the landscape for one scene, the crew watched in horror as a jeep driven out from base camp by some unwitting soul sped for miles right through the middle of it.

Lean, of course, specialized in epics. *Doctor Zhivago* and, though it has aged, *The Bridge on the River Kwai* are two others with a lot to offer kids. *Lawrence* is the best of them, spare for all its grandeur, thinking all the while. It may be a little on the long side, but with video you can take a break as audiences did in theaters years ago. Anne Coates, the film's editor, remembers working around the clock, seven days a week, to get the film ready for theaters. She and her staff had only seen the film in parts. They had been invited to see the whole thing at once, but no one had the time.

There is much violence, especially in the battles, but none of it is dwelled on in great detail. At the end of his own rampage, Lawrence holds a bloodied dagger, but as with everything else in this movie, there is a purpose. When he is captured by the Turks, there is the connotation of sexual assault, but this will be lost on most children. There is no profanity. Ages eight through twelve are fine, though some parents will disagree.

49. A LEAGUE OF THEIR OWN

Geena Davis, Tom Hanks, Lori Petty, Madonna, Rosie O'Donnell, Jon Lovitz, Megan Cavanagh, Garry Marshall

DIRECTED BY PENNY MARSHALL

1992. 128 minutes. PG

Kids will get a kick out of Marla Hooch's baseball tryout. The scene is Fort Collins, Colorado, spring, about 1943, and with snow on the ground they play ball in the high school gymnasium. The stocky young Hooch (Megan Cavanagh) waves her bat at a pitcher using a ramp for a mound and some fielders scattered around the basketball floor. Swing after swing, she sends line drives rocketing off brick walls, shattering windows, and ricocheting around the stands. She can hit well, all right, but the scout Ernie Capodino (Jon Lovitz) thinks she is no home run in the looks department, which is too bad because that's part of the package Capodino is looking for.

But if there's one message in Penny Marshall's film, it's that being yourself counts much more than how you look. It's wartime, and with the Joe DiMaggios and Bob Fellers gone, the candy bar baron Walter Harvey—modeled after the chewing gum king and former Chicago Cub owner Phil Wrigley—decides to spruce up Midwestern ballparks with the four-team All-American Girls Professional Baseball League. Combing barnyards for talent, Capodino, a big-city boy, sidesteps the livestock ("Get away from me!" he screams at the chickens) and recruits tall, good-looking Dottie Hinson (Geena Davis), a fine catcher, and her feisty younger sister, Kit (Lori Petty), a pitcher who bridles at being in Dottie's shadow.

Kit will captivate any kid who feels outshone by an older and possibly more gifted sibling. The sisters are pals, though, and both are assigned to the Rockford Peaches. This being a Penny Marshall film, you can be sure the homely Hooch makes the Peaches, too. Harvey the candy man (Garry Marshall, Penny's brother) plays the beauty-and-the-bats angle for all the media attention he can get, going as far as sending the players to charm school. But not all of them can be Miss Georgia, as is one Peach, or the sexy center fielder Mae Mordabito (Madonna). As a bonus, Hooch also gets a man and a fancy wedding.

This is one of those family movies kids and parents can watch together and enjoy about equally. One reason is that the film presents images of strong women without being preachy. Marshall said the moral was that everybody should get a chance according to her talents. In real life the league continued until 1954, but in the movie Harvey makes it clear that after the war the women's jobs were over and they should get back to the kitchen. The film plainly objects to that way of thinking, but it also recognizes the attitudes of the period. In the end we can be grateful for the league and what it accomplished.

Marshall, one of relatively few women directors then and now, had a cast of thirty-two actresses. "I hadn't worked with so many women before," she told the *New York Times* in 1992. "I thought it was something I should do. 'Cause I keep getting asked about it. But I wasn't doing it just to do a women's picture. 'Women's issue' is a turnoff altogether. The problems as they're presented in the movie apply to both men and women. It's about not being ashamed of your talents. It's a universal thing."

Marshall began her career as an actress, most notably as Laverne in the sitcom *Laverne and Shirley*, a character of the people if there ever was one. Much of Laverne's vulnerability and self-doubt transfers to Marshall in the director's chair. Everybody who works with Marshall talks about her attention to detail and tendency to shoot scenes repeatedly. "She can drive me crazy, making you do things one hundred thousand times," Tom Hanks said in an article in the *Times*. "But Penny's passive personality gives a collective feeling on the set instead of the idea that the director is God."

Four years earlier Hanks and Marshall made *Big*, about a thirteen-year-old boy who gets his wish to turn into a thirty-year-old man (see page 33). In *League* he is the boozy Jimmy Dugan, manager of the Peaches. Jimmy was a major league home-run champion six times, but now he drunkenly urinates in front of the women in the locker room and passes out in the dugout during the team's first game. What can we say for Dugan, who's trying to get back into Harvey's good graces after some drunken escapades? He's just a man, like any other, and Hanks plays him naturally and understatedly.

The film has all the good old movie satisfactions: the big games won, the heartwarming relationships, true tenderness in a tough world. In the last scenes some now elderly real-life players join a tribute to the experience at a reunion in Cooperstown, New York, home of the Baseball Hall of Fame. Marshall does a smart thing when she adopts a breezy attitude about the issues and lets Hanks and her other stars play ball. Madonna as a center fielder? "Her familiar attention-getting tactics are nowhere in evidence, except in those scenes that affectionately mock her familiar image," Janet Maslin wrote in the *Times*. And she can go to her left.

The subject of sex comes up now and then but never too salaciously and always naturally as a part of life. There is no actual sex, however. Kit the pitcher gets into a scuffle with an argumentative teammate (Rosie O'Donnell). No one resorts to pure obscenity. Age eight is arguably a good age to start with this film.

50. LILO & STITCH

With the voices of Daveigh Chase, Chris Sanders, Tia Carrere, Ving Rhames, David Ogden Stiers, Kevin McDonald, Zoe Caldwell

DIRECTED BY DEAN DEBLOIS AND CHRIS SANDERS
2002. 89 minutes. PG

One day tiny Lilo, about eight, and her teenage sister, Nani, find a huge bald man with an earring and dark glasses on their front porch. "Your knuckles read 'COBRA,'" Lilo says. His full name is Cobra Bubbles and he's a social worker, though not a typical social worker.

"Did you ever kill anyone?" Lilo asks. Bubbles says they are getting off the subject. Lilo and Nani live alone together after the death of their parents, and Bubbles is looking into conditions around the house. "I am the one they call when things go wrong," he says.

One problem is that Nani left Lilo alone while she ran a few errands. Inside the house Lilo hides out while Elvis Presley blares on the record player and lids leap off pots on the stove obviously turned on high while Nani was absent. To impress Bubbles, Lilo says she takes naps, eats four food groups, and looks both ways before she crosses the street. She also says she punishes her friends according to a book called *Practical Voodoo* and gets disciplined herself by Nani, who hits her with bricks. At the end of the interview, Bubbles takes Nani aside. "In case you're wondering, this did not go well," he says. Nani has three days to change his mind or Lilo will be removed from her care.

Nani is a sweet kid trying to do her best in difficult circumstances, which makes her a young heroine for the twenty-first century in a story that appeals to older children as well as those who customarily troop off to these films starting at about age five. In the last few years animated features have tried to cross over to younger teenage audiences with mixed success. Recent Disney films like *Treasure Planet, Atlantis: The Lost Empire,* and *The Emperor's New Groove* have fallen flat. *Lilo & Stitch,* on the other hand, worked with adolescents who share the sisters' concerns about security, family, and friends.

The style and feel of the film work well to support this. Dropping computer animation for the most part, Disney went back to watercolors. Devised by a mad scientist many planets away, Stitch may be computer-generated sci-fi, but Lilo and Nani are warm and familiar and their surroundings soft and round. Watercolors help achieve this. As one artist describes it, "We would paint *Lilo & Stitch* just the way it was done back in the 1930s and 1940s, slowly building wash layers, one over the other, until the painting evolved gradually as if it were rising through the mist." Artists learned the technique. "There were a lot of nervous painters who never had used this medium before," one of them says.

Banished from his own planet as an incorrigible troublemaker, Stitch hijacks the spaceship taking him into exile and lands it in

Hawaii. Designed as a device that attacks and destroys, he turns out to be a lonely, troubled little thing much like Lilo. But in his creation for the movie his body was a "multi-tool of iron cartilage and titanium glands lashed together with the strongest molecular bonds imaginable, its limbs folding and unfolding with artificial precision," in the words of one of his designers.

Thrown into an animal shelter on earth, Stitch discerns that he's not that huggable and he sucks up some of those limbs so he will resemble a dog and be adopted by Lilo. Nani figures her little sister could use a pet to ease her loneliness and soften some of the angry behavior that makes her a pariah at school. The girls go at life full throttle and everything around them takes on the nicely used look of a favorite pair of shoes. Steven Spielberg's movies are notable for their domestic messiness, and this film has the same kind of chaotic housekeeping. The scene is Hawaii, a warm place to open up life and strew things about. Computer-generated films of the last ten years like *Monsters, Inc.* and *Toy Story* grab older audiences with their wit, knowingness, and reality. This one does the same, but with a look that goes back decades.

When the idea for *Lilo & Stitch* was developed in the late '90s, Disney had released *The Hunchback of Notre Dame, Hercules,* and *Mulan,* none of them striking successes at the box office. At the studio filmmakers work as teams, going from one project to the next. In the book *Lilo & Stitch: Collected Stories from the Film's Creators,* the director Chris Sanders wrote that each of these movies "had seen an increase in complexity and an improved level of finish, but in the process we wondered if they had lost some of the imperfections that gave them character. And what about spontaneity and risk? Were we engineering them away? While we were proud of the films of our era, we all expressed a secret desire to make a *Sleepy Hollow* or a *Dumbo*—small, strange movies with more heart than budget, made when animation was an unexplored frontier."

Disney had become leery of the elaborate, epic-scale film. "So when we learned that our budget and time frame were to be considerably modest compared to films in production, we simply smiled and embraced the notion of making a smaller, gutsier film," wrote Dean DeBlois, the movie's other director.

Spoken like a true Disney company man, but they made it work. DeBlois talks about a "contained and specific" story that nevertheless has to mesh the science and politics of Stitch's colder alien world with the everyday tribulations of an orphaned teenager trying to care for her little sister.

On Earth Stitch identifies with the story of the ugly duckling and develops a need to be part of a family. "But the sentimentality does not feel dishonest or heavy-handed, and Stitch's inevitable domestication does not entirely rob him of his demonic charisma," the critic A. O. Scott wrote in the *New York Times*. A big chase scene involving aliens sent to retrieve Stitch ends in peaceful resolution. And we learn more about Bubbles. Actually, he's CIA and dealt with these same aliens in 1973 in Roswell, New Mexico. "Ah, yes, you had hair then," one alien remembers.

The film should appeal to those from six to twelve. The parental loss has already occurred so the youngest viewers have no traumatic deaths to deal with. Lilo is a sad figure, but she rallies steadfastly and often humorously. There is some action-thriller business now and then, but nothing threatening. Nani has a nice young boyfriend, but sex is never contemplated. Nor is a profanity uttered.

51. THE LION KING

**With the voices of James Earl Jones, Jeremy Irons,
Jonathan Taylor Thomas, Matthew Broderick,
Moira Kelly, Ernie Sabella, Nathan Lane,
Whoopi Goldberg, Cheech Marin**

DIRECTED BY ROGER ALLERS AND ROB MINKOFF
1994. 89 minutes. G

It's always interesting to watch Disney do battle with darker material in an effort to stay mainstream and family-oriented. The struggle goes back to *Snow White and the Seven Dwarfs* (1937, see page 249), when the studio had the violent brothers Grimm to contend with in Disney's first animated feature. Thereafter blacker predilections have been skirted or brightened in films from *Pinocchio* (1940, see page 215), to *Pocahontas* (1995). With *The Lion King*, however, Disney invented its own story that, whether or not the studio was fully aware of all the examination it was inviting, is positively Shakespearean in its tragic images.

Or so the analysts would have it. Kids get the big, superbly drawn and animated Disney package with all or most of the theorizing flying clear over their heads. As in many Disney films, they are presented with traumatic moments, which, life being life, is as it should be. Matters are horrific indeed as Mufasa, the lion king, is murdered by his brother, Scar, who wants the crown. The bewildered cub Simba is left to plead with his father's body to come back to life. So once again Disney violently does away with a parent in front of the little ones (at least Bambi's mother was shot offscreen), and adds an extra twist when Scar convinces little Simba that he is responsible for his father's death and should flee forever.

As we see in many films in this book, a traumatic experience liberates the little one to venture forth on his own. That's appealing, if frightening to children, but here Scar's cruelty makes film guides question the movie's G rating and advise parents to gather five- and six-year-olds in laps to get them by this upsetting rough spot. After that there is plenty of violence ahead, especially at the end when the grown Simba settles the score with Scar, but nothing else as disturbing as the loss of a parent and home. And to lighten the load and get the little ones back on track, Disney does as it often does at dark moments and trots out a couple of sunny sidekicks, the meercat Timon and the warthog Pumbaa.

The Lion King is notable in that it departs from the Broadway musical approach introduced by *The Little Mermaid* (see page 164) at the start of Disney's second great age of animated features in 1989. The songs by Elton John and Tim Rice are catchy enough, but we have plainly moved on to a more involved kind of storytelling. Analysts see a bit of *Hamlet* and *Richard II* in the rise of Scar, the usurper. When the dead Mufasa materializes in the heavens to counsel his banished son on the responsibilities of leadership, they are reminded of exhortations in *Henry IV* and *Henry V*. In exile, Timon (as in Shakespeare's *Timon of Athens*) and Pumbaa initiate the young Simba to the ways of "hakuna mutata," or taking life easy and having a good time. These antics may be tolerable in youth, but suddenly Simba springs forth a full-grown male (with the voice of Matthew Broderick) and he must confront his life's calling.

The Lion King is all about hierarchy, male dominance, one's place, and the rightness of an immutable order. There is much talk about the so-called circle of life, or food chain, which works out for the meat eaters at the top until, as Mufasa explains to Scar, lions die and return to the grasses where in theory they are eaten by antelopes and other grazing animals they have consumed all their lives.

Given that scenario, it's interesting to note that Mufasa's end is partly the doing of stampeding wildebeests, a staple of a lion's diet. In Disney's traditional rosy view of how things work in the jungle, wildebeests and the rest of the dined-upon are expected to gather in obedience and admiration under the soaring pinnacle on which Mufasa presents the baby Simba to all his subjects. The scene, kind of an insignia for the film, is repeated when Simba and the lioness Nala present their own offspring to the throng, another circling of life.

In a cutesy Disney touch, Simba's mate Nala, who dominated him in rough-and-tumble play when they were tiny, still overpowers him when they encounter each other as adults after years of separation. It is Nala who impresses on him that he must take life seriously and return to take the throne from Scar, who has made a mess of the pridelands after the death of Mufasa. According to Nala, Simba's life of ease amounts to irresponsibility and dereliction of duty. But the film makes no attempt to grant even a female as strong as this one a place in a purely male hierarchy.

Furthermore, within the male world, rank and purity of line must not be trifled with or ruin is the result. Under Scar the pridelands have dried and turned to moonscape and the people are hungry and threatened. Partly this is because he has formed an alliance with hyenas, an ugly, treacherous, and decidedly inferior lot from the outskirts of the jungle community. Scar has found them useful in his drive to power, but give these beasts even a modicum of authority and decline is sure to follow.

Scar, swaybacked, scruffy, and evil-looking, is the most interesting character in the film. For all their good looks and pedigree, Disney heroes like Mufasa and Simba are bores by comparison, sometimes vacuous and frequently ponderous and pompous. Scar is a sly, camouflaged kingdom-wrecker, right down to the slithery tone of voice employed by Jeremy Irons. African-American critics observe that he has a darker complexion than the other lions and suspect racism.

Many others noted the rampant commercialism of a film that made $300 million at the box office and generated every kind of merchandising spin-off imaginable. Nevertheless, as the *New York Times* critic Janet Maslin put it when the movie opened in 1994, "More so than the exuberant movie miracles that came before it, this latest animated juggernaut has the feeling of a clever predictable product. To its great advantage, it has been contrived with a spirited, animal-loving prettiness no child will resist.

"Let's put this in perspective: nobody beats Disney when it comes to manufacturing such products with brilliance, precision, and loving care."

To sound the warning once more, small children will be upset at Mufasa's death, little Simba's grief, and his expulsion from home.

52. LITTLE FUGITIVE

Richie Andrusco, Rickie Brewster, Winifred Cushing, Jay Williams

DIRECTED BY MORRIS ENGEL, RAY ASHLEY, RUTH ORKIN
1953. 75 minutes. Black and white. No rating

For the second time in this book, a young one flees home after being tricked into thinking he is responsible for killing a family member. Because there's royalty involved, the flight in *The Lion King* (coincidentally the entry before this one) takes on Shakespearean dimensions. In Morris Engel's small jewel of a film, the fact that seven-year-old Joey (Richie Andrusco) is led to believe that he has shot his twelve-year-old brother, Lennie (Rickie Brewster), with a .22-caliber rifle is of fleeting consequence. After shedding a tear or two of grief and alarm at what he is supposed to have done, little Joey straps on his cap gun, slips out the window of his Brooklyn apartment, and runs away for a generally upbeat couple of days in the amusement park at Coney Island.

Ray Ashley and Ruth Orkin, Engel's wife, are also credited with writing and directing the film, but it is chiefly remembered for Engel's extraordinary photography. Today the whole notion of the story seems a little horrifying: a seven-year-old disappears for two days wandering amid adult strangers, sleeps on the beach, and eludes efforts to return him home. In 1953 the world was safe enough for kids to do that kind of thing without automatically falling victim. The movie is a summer idyll, a grand adventure. For some contemporary young children it may have too little action (and it is in black and white). But after a while most kids will be hooked as Joey pitches and bats baseballs, rides ponies, makes some spending money by returning bottles for deposit refunds, engages various grown-ups, and, most appealing to kids, figures out things for himself.

Engel's movie cost $30,000 and was shot in Brooklyn, New York, and at Coney Island from July to September. It has been hailed by the likes of François Truffaut and Stanley Kubrick, but what makes it work for kids is the utter simplicity and reality of the story. As a still photographer of city street life, Engel made black-and-white images of gripping vibrancy and texture. For his first movie he did away with the tripod and took up a light, handheld 35-millimeter camera designed especially for him by a friend, Charlie Woodruff. So what should they film? "We decided to make a movie about kids because I was comfortable working with kids," Engel says in a commentary on the DVD. A friend came up with the idea of the boy running away, but he needed a reason. Engel hit on getting him to think he had killed his brother.

And where are the boys' parents, you may ask. There doesn't appear to be a father, and the mother has been called away for a couple of days to attend a sick relative. These days that might be called neglect or reckless endangerment, but in the context of a New York working family in the 1950s that's the way it is and it makes sense. Lennie is left in charge of Joey, which causes resentment and leads to a very nasty prank pulled off by Lennie and his friends.

Out in a field Joey naturally wants to shoot the gun like the big kids. He grapples with it and finally squeezes off a shot. About a hundred yards away, Lennie hits the deck, smearing himself with ketchup. One of his friends tells Joey he could get the electric chair for murder. But as traumatic as it might be, accidentally potting your brother was no reason for a hardy little city kid not to bounce right back. Engel, in fact, was more worried about the boys handling the rifle and Richie Andrusco accidentally falling out the window during his escape.

At Coney Island the film becomes pure art as Joey explores a gritty and welcoming land, from barkers on the boardwalk to the jam-packed beach. The adults he encounters are unfailingly kind and decent, which is a nice element for young viewers. Engel cast the two boys himself. As Lennie, Brewster was already a pro and took direction perfectly. Andrusco, Engel says, had "an animal strength and a seven-year-old's indifference to the camera." Directors habitually complain about working with animals and children, but in this particular case Engel was able to work around childish vagaries.

One day Andrusco announced he "didn't want to make no more movie." Engel said fine and told him to wander and play as he liked, which was pretty much what the movie was letting him do to begin with. In that mode, the film plays off the boy's phenomenal energy. At the end of Joey's first day at Coney, Engel faced the question of letting a small child sleep there unattended out in the open. Would audiences accept that? Finally Joey lies down, simply and gently done in by his own exhaustion. At dawn he is off again.

There are no more than 2,000 words of planned dialogue. Almost everything was done in one take. Relatives and friends were invited to appear in the film, but only a couple of cousins showed up and were put to very good use as a couple kissing under the boardwalk. Critics complained that Engel was more concerned with bringing Coney Island to life than attending to his characters. On the DVD he says friends told him the film needed more story, ironic for a film nominated for an Academy Award for best story (a discontinued category).

But no one would argue that the film's major strength lies in its riveting photography of people and place and era and season and countless acutely observed rhythms and details. Engel credits much of the effect to his soundman, Eddie Manson, who fashioned the haunting musical accompaniment with a single harmonica, and gave the city and Coney Island much of their atmosphere. During a thunderstorm, the heavy rain drums the boardwalk and drips come from everywhere. Saul Bellow wrote that Engel "could penetrate the hard surfaces of appearances, make the stones eloquent, cause subways and pavements to cry out to us."

In Engel's film the city is worn and pure. It was his first and last major success. He had great difficulty getting *Little Fugitive* distributed, but it did get into major festivals abroad where its stark, rich style won attention. "Our New Wave would never have come into being if it hadn't been for the young American Morris Engel," Truffaut said. Now in his late eighties, Engel always kept his head. Truffaut was being ridiculous, he said, but he'll take the compliment. On the DVD he says that Stanley Kubrick inquired about borrowing his portable camera. "That was the last of Stanley," he says.

The very young could be distressed by Lennie's shooting and the blaming of Joey. Age eight is a good time to start, but be ready to fend off the complaints of action-seekers initially put off by the leisurely pace. They'll be caught up soon enough by the sights and sounds and the film's wonderfully evocative richness.

53. LITTLE MAN TATE

Jodie Foster, Adam Hann-Byrd, Dianne Wiest, Debi Mazar

DIRECTED BY JODIE FOSTER
1991. 99 minutes. PG

This movie belongs to a child from start to finish. Adults in the film are perfectly estimable people, but our attention never strays from the freckled, contemplative face of Fred Tate (Adam Hann-Byrd), a seven-year-old prodigy. Fred is a quiet, lonely kid, but he is a very large figure. For one thing, he has needs enough for two mothers. Not one for relationships, his birth mother, Dede Tate (Jodie Foster), never mentions his father. Fred is called an immaculate conception, which, as Dede admits, presents her with an added layer of parental responsibility.

Fred's IQ is never mentioned, but he can multiply two columns of twenty-digit numbers in five minutes and plays the piano at competition level. Dede, a starchy cocktail waitress, is no dummy but she can only wonder at such abilities and feel not a little overwhelmed. As a child Foster was regarded as something of a prodigy herself. This is her first film as a director, and on the DVD she says that prodigies rarely do much in later life because their gifts stymie their development as people.

Dede is determined that this must not happen to Fred. At school he is shunned and called a freak by the other kids, who fail to show up at his birthday party. Dede is angry and helpless. An edgy, assertive free spirit, she hasn't the tools to reach Fred on an intellectual level, which leaves her conflicted and threatened.

We sense that this is another case of the child taking control of the parent. Fred has heard about this place for kids like himself called the Grierson Institute. Dede is resistant, but she schedules an appointment with Jane Grierson (Dianne Wiest), the prim director. After a few moments of testing Fred, Jane decides she has a project on her hands: Fred must be exposed to the mental stimulation he will never get with Dede.

On the DVD Foster describes Jane as all grids and categories. Dede, by contrast, is identified by the Tates' sprawling old Manhattan apartment jammed with stuff and personality. Dede instinctively dislikes Jane, who judges Dede solely by her stewardship of Fred. Foster says that women in American society identify themselves by their children. Therefore, Dede feels that Jane is trying to take her identity away from her.

Dede is also smart enough to realize she has no choice when it comes to Fred. He will live temporarily with Jane and attend a summer college session while Dede goes to Orlando with a friend and her children. Now poor Fred has two mothers, one for the head and the other for the heart. However, in Jane he has not only a parent but someone he must prod along as he occasionally steered Dede. Also gifted as a child, Jane was neglected by brilliant high-powered parents too involved with their own lives to nurture hers. Now she's repressed, completely hemmed in by her mission to serve kids like Fred on an intellectual level. She would like to reach them in more personal ways, but, just as Dede hasn't the mental gifts, Jane hasn't the emotional capacity.

"Why do you always talk about college?" Fred asks her one day as she preps him for an appearance on a whiz-kids television show. "Why doesn't anyone ever come over? Why don't you have children of your own? What's wrong with you?"

Kids watching all this will be fascinated with Fred, who sweetly tries to take whatever comes but gradually begins to feel caught between two caretakers who have assigned themselves different areas of responsibility but haven't the ability to make him whole. Unlike most of the other kids he runs into in genius school, Fred has an uncommon degree of wisdom. "It's not what he knows; it's what he understands," says one of Jane's testers.

All he really wants is to be normal. Later in life he will love jazz, for him a great normalizer as well as intellectual and spiritual stimulant. Foster says that music is vital to her. Watching the movie, one thinks of parallels between her and her subject. On the DVD she says that she is the films she directs. She also continually refers to her experience as the gifted child of a single parent. Foster biographies mention intelligence, intensity, determination, artistic daring. Perhaps there is a mix of Jane and Dede.

As a fourteen-year-old, she was already famous for her portrayal of a prostitute in *Taxi Driver* (1976). By the late '80s she had graduated from Yale and won her first Oscar in *The Accused* (1988). In 1991 she won another as the FBI agent Clarice Starling in *The Silence of the Lambs*. That same year saw the release of *Little Man Tate*. Actors as directors often flop in Hollywood, so there were some misgivings among friends and colleagues when she undertook the project. Luckily it landed at Orion, an independent studio, now sadly out of business. There she was told not to worry about all the mistakes she was going to make (not to mention all the money the movie wouldn't make) and go ahead and shoot the film the way she wanted.

In a way, the shoot fits the movie. With very little money, Foster couldn't afford rehearsal time, which meant that there could be no improvisation and scenes had to be done in one or two takes, which is the way Foster likes to work anyway. This required precision, with everything blocked out—a little like Jane's grids. Foster says that it helped to have Adam Hann-Byrd interact with her in a scene so she could get a feel for him and Dede together. She found him in a New York City school. He had no acting experience, but he did have focus. At his audition, fire engines arrived directly across the street as he was reading his lines, but it didn't distract him a bit.

She also found he was a lot like Fred. "Adam is not a terrifically comfortable person," she says, "a little twitchy, a little awkward." To break the ice, she took him to dance class where they could laugh and throw each other around. Dede likes to dance. At the end of the film Fred has another birthday party and everybody from his school comes. He cuts a rug with his mother, and even Jane gets out there with him. In a voice-over narration he says that just when he began thinking he was the smartest one at Grierson Institute, a six-year-old comes along and gets into law school. By now, though, who cares?

The film may move a little slowly for some kids, but Fred is a compelling, endearing figure, and this is a first-rate family film. Fred's loneliness and distress may bother some children in places. There is no sex and some light profanity. Age nine or ten may be about right.

54. THE LITTLE MERMAID

With the voices of Jodi Benson, Pat Carroll, Rene Auberjonois, Christopher Daniel, Buddy Hackett, Samuel E. Wright

DIRECTED BY JOHN MUSKER AND RON CLEMENTS
1989. 82 minutes. G

Children won't hang on every little detail of how this film came about, but they might appreciate the ways it differs from films of Disney's first great era of feature animation, which began with *Snow White* in 1937 and ran through *Sleeping Beauty* in 1959. That year the studio shifted emphasis to pursue television and live-action movies like *Mary Poppins* (see page 185). By 1989 the sweet, sometimes somnolent, usually passive Disney animated heroine had become a sassy, adventurous teenage mermaid named Ariel (the voice of Jodi Benson), who yearns to go off on her own. What's more, her father, Triton (Kenneth Mars), the king of the sea, finally allows her to leave, which is Disney's message to parents about the importance of letting go of their children. Older kids can appreciate that.

The Little Mermaid began Disney's second era of feature animation, which included *Beauty and the Beast* (1991), *Aladdin* (1992), and *The Lion King* (1994) before moving on to a third era of computer-generated film that started with *Toy Story* (1995). *Mermaid* was the first of several films to bring the feel and style of the Broadway musical to feature animation through the songs of the lyricist Howard Ashman and the composer Alan Menken.

Traditional elements are all here: a classic fairy tale by Hans Christian Andersen, a handsome prince, a wicked witch in the form of Ursula the octopus, a crab named Sebastian as a Jiminy Cricket stand-in. Andersen's mermaid fails to keep her legs and wastes away. That's not about to happen this time. Now there's a little star who belts out her longing to have a life on land—"Bright young women / Sick of swimmin' / Ready to staaaand!"—as if it's a Broadway opening night.

This was one of a new breed of Disney film aimed at viewers of all ages. "Teenagers will appreciate the story's rebellious heroine, a spunky, flirty little nymph who defies her father's wishes when she leaves his underwater kingdom to explore the world," Janet Maslin wrote in the *New York Times*. "Adults will be charmed by its bright, outstandingly pretty look and by its robust score. Small children will be enchanted by the film's sunniness and by its perfect simplicity."

There are darker moments, as there have to be. To receive legs and pursue a romance with the prince on land, Ariel makes a Faustian bargain and gives her voice to the vindictive Ursula, who extracts it from her like a tooth in a lusty production number that could alarm very young children. When the agreement is made and the deed is done, it is a poignant moment with a real sense of loss. Ariel laments that after she moves ashore, she will never see her family again. Ursula says yes, that's true, but she will have her man.

Some women criticized the character for needing a man to fulfill her life. Others thought Ariel had too much cleavage. On-screen she manages a three-pronged agenda: winning the prince, overcoming Ursula, and assuaging her father. In true fairy-tale style, the prince, a handsome, bounding fellow more or less along for the ride, comes within a whisker of marrying the wrong woman (Ursula in disguise), but Ariel salvages the situation aided by the kind of last-second luck due all heroines headed for a glorious ending.

The film was the first of a half-dozen or so Disney animated epics to make hundreds of millions of dollars at the box office and hundreds of millions more on home video through the 1990s. Before *Mermaid* the studio's animation division had atrophied with a seniority system that stifled innovation and drove away younger talents like Don Bluth and Tim Burton. Then Michael Eisner was brought in to run the studio in 1984, and with him came Jeffrey Katzenberg, the supporting hand behind Disney's second era.

But it was Roy Disney, Walt's nephew, who convinced Eisner and Katzenberg to revive animation. Two young animators who had stuck it out during the dead years, John Musker and Ron Clements, wrote and directed *Mermaid*. Animated films usually have storyboards, but this one had a script, one indication that it would be approached in ways similar to a live-action feature.

In an article in the *Times* just after the film was released, Clements told Aljean Harmetz that a contemporary story can be stylized and caricatured, but to be convincing a tale must achieve realism. "We wanted as realistic an environment as possible to make the audience forget it was watching a cartoon," he said. "It's easy to sustain audience interest for an animated short. But beyond ten minutes, the audience has to forget the medium and get involved in the characters and story."

Musker said that the vibrant Ariel gave them problems depicting the prince. "The more active we made her, the tougher it was to make him active," he said. "Trying to keep him from being stiff, we made him one of the guys. We were going for a Jimmy Stewart or Henry Fonda prince, and we didn't make it."

The prince is almost incidental, given Ariel and the music. The songs were written to drive the plot. Ashman, who collaborated with Menken on *Aladdin* and *Beauty and the Beast* before he died of AIDS in 1992, told Harmetz that ballads were next to impossible in the modern era. "Kids have such a short attention span," he said. "Cinderella sings a ballad while she's scrubbing the floor. It's a brilliant piece of animation with her face reflected in dozens of bubbles, but the kids run up and down the aisles and get popcorn."

Broadway shows typically have an "I want" song, allowing the heroine to set out her desires and tell us what she'll be striving for. In *The Little Mermaid,* Ariel longs for the prince in the ballad "Part of

Your World." To keep the kids amused, and presumably in their seats, Ashman put her in a grotto full of eye-catching artifacts from wrecked ships.

As noted, one raucous musical scene with Ursula might bother some of the youngest ones. In other respects, the film is perfect from age four up.

55. A LITTLE PRINCESS

Liesel Matthews, Liam Cunningham, Vanessa Lee Chester, Eleanor Bron

DIRECTED BY ALFONSO CUARON
1995. 97 minutes. G

"Give Hollywood a kick in the right direction," read the letter from Peggy Charren in 1996. Founder of Action for Children's Television, Charren built her organization on the scarcity of truly first-rate material for kids, and here she was putting in a good word not for a TV show but for the Mexican director Alfonso Cuaron's remarkable movie, which had just been released on video.

In theaters Cuaron's adaptation of Frances Hodgson Burnett's story about a little girl who loses her father and then regains him had itself been lost amid a summer flood of big films like *Batman Forever, Die Hard with a Vengeance, Pocahontas,* and *Casper.* When watching films at home, the family tends to settle into a "girls'" film like this one, with boys joining in as often as not.

Cuaron does a spectacularly colorful and affecting job with a story that had two good but relatively standard treatments in earlier films, one starring Mary Pickford (1917) and the other Shirley Temple (1939). Burnett stranded rich kids in fearful and lonely English settings of wealth and power, only to rescue them in somewhat unlikely but uplifting scenarios (we'll see another example in

---

The Secret Garden, page 234). In this case Burnett's depository was "a big, dull, brick house, exactly like all the others in its row," but Cuaron energizes the scene by moving the story from London to New York.

As he is about to go off to fight in World War I, the well-to-do Captain Crewe (Liam Cunningham) puts his daughter Sara (Liesel Matthews) in Miss Minchin's Seminary. Sara's mother is dead and father and daughter have been living in India. "I was twenty pages into the script and I called my agent and said I found a film I want to do," Cuaron said in a recent interview from London, where he was preparing to direct *Harry Potter and the Prisoner of Azkaban,* the third film of the series. "The pages were vibrating in my hands."

By now we know him as something of a chameleon. "Mr. Cuaron's devilish talents, and his compulsion to subvert the very genres he's appropriating, serve him in good stead," the critic Elvis Mitchell wrote in the *New York Times.* Mitchell was referring to Y *Tu Mama Tambien* (2002), Cuaron's steamy road movie about a distressed young wife who runs off with two teenagers for a sojourn at the beach. In 1997 Cuaron appropriated Dickens's *Great Expectations* for a stylized and generally successful modern rendition that was no David Lean production (see page 112) in heft and dimension but wasn't intended to be. Nor was his take on *A Little Princess* intended to reflect Frances Hodgson Burnett's.

"Alfonso walked in, this hip young filmmaker, and I figured he would have absolutely no connection to this movie," Mark Johnson, the film's producer, told Bernard Weinraub in the *Times* in 1995. "Within twenty minutes I knew he was the right guy. It wasn't only his passion, but he was very articulate about what the movie had to say about the imagination and storytelling." Cuaron said he made the movie for his ten-year-old son. "Maybe you have children. You were a child once, a long time ago," he said on the telephone from London. Sara Crewe is ten when her father drops her off with Miss Minchin (Eleanor Bron), the witchlike money-grabber who makes a business of warehousing children of the rich. Cuaron immediately injects the magical and mystical into a story of gloriously colorful dreams and departures.

In the '90s Cuaron chose Liesel Matthews from among ten

thousand children screened for the role of Sara, and she is a scrumptious little girl, the perfect courageous and enlightened princess. Once more a child uses the pain of separation to find identity and come into her own, this time blossoming as a natural storyteller and leader among her neatly uniformed schoolmates who regularly gather by her bedside to hear her fanciful flights into whimsy and legend. (In 2002, the eighteen-year-old Matthews, a member of the Pritzger family, owners of the Hyatt hotel chain, made news by suing her father for allegedly draining more than $1 billion from her trust funds.)

Sara need only imagine to take us from Minchin's to the battlefield where her father reads her letters in teeming rain and great peril. One letter, she hopes, "kindles your heart, puts a smile on your face." Tragedy is ahead, or what we suppose is tragedy. Smaller viewers will need a comforting arm around them as Sara learns that her father is dead and she is banished to the garret after Minchin learns that along with his life Captain Crewe has apparently lost his money.

Cuaron's film does a spectacular job with the attic world where Sara befriends the little black servant girl Becky (Vanessa Lee Chester) and weaves richly magical connections to the refuge that gradually presents itself in the house next door. "In this film's harmonious world, anything from a bird to a balloon to the weather can conspire to intensify the character's thoughts," Janet Maslin wrote in the *Times*. "Mr. Cuaron makes that clear from the opening sequence, a brilliantly colorful staging of an Indian myth (among the film's clever amplifications of the original material) that sets the tone of inviting artificiality."

The story deals with race and class and loyalty through radical shifts in fortunes, but the film also teaches kids about artistic style. In this context the "artificial" generates fantasy with bits of colorful, symbolic whimsy used to carry and heighten the emotions. Rarely has swirling snow been as evocative as it is when mixed with the reds and oranges of Sara's imagined flights from the dark reaches of the garret.

One is always aware of color in this movie, and primarily the color is green, all shades of it. Production notes say that it was the only color that can be lit in warm and cold tones, providing great flexibility. Most everything from clothing to furnishings in the rather opulent Miss Minchin's has a green hue, an effective way to relieve the usual monochromatic black-and-white or sepia look of turn-of-the-century tableaux.

The story is told from the perspective of small children in a world where they are regarded as grown-ups. The school is made artificially huge, with exaggeratedly large staircases and high ceilings. The idea was to overwhelm the girls, make them feel even smaller in keeping with Minchin's policy that they be treated as small adults.

The production notes say that all classic stories need a building like Miss Minchin's for the story to emanate from. With Harry Potter, Cuaron has moved on to Hogwarts. After that, who knows? "I enjoyed *Shrek*," he said. "I'd love to do something like that."

Small children may be greatly upset when Captain Crewe leaves his daughter and later when it is thought he has been killed in the war and Sara loses everything, right down to her locket with her parents' pictures, which is stolen from her by Minchin in the name of paying for Sara's keep. Great violence is implied but not shown in scenes from the battlefield. There is no sex or profanity. About seven seems the right age to start.

56. LITTLE WOMEN

Winona Ryder, Claire Danes, Trini Alvarado, Kirsten Dunst, Susan Sarandon, Christian Bale, Gabriel Byrne, Eric Stoltz

DIRECTED BY GILLIAN ARMSTRONG
1994. 115 minutes. PG

This is a strong film, "so potent that it prompts a rush of recognition from the opening frame," Janet Maslin wrote in the *New York Times*. Nominally, it is one of ten screen adaptations (five of them for television) of Louisa May Alcott's beloved semiautobiographical story of the four March girls proceeding into womanhood in Concord, Massachusetts, and environs during the 1860s. The 1933 film with Katharine Hepburn and Joan Bennett, directed by George Cukor, is a fine relic from the days when Hollywood grown-ups played children and the women weren't so little. Gillian Armstrong's movie, by contrast, fairly flies with the likes of Winona Ryder and Claire Danes and Kirsten Dunst.

Young children may need hand-holding when the four sisters become three. As she lies dying of complications from rheumatic fever, Beth March (Danes) observes that she's the sister who loves being home and now she's the one who is going away. It's a great scene, as full of life as it is of death. Before it was shot, Danes and Ryder, as the tomboy and aspiring writer Jo March, geared up long and hard to achieve the emotion. Then something went wrong with the film negative, and the scene needed to be redone. In a DVD commentary, Armstrong said that Ryder didn't speak to her the next day.

The father of the family (Matthew Walker) is away in the Civil War and is such a cipher that he all but disappears after his return. With the exception of Laurie (Christian Bale), the March girls' good pal and all-purpose love interest, men are trappings in this story, and that even includes the professor (Gabriel Byrne) who is paired with Jo at the end of the film. This is a woman's story, roaringly female.

With the male provider gone for a long period and the family in reduced financial circumstances, Marmee (Susan Sarandon) and her four daughters bustle about their large house, which is always about to burst with activities and heartfelt interaction. Kids or anyone watching this film today will be aware how people from an era before television and the automobile took active measures to entertain and inform themselves. All of them read constantly, which is harder work for some than it is for others. A Dickens enthusiast, Jo stages attic theatricals with costumes and makeup. Next door, Laurie, from a well-to-do family, plays the piano and plans musical study abroad.

In the Cukor film, the Depression cast an air of reality over the March's comfortable impecuniousness, and the rush of 1930s modernity had viewers nostalgically longing for a gentler time not so long in the past. By the 1949 *Little Women*, directed by Mervyn LeRoy,

---

postwar prosperity had taken hold and the Marches indulge in a ripping good shopping spree.

Armstrong's film and its characters hew more closely to Alcott's
own interests and personality. Transcendentalism is added to the
book's issues of women's suffrage and high ideals. This is a 1990s
film born on a story that in Armstrong's opinion owes its timelessness
to its honesty and humor. On the disc Ryder says it's about goodness,
being a good person, following your heart, breaking hearts, yours
and other people's. Eric Stoltz, who plays a young scholar who marries Meg March (Trini Alvarado), says it's about doing the right
things in their lives. Danes says it's about learning about yourself at
this age. In most stories set in the 1800s, girls were never allowed to
be adolescents. In this film they are.

Armstrong says the cast worked on adopting the etiquette of the
day, which would have been important even to nonconformists like
the Marches. "In the 1860s, educated speech was of the utmost
importance in the March class of New England society," Anne Hollander, an art and film historian, wrote in the *Times*. Here a first-rate
cast does what it can, but this is the 1990s. "Ms. Sarandon's Marmee
says 'different than,'" Hollander wrote, "and Ms. Ryder speaks in
the same modern squawk she has used in all her films." Armstrong
says that Ryder was actually pretty good with accents, but she does
sound a bit mannered at times. In all, it only seems to add charm to a
highly spirited performance.

Armstrong, an Australian, was offered the film three times before
she took it. Earlier she had made *My Brilliant Career,* about another
strong-headed young woman who wants to write and who rejects an
attractive would-be husband because she doesn't love him. Jo does
much the same in *Little Women* and Armstrong felt she had done this
kind of story already. Ryder, who was the reason Columbia wanted
to make the picture, helped change her mind. She also recommended
Bale and Danes, a teenager who had made a big impression on the
acclaimed but short-lived television show *My So-Called Life.* Danes
auditioned for the role of Beth. "It was one of those rare instances
when you hear an actor read and know she's destined for greatness,"
Armstrong says.

Sarandon wanted the role of Marmee, though her agent didn't like her playing a woman as old as Ryder's mother. Dunst is Amy, the littlest March, and she all but steals the film before Amy grows into the much more sedate Samantha Mathis. Dunst came to the project fresh from the very unchildlike *Interview with a Vampire*, with Tom Cruise and Brad Pitt. The studio wanted name actresses to go with Ryder. Danes, a virtual unknown, had a second strike against her. "They also freaked out because Claire was taller than Winona and wouldn't seem like her little sister," Armstrong says. So sometimes they shot Danes on her knees.

This is a superb film for the whole family starting at about age seven or eight, maybe younger, depending on the child. Also try the 1933 film with Hepburn as a strapping, theatrical Jo of the old school and a very adult Joan Bennett playing little Amy in the days before kids usually played kids. There is no sex, violence, or profanity.

57. THE LONGEST DAY

John Wayne, Rod Steiger, Robert Ryan, Peter Lawford, Henry Fonda, Robert Mitchum, Richard Burton

DIRECTED BY KEN ANNAKIN, ANDREW MARTON,
AND BERNHARD WICKI
1962. 180 minutes. Black and white. No rating

Darryl F. Zanuck, who produced the movie, is an uncredited fourth director of a film that could be described as the Normandy invasion without the horrific, if realistic, R-rated slaughter of Steven Spielberg's *Saving Private Ryan*. How realistic is *The Longest Day*? In his autobiography, *So You Wanna Be a Director,* Ken Annakin quoted Zanuck as telling him, "What I want from this film is absolute truth. It must be war as it really was, not Hollywood war." Nevertheless this was 1962 and the so-called code of decency, in effect until 1966, wouldn't have allowed the graphic dismemberment we see in the Spielberg film. "We were still under a certain censorship for killing and brutality, but that wouldn't have been Zanuck's cup of tea anyway," Annakin said in an interview in 2001.

That's good for kids because along with a big action film that's on the go from start to finish, they view a spectacular and historically important event without the gore. Much of the landing and the struggle to claw inland is shot from helicopters, high enough to catch the vast panorama but close enough to convey the reality that Allied troops were going down in heavy German fire from the bluffs overlooking Omaha, Juno, Sword, and Gold beaches.

Ten thousand extras stormed ashore in *The Longest Day.* Some big Hollywood names got their fatigues wet. Henry Fonda is Brig. Gen. Theodore Roosevelt Jr., who hits the beach with his boys despite misgivings in Washington about risking the son of a former president in combat. Normally a GI in other war flicks, Robert Mitchum gets a general's star in this one and prods his terrified and demoralized troops into staging the breakout that starts the Allies on the long road to Paris. Parents who have seen the film will recall the man with the bulldog, the beachmaster Captain Colin Maud (Kenneth More) of the Royal Navy. And there is the Duke (John Wayne) as Lt. Col. Benjamin Vandervoort of the 82nd Airborne Division, who breaks an ankle in a drop into the key village of Saint Mère-Eglise.

Zanuck flew the big names on and off location in France according to their availability. Not a director, Zanuck wanted to play at being one and asked Annakin to set up some invasion shots for him. At the appropriate moment, he would step in to yell "Action" and "Cut." Not thrilled at the prospect, Annakin went along; but usually Zanuck, who was running 20th Century Fox, was too busy to show up.

While *Saving Private Ryan* gives us an exclusively American view of the invasion, *The Longest Day* lends an international perspective.

Peter Lawford of Hollywood "Rat Pack" fame sashays into the fray as the British commander Lord Lovat, dapper in beret and white turtleneck and only vaguely cognizant of withering German machine-gun fire. The real Lord Lovat showed up to watch the filming. "Look at how that idiot walks," he roared at the sight of Lawford mincing cockily as if he were in Vegas. Coming ashore with his commandos (real ones on loan from the British army), Lawford forgot to zip up his wet suit and sank in eight feet of water. Later he threatened to sue the wardrobe lady.

We also view the action through the eyes of the Germans. Most memorably there is the look of total shock on their faces as the gigantic Allied armada materializes in the mists offshore. Werner Hinz is a fine Field Marshal Erwin Rommel; Curt Jurgens, the quintessential portrayer of top German brass, is the droll Maj. Gen. Gunther Blumentritt.

Early '60s pop figures toil in the enlisted ranks. Paul Anka, Fabian, and Tommy Sands are Army Rangers. Red Buttons is a voluble private; Sal Mineo is a doomed GI named Martini. Another private is played by Sean Connery, who was about to become James Bond in *Dr. No*. Annakin says that Zanuck hated Connery's accent and thought he looked like a slob. It's safe to say he was the last studio head to feel that way.

War is war, of course, but here we have a serious entertainment that covers a huge subject about as palatably as possible for kids. The violence is fairly circumspect, which clears the way for children starting at about age ten. There is no sex or profanity.

58. THE LORD OF THE RINGS: THE FELLOWSHIP OF THE RING

Elijah Wood, Ian McKellen, Viggo Mortensen, Liv Tyler, Cate Blanchett, Sean Astin, Christopher Lee, Ian Holm, Hugo Weaving

DIRECTED BY PETER JACKSON

2001. 178 minutes. PG-13

A month before the movie opened in December 2001, an interviewer asked the English actor Ian McKellen, who plays Gandalf, if he looked forward to "playing a craggy old guy to a theater of overstimulated ten-year-olds." McKellen answered that the very young could see the film, but about the only thing that linked the *Rings* films with children's movies like *Shrek* and *Harry Potter and the Sorcerer's Stone* was its intense marketing.

Peter Jackson's epic, the first of a trilogy adapted from J. R. R. Tolkien's books, is a slew of things to a variety of people. (The second installment, *The Two Towers,* has also been released on DVD, and the third, *The Return of the King,* is to open in December 2003.) Yes, it could be called a kids' movie, but this is a tale of warring factions, and the violence is frequent, very realistic in a fantastical way, and altogether unsuitable for little ones. Age ten, in fact, is perhaps the floor here, though parents could decide younger children are up to it. Other elements of the film—notably little Frodo Baggins (Elijah Wood) in his half-pint Hobbit realm, for instance—delight all ages.

Jackson's movie is in the service of arguably the most popular books of the twentieth century. On the literary side, only *The Hobbit,* a fourth Tolkien work that preceded the *Rings* trilogy, is meant for children. Parents and children who have dipped into the other Tolkiens (more than a thousand pages' worth) appreciate the challenges of bringing such a dense, incredibly detailed work to the screen. The story of that is a saga unto itself.

Rings the movie is labeled fantasy, a genre that with the exception of *King Kong* and a few other films has generally leaned toward the ridiculous. Jackson, a New Zealander, is quick to point out that *Rings* is mythology, not fantasy. He started developing the film conversion in 1996 in partnership with Miramax, which laid out $20 million to start the project. But how to approach the huge literary outpouring of the renowned Oxford philologist who took it upon himself to create an entire English mythological tradition that had been essentially lost after the Norman invasion of 1066? With an entire world to establish on-screen, too much compression would be disastrous. Jackson decided on a trilogy.

Miramax is run by Harvey Weinstein, himself a moviemaking legend if not an enthusiast of endless epics with enormous budgets. At first he suggested two films, and Jackson and his team of thirty writers and designers set to work. By the time they finished the scripts, the budgets for each movie had risen to $130 and $140 million. Weinstein's sights, on the other hand, had lowered. Jackson said he was told there was $75 million for one film.

Shoehorning to the point of evisceration obviously was pointless. Jackson headed back to New Zealand with the project "turned around" (killed), as they say in movie parlance, but intermediaries persuaded Weinstein to relinquish the rights. A relatively small film company, New Line, decided on a make-or-break plan to produce all three films as Jackson originally envisioned. The budget was $270 million.

As a setting for a world both recognizably earthly but jungled and craggy and otherwise unfamiliar in ways that suggest the mythical, Jackson chose his native New Zealand. All three films would be made at once, with many scenes shot simultaneously all over the country. The project would last eighteen months, which for the actors represented not so much a job as a commitment to uproot their lives and virtually disengage from everything else.

Jackson avoided major stars because they would deflect attention from a complicated story that had to be established quickly and clearly. The critical casting decision was the choice of Wood, an American, to play the tiny Hobbit man/boy Frodo Baggins, who is charged with saving Middle-Earth by destroying the ring of power sought by the black lord Sauron. Jackson originally felt that an English actor would be better suited for such English material, but auditions of three hundred candidates in London turned up no one. Then a video arrived from Wood, who rented what he considered a Hobbit-like costume in Los Angeles and read some selections from Tolkien's books. Jackson says that no one but the consummately English, Shakespeare-trained McKellen was considered for Gandalf, the agent of higher powers sent to help Middle-Earth.

Violence notwithstanding, kids unfamiliar with the books will enjoy a first-rate action-adventure full of characters and situations they will understand. Tolkien readers generally approve of the first *Rings* film, though they feel the battles and cliff-hanging escapes might take too much precedence over much of the ornately filigreed literary legend steeped in reams of historical documents, footnotes, ancient tales, and complex linguistics. Purists also note the expanded participation of the beautiful Arwen (Liv Tyler), the immortal elf in love with the warrior Aragorn (Viggo Mortensen). But, hey, this is a movie.

Jackson says the film is more popular with the uninitiated. One of his jobs was to winnow Tolkien without alienating the loyal. That meant staying true to the author's Christian-rooted ideas of good and evil. Tolkien wrote shortly after World War II when the crimes of Hitler and Stalin were fresh. He also loathed machines and technology. "He said that the most evil creation visited on this world was the internal combustion engine," Jackson told the interviewer Charlie Rose. One wonders how the author would have felt about the computer-generated graphics that integrate much of the action with the spectacular landscapes.

Some moviegoers complain that the film ends abruptly with no big-bang finale that kids and the rest of us crave and expect. That's true but remember that the first film leads into the second and the second into the third. After the first movie, Jackson talked about his expectations for the next two. "They have to be better, don't they?" he said to Rose. Critics generally agreed that *The Two Towers* equaled or surpassed *Fellowship*. By now a verdict should be imminent on *The Return of the King*.

Some children under ten, to set an arbitrary age, will take the film's carnage in stride, but don't count on it. This is clearly stylized, digitally assisted violence, but a very high body count and all the menacing creatures could prove disturbing. The Two Towers is also extremely violent. Be very careful about any child under twelve or so. There is no sex or profanity.

59. LOST HORIZON

Ronald Colman, Jane Wyatt, Edward Everett Horton, Sam Jaffe, H. B. Warner, John Howard

DIRECTED BY FRANK CAPRA
1937. 138 minutes. No rating

Capra's tale about a mystical otherworld called Shangri-la includes a technical curiosity that should be explained to kids beforehand lest they think something has gone completely weird with the movie. Like other older films, *Lost Horizon* was shot on nitrate stock, which deteriorated to the point of disintegration. By 1967, there was nothing left of the original camera negative. Various prints and parts of prints had become scattered, and it took years to find enough elements to make a complete movie—or almost a complete movie. Actually, the recovered parts turned out to be seven minutes shorter than the sound track. To stretch the movie to match its sound, still photographs are used to bridge the gaps.

In the bargain kids will get several little slide shows, so to speak, within the movie. The stills appear only a few times, and they are exquisite. Far from detracting from the action, they and the audio carry it along perfectly well. They also illustrate a clever way to preserve a film. But it's good to know all about this beforehand so it doesn't prove too disruptive.

As for the moving parts, digital repairs revive a striking piece of work. A story about trekking up a towering peak in a raging blizzard, ducking through a tiny slit, and emerging in a warm, sunny valley makes a nice fantasy. The idea was suggested by James Hilton's novel about George Leigh-Mallory, who disappeared from the face of Mount Everest in 1924. In the film, a half-dozen or so freezing survivors of a plane crash follow an elderly Asian guide (H. B. Warner) to salvation. In the fragrant warmth of Shangri-la, moderation is the rule and the inhabitants step away from confrontation. A pacifistic society has managed to detach itself from man's greed and brutality. How will the newcomers react?

They are led by Robert Conway (Ronald Colman), a celebrated British author and statesman of peaceful inclinations himself who is trumpeted back home as a probable foreign secretary. Before the crash he had been dispatched to China to rescue a group of his countrymen from a violent political upheaval. Conway herds them aboard an aircraft presumably bound for Shanghai. Come daylight, they realize they are flying in the opposite direction. Peaks appear as winds rise and snows worsen. Down they go, bouncing and plowing to a stop on the side of a mountain. No one suffers a scratch except the pilot—the one of them who could supply some answers—who is dead.

It's damn cold, and here and in all the mountain scenes that follow the film created some startling special effects—right in sunny California. Capra rented the cavernous Los Angeles Coal and Ice Storage Company and fed three-hundred-pound blocks of ice to a blower that produced snow by the ton. Four miles of ammonia piping kept the temperature in the twenties. For shots of hiking across open mountain faces, he hired a documentary filmmaker to put people in the outdoors and trek for real.

Along with his feature films, Capra made his own patriotic documentaries during World War II. Some of this zeal spills over to *Lost Horizon*, which has some propagandist overtones. In 1938, when the film was released, a caption read, "Our story begins in the war-torn Chinese city of Baskal, where Robert Conway has been sent to evacuate 90 white people before they are butchered in a local revolution." After war broke out, the caption stated that Baskal was "beset by invaders from Japan" and the white people are about to be "butchered by the Japanese hordes."

But these are footnotes. *Lost Horizon* is full of Capra's usual energy and enthusiasm. Some first scenes set in London were discarded after a preview audience laughed at their overwrought melodrama. At the screening, Capra was so upset he rushed out into a rainstorm and didn't come back until the movie was over. The rest of the film got it exactly right. "There's a wish for Shangri-la in everybody's head," the two-hundred-year-old High Lama (Sam Jaffe) says. Children will love the notion of a secret place where people never grow old and there is warmth and kindness and safety. The unreality of that is worthy of discussion, but it's a nice notion to hold.

Many older kids will grasp the film's ideas; younger ones will enjoy the trek and spectacular settings. Capra's utopia is both wonderfully tucked away and grandly spacious. The High Lama has read Conway's books and regards him as his successor. Conway is enthralled, but the pull of his prior life is too strong and he leaves. Once gone from Shangri-la he realizes his mistake and desperately fights to return to a life and philosophy he can't abandon. Capra doesn't deny him. Kids will love the movie for that.

Children will begin to like the film at about age eight and probably go on liking it until whenever so-called cool and sophistication rules out an admittedly very old movie with some very old ways of expressing itself. Even then many kids will sit still for it on the right occasion. Anyway, there is no violence, sex, or profanity.

60. THE MAGNIFICENT SEVEN

**Yul Brynner, Steve McQueen, Eli Wallach,
Charles Bronson, James Coburn, Horst Buchholz,
Robert Vaughn, Rosenda Monteros,
Vladimir Sokoloff**

DIRECTED BY JOHN STURGES
1960. 126 minutes. No rating

The stars of John Sturges's film didn't have their hopes up when it was released. "We had no script, a Japanese story that doesn't necessarily appeal to Americans, a Mongolian guy playing a cowboy," says Robert Vaughn, who portrays one of seven gunmen hired to protect a Mexican farming village against an outlaw band. He could have mentioned a German (Horst Buchholz) playing another gunfighter and a New Yorker if there ever was one (Eli Wallach) as a Mexican bandit chief.

In fact, the film opened quietly in the United States but caught fire in Europe, which inspired Universal to get behind the picture in this country. Three sequels followed and a television series. Today the film is a classic—and one that, despite its violence, even young children can enjoy and appreciate.

Vaughn was speaking apocryphally about the script. Actually it was a fine one, full of sage observations and swift ripostes. The Japanese story, of course, was Akira Kurosawa's epic *The Seven Samurai* (1954), about a roaming band of knights who defend a village against forty mounted bandits in the fourteenth century. The "Mongolian" Vaughn refers to was Yul Brynner, in the role of Chris, the lead gunfighter. Actually, Brynner was born in Russia.

Traditional westerns like *Rio Bravo* (1959), with their shining ideals and upbeat endings, were on their way out in 1960, giving way to the more stark, nihilistic "spaghetti" variety of Sergio Leone. *The*

Magnificent Seven is somewhat transitional. Ideals come grudgingly in this film. In fact, they are towering, but everybody has to dig hard and pay plenty to keep them in focus.

Early in the film, Chris, a fierce, quiet stranger all in black, and another gunslinger named Vin (Steve McQueen) are hanging around the hitching rack when they decide they don't like the idea of a man being denied a boot-hill burial just because he is an Indian. Driving the hearse themselves, the pair team up and engage in the film's first gunplay to get the Indian planted as is his right.

Watching this scene are three Mexican farmers in town to try to buy guns to defend themselves against a bandit named Calvera (Wallach) and his thirty-five men, who regularly ride into their village to steal food and terrorize the people. Chris suggests that since the farmers know nothing about guns they should hire people who do. About all they can scrape up will pay seven men $20 each for what Chris figures will be six weeks' work.

The next part of the film concerns itself with that time-honored procedure in many movies: recruiting just the right experts. All but one of the men Chris picks are fast guns he either knows or recognizes as people who can get the job done. Vin is in, though the money will hardly buy bullets. Lee (Vaughn) is a dude with demons. Half-Mexican himself, O'Reilly (Charles Bronson) has enough softness to attach himself to the children of the village. Britt (James Coburn) is as fast with a knife as he is with a gun, a kind of counterpart to Kurosawa's swordsmen. Harry (Brad Dexter) is the one among them who thinks that there has to be a pile of money in it somehow (Aztec treasure perhaps). The seventh is Chico (Buchholz), a stubborn, hotheaded aspiring gunfighter who is finally allowed into the group despite his inexperience.

When they reach the village, battles ensue and individuals emerge. By now children will be aware of the sturdier individuals and their values—Chris's calm steadfastness and sense of justice, for example—but gunslingers and townspeople are put to the test. Chris is offended to learn that the farmers have hidden their women from the seven. Such lack of trust in the people they have hired to save them puts the mission on slippery footing right at the start. Later he will demand perseverance and threatens to shoot villagers who defect, an interesting edict that might be discussed in relation to similar events during the war in Iraq.

Outmanned and outmaneuvered by Calvera, the seven themselves consider quitting. "We took a contract," Chris says, as he tries to hold the group together.

"Not that any court would enforce," someone answers.

"That's the kind you have to keep," Chris says. Later, though, he recognizes a hopeless situation and orders the others to withdraw.

These are not stick figures. In a documentary on the DVD, Chris is described as a dirty bum. The only things clean about him are his gun and his soul. Deathly afraid that his gun hand is slowing, Lee calls himself "a deserter hiding out in the middle of a battlefield." The villagers tell him they live with that kind of fear themselves. O'Reilly is adored by three village children, who call their fathers cowards for not wanting to fight. He spanks one for even thinking such a thing. Their fathers show courage instead by bearing responsibility for their families. Perhaps the most interesting character is the voluble Calvera, something of a psychiatrist and philosopher who wonders why Chris would commit himself to the village and its people.

Kurosawa admired the films of John Ford and modeled aspects of *The Seven Samurai* after an American western. A major difference is how the seven are hired. In Kurosawa's film, they are employed to save the village, but in Sturges's movie, shot in Mexico, the process is more convoluted. Mexicans felt slandered by their depiction in *Vera Cruz* (1954), to the point of ripping out seats and throwing them at the screen. When Sturges went to make *The Magnificent Seven*, censors objected to Mexicans being depicted as people who need others to fight their battles for them. Thus the villagers buy guns with the intent of fighting for themselves. It is left to Chris to suggest hiring others who were better at this kind of thing.

And it's Chris who summarizes what glamorized gunfighters come out with at the end: no wife, no kids, no prospects. Some wanted to make Chris an older Spencer Tracy type, no longer up to the physical task of gunfighting but patriarchal. Sturges and Tracy had worked together in *Bad Day at Black Rock* (1954), but here the filmmakers went for the lean, taciturn Brynner. Sturges, a respected craftsman, put young faces in the middle of the picture. Some went on to big careers. McQueen, who had emerged in the television series *Wanted: Dead or Alive,* wasn't given much to say as Vin, but he was always trying to upstage Brynner with gestures and mannerisms. Brynner kept his black hat on his famously shaved skull. All he had to do to upstage McQueen, he said, was take it off.

The film has something to say about courage, resolve, and loyalty. Obviously there are many gunfights with a good many deaths, but these aren't as graphic as they would be today. The film's strong sense of decency and morality should carry the day. As an action film, it's a crackerjack, even now.

61. MARY POPPINS

Julie Andrews, Dick Van Dyke, David Tomlinson, Glynis Johns, Karen Dotrice, Matthew Garber

DIRECTED BY ROBERT STEVENSON
1964. 140 minutes. No rating

Put together a collection of one hundred movies for younger children and at least a dozen of them have to be from Disney. After that, the compiler is more or less obliged to stave off Disney titles as if repelling boarders. This may sound un-American, but good riddance in a lot of cases.

No one would denigrate Walt Disney's innovative bursts, from his first cartoons, called Newman Laugh-O-Grams, in Kansas City about 1920, through the first animated features of the 1930s (*Snow White and the Seven Dwarfs* and *Pinocchio*, see pages 249 and 215) and all his singular cinematic achievements before his death in 1966. But it comes as no news that a Disney product can be bland and banal. Like many innovators, Walt Disney was happiest innovating, after which his interest moved to the next innovation. In his wake the Disney studio tended to settle into grooves for long stretches, and this is particularly true of the breed of cheery live action family films it turned out in the '50s and '60s.

Now and then some exceptional films emerged—*20,000 Leagues Under the Sea* in 1954, for one (see page 287), and *Swiss Family Robinson* (1960) for another (see page 275)—but as often as not "product" was the word for it.

Mary Poppins just explodes from the pack, an original and a winner in every respect for kids from about four up. Robert Stevenson's adaptation of P. L. Travers's classic tale of the flying nursemaid has terrific effects and music, but its great strength is Julie Andrews in the title role. With her long, lovely face and pleasingly starchy manner, she is fascinating to watch as she flies her umbrella into the London household of George and Winifred Banks (David Tomlinson and Glynis Johns) and their young daughter (Karen Dotrice) and son (Matthew Garber).

Andrews won the Oscar as best actress. It was her first movie role, the beginning of her intermittent appearances on the screen. That same year she appeared opposite James Garner in Arthur Hiller's *The Americanization of Emily* (a good bet for kids from eleven up). The next year she would gain immortality, as they say, as another nanny in Robert Wise's *The Sound of Music* (see page 256). That got her a second consecutive Oscar nomination. Her third would come for *Victor/Victoria* (1982), directed by her husband, Blake Edwards. Other than these few films, however, this aspect of her career languished in the late '60s and '70s—along with the movie musical—as she moved on to successes in television.

The *Poppins* Oscar involves a nice piece of turnaround. Eight years earlier, Andrews was Eliza Doolittle in *My Fair Lady* on Broadway, one of the great matches of character and star in stage history. When it came to making the movie, the studio head Jack Warner decided on Audrey Hepburn for the role. Hepburn was appealing, certainly, but she couldn't sing a lick. *My Fair Lady* beat *Mary Poppins* (and *Becket, Dr. Strangelove,* and *Zorba the Greek*) as best picture in 1964, but Hepburn wasn't nominated. Some said that

Andrews's victory was intended as a slap at Warner, but her performance as Poppins stood on its own.

The voice and manner do it. It's hard to take your eyes off Mary Poppins. Dick Van Dyke is also effective as Mary's friend Bert, the chimney sweep and jack-of-all-trades. Under heavy makeup and with a flowing beard, Van Dyke is also old man Dawes, patriarch of the bank that employs George Banks, the stodgy (at first) dad who holds that a British nanny should be a general, the better "to mold the breed." In Mary Poppins he gets a governess who knows her own mind, but leaves the children plenty of room to indulge their whimsy.

Mary's specialty is gliding through the skies under her umbrella and inserting herself into households where children need liberation from suffocating parents. Not knowing quite what to make of Poppins, George Banks finds himself not only hiring her against his better judgment but knuckling under in dithering ineffectuality every time he tries to assert his stringently hidebound views of child rearing.

Poppins ignores him. Since she is magical—able to straighten a monumentally messy room with a wave, for example—special effects play a large part. The film famously blends animation and live action when Mary and the children follow Bert into one of his sidewalk chalk drawings and spend the day gamboling with animated characters, including a group of dancing penguins.

This was still a grand era for the movie musical. At his most pedantic, father Banks expresses his views in a patter song style very similar to that used by Rex Harrison as the pedantic Henry Higgins in *My Fair Lady*. The movie was nominated for thirteen Oscars all told. The Sherman brothers, Richard and Robert, won one Oscar for their score and another for best song, "Chim Chim Cheree." Sets are spectacular and the look sumptuous (Disney never scrimped on budgets), giving an impression of London that is convincing and unreal at the same time. Rooftops are wonderfully stylized and complex, particularly during an electrifying production number called "Step in Time" with a dozen dancing chimney sweeps.

Amid its upbeat fancy, the movie also deals some serious reflection on the role of a man like George Banks. Behind all the self-righteous rectitude is a lonely fellow isolated by his responsibility. When he takes his children for a visit to his office his son acts frivolously, in the view of George's bosses, and he is fired. This is a catastrophe, the removal of everything that matters. Summoned to a 9 P.M. firing, George walks to his fate through wet empty streets as if approaching execution. At the bank, the red flower in his lapel is stripped and torn in two, his big black umbrella is inverted, and someone punches a hole in his bowler. Ignominy.

Pretty hilarious actually. Earlier at home Banks has gotten his first inkling of what his severity is doing to his children. The drumming-out ceremony at the bank releases his feelings and he practically skips out of the place. Later everybody goes off to fly a kite in the park, which is fine. But then Banks meets his former employers, who offer him his job back. He humbly accepts as if nothing had happened. What one won't do for a happy ending.

This is a perfect family film, no reservations whatever. The suitable age starts at four or five. Some critics call it the best children's film ever, along with The Wizard of Oz.

62. MONSTERS, INC.

With the voices of John Goodman, Billy Crystal, Steve Buscemi, James Coburn

DIRECTED BY PETE DOCTER,
WITH LEE UNKRICH AND DAVID SILVERMAN
2001. 92 minutes. G

Monsters, Inc. is among the most wildly popular kids' films of all time (five million videos sold in one day). This is the fourth totally computer-animated film to come from Pixar, the northern California studio that works in partnership with Disney (the first three being the two *Toy Story* movies, see page 284, and *A Bug's Life*). Pete Docter, the director, has fond if somewhat ambivalent feelings about the Disney connection. Like many who work at Pixar, he is a graduate of the California Institute of the Arts (Cal Arts for short), which is especially strong on the training of animators and was in large part set up and sponsored by the man himself, Walt Disney.

Docter, age thirty-three, was in the class of 1990. "When you're there it's almost anti-Disney," he says. "There's a real sentiment against the traditional stuff. In a lot of ways, it's still a sixties school. Rebellion is where it's at." But in the next breath he's almost apologetic. "*Dumbo* is my favorite all-time film," he says. "We think of our films in terms of that lineage. We're huge fans of those films. I admire the simplicity, the personalities they capture, and the animation. We try to do the same thing here, only with cutting-edge media."

Computers render three-dimensional settings and movement of such striking detail that the film seems like live action—well, animated live action. But Docter says the story, not the technology, is the vital element. At Pixar, ideas are group projects, hatched and developed among filmmakers whizzing around on scooters. Most of them have kids of their own to keep them on track. And they remember their childhoods. "With *Monsters* I was trying to tap in to what we did in *Toy Story*," Docter says. "There we hooked into something we all believed in as kids. We knew that when we closed the door, the toys came to life. This time, I knew there were monsters hiding in my closet. That gave us a leg up on what counts with kids." After that, the plot is not so simple.

At Monsters, Inc., a gigantic plant with towering smokestacks in the city of Monstropolis, vast assembly lines of thousands of closet doors whiz around on conveyors like garments in a huge dry cleaner's. Through those doors and into children's bedrooms plunge multi-limbed, many-eyed creatures with backbones as spiny as the Apennines and teeth as big as fence pickets. Their job is to elicit the loudest shrieks possible from kiddies tucked into their beds, and since Monstropolis converts the screams into electric power, the scarers, as they are called, are slaves to quotas.

Above all, scarers are taught to close doors tightly behind them when they are done scaring and leave a child's room. Otherwise the worst could happen: a kid could follow them through the other way, back into Monstropolis, where children and all objects related to children are regarded as toxic hazards. Alarms shriek and helmeted, rubber-suited agents of the CDA (Child Detection Agency) rush to decontaminate. *Monsters, Inc.* opened in theaters during the anthrax scare in 2001, but audiences didn't seem put off by responses to a "2319," or report of a human toy or maybe piece of clothing that might endanger Monstropolis. When one poor scarer returns with a sock in static cling on his furry back, he is shaved from head to toe and scoured.

Some critics said they couldn't imagine children warming up to such a story. The problems, they felt, had to do with the colder realities of Pixar animation and the fact that in this scenario children themselves are held up as all that is to be dreaded. Of course, it's this last element that works so well with kids, who are absolutely thrilled that the monsters employed to scare the daylights out of little ones in their beds turn out to be more scared of them than they are of the monsters.

Another thing about those kids in the movie: they don't frighten as easily as they used to. Good scarers are hard to find. Having run into a situation he clearly couldn't handle, one scarer emerges in shell shock. The ideal scarer, according to P. J. Waternoose (James Coburn), president of Monsters, Inc., is a big blue bearish figure named Sully (John Goodman), who is built along the lines of the Sesame Street cookie monster, only several feet taller. Sully, a kind of walking shag carpet, ranks No. 1 among scarers at the plant, but what delights kids watching the movie is that he's the sweetest guy imaginable.

Therefore, it stands to reason that Sully is the one to discover that the human infant, called Boo, who inevitably follows him back through the door and unleashes panicky bedlam in Monstropolis, is really harmless. This is a jaunty tale, told with absolute assurance by people who have kids and understand them. It has its share of standard plotting: the bad guy—or in this case, lizard monster (Steve Buscemi)—with his scheme to take over the plant, a chase on a roller coaster of speeding doors, a basically happy but somewhat bittersweet ending that sets up a sequel. Its message is to relax, keep an open mind, and realize that appearances are often far from reality.

The film is especially good with little touches. In a city street a frustrated fire-breather keeps setting fire to the newspaper he's trying to read. When Sully's scream total dips he gets lucky and hits a slumber party. At Monster's, Inc. the slogan "a better tomorrow today" spoofs General Electric. At first terrified of Boo, Sully lobs Cheerios into her mouth from across the room. "A killing machine," says his smart-mouthed sidekick, Mike (Billy Crystal), of their little guest. But Sully and Mike come to know better.

As in all Pixar films the characters seem lifelike. Along with freedom of movement, computer animation raises expectations of nothing less than perfect photographic reality. That's not possible, but the effect is not cold and unnatural; rather it's different and not necessarily unpleasing. Pixar clearly knows what it's doing. "Others try to pander," Docter says. "We just make films for ourselves."

At one point Sully and Mike are "banished" and become outcasts, an interesting notion to explore with kids but perhaps upsetting to the very young. Otherwise the action could be a trifle intense for, say, three- to five-year-olds, but all the scares are clearly in fun. Industrial underpinnings or no, this is a film for small children. Parents won't mind it either.

63. MR. SMITH GOES TO WASHINGTON

James Stewart, Jean Arthur, Claude Rains, Edward Arnold, Thomas Mitchell

DIRECTED BY FRANK CAPRA

1939. 125 minutes. Black and white. No rating

Gazing out his office window, the awed Senator Jefferson Smith (James Stewart) pays homage to the shining dome of the capitol building "sparkling away under the old sun out there." Well, darned if it doesn't. The gawkily boyish Smith also shows enthusiasm over the Lincoln Memorial a couple of times in Frank Capra's film. There old Abe resides "in this temple as in the hearts of the people for whom he saved the union," as it says in the inscription.

Capra scouted Washington for locations, and he has Smith take much the same tour at the start of the movie. Their mutual sentimentality is done up in waving flags and a blaring national anthem, which may seem a little cornball to kids today. Just point out that the emotions are no more pronounced than the patriotic feelings that began flowing after the terrorist attacks of 2001. It's all a matter of adapting to the period and style.

Capra, born in Sicily and the son of an immigrant orange picker, intended the movie to celebrate democracy as war clouds were gathering. He also wanted to uphold integrity of government, the message being that we had better be careful or freedom could be taken away from us. But the most interesting aspect of this film is the uproar it stirred up in official Washington and its press corps, who are depicted, respectively, as venal frauds and blathering hacks.

One of this country's greatest filmmakers, Capra often had to struggle in his career. In his early days he was fired repeatedly and succeeded only with dogged persistence. His movie gives us big, broad characters expressing themselves clearly enough for even small kids to understand. Jefferson Smith of Montana is chosen by the state's canny old political patriarch, Senator Joseph Paine (Claude Rains), to finish the term of a deceased colleague. Of noble intentions once himself, Paine is now party to a crooked big-money scheme put together by Jim Taylor (Edward Arnold), a press tycoon who buys politicians. Smith is seen as just the yokel they need to support their interests, but Paine and Taylor have the wrong man. In Smith, Capra gives us a little guy, but one who has the guts to stand up to entrenched power. Only after much humiliation from an establishment and a press corps that ridicules his naïveté does he realize that he has the strength and ability to fight back.

This is arguably Stewart's greatest role. Capra and his boss, Harry Cohn, the head of Columbia, originally wanted Gary Cooper, the star of *Mr. Deeds Goes to Town,* another great Capra family film, about a millionaire who wants to give his money away to the needy. But Cooper was under contract elsewhere. *Mr. Deeds* also starred

Jean Arthur. In *Mr. Smith* she is Saunders, the senator's brash aide who eventually falls in love with him. For all her remarkable vitality on-screen, the insecure and self-deprecating Arthur dived into her trailer after every scene. "She was unbelievably difficult to work with, hard to rehearse, very shy," Frank Capra Jr., the director's son, says on the DVD.

Washington has jaded Saunders. "My eyes were big blue question marks; now they're big green dollar signs," she tells Smith. But she can't help being nice to the new boy. Saunders encourages Smith to introduce his own pet scheme for a national boys' camp. The very idea brings guffaws from senators and the press. Then the camp gets in the way of Paine and Taylor, setting up the struggle between them and Smith that leads to Smith's filibuster and all sorts of down-and-dirty retaliation designed to smear his integrity, force his resignation, and drive the boy wonder into oblivion back in Montana.

During the film, the senators carry on like arrogant schoolboys. The press passes it on to the public. "We tell them what phonies and crackpots make their laws," a reporter tells Smith. Capra had heard that left-handed people were eccentric, so he hired the left-handed Thomas Mitchell to play the reporter Diz Moore, who isn't quite a fall-down drunk but has all the stereotypically raffish characteristics of loudmouthed newspaper scribblers.

When the movie was finished, it was screened for a senatorial crowd at the Washington Press Club. They didn't like what they saw. Capra was a two-time Oscar winner and Harry Cohn's favorite at Columbia, but Cohn ducked out at the first signs of outrage from the audience. Poor Capra stuck it out for the screening and a dinner afterward, where he took a lot of verbal abuse. Alben Barkley, then a real-life senator from Kentucky and later Harry S Truman's vice president, attacked the film as a gross distortion. But when the public liked *Mr. Smith,* official Washington and the press backed off.

"He should have seen trouble coming, but he didn't," Capra's son said of his father. The House Un-American Activities Committee tried to read something sinister into Sidney Buchman's screenplay, but it was hard to pinpoint anything communistic or otherwise seditious in *Mr. Smith Goes to Washington.* Capra did detect some mischief in the Senate chamber, which he studied before he made an exact replica in Hollywood. In the real chamber—and kids will appreciate this—he found senators' initials carved in the desks and the clock locked to prevent them from pushing the hands forward so they could get out early.

Kids should start to like this film by the age of eight or thereabouts. Whatever their age, they may find it a little outmoded, but that shouldn't matter. There is no sex or profanity and only a bit of violence when Smith slugs a few reporters for making a fool out of him in the papers.

64. MRS. DOUBTFIRE

Robin Williams, Sally Field, Lisa Jakub, Mara Wilson, Matthew Lawrence, Pierce Brosnan

DIRECTED BY CHRIS COLUMBUS
1993. 125 minutes. PG-13

This is another movie that film critics attack and kids like (not to suggest a parallel with *Harry Potter and the Sorcerer's Stone,* also directed by Chris Columbus, see page 121). The transformation of Daniel Hillard (Robin Williams) into a large English nanny struck reviewers as more of a stunt than an act of love by a man threatened with divorce who claims that he literally can't survive without being in contact with his children. Hillard's disguise is incredible, but are we really to believe that his estranged wife, Miranda (Sally Field), wouldn't recognize him? How could Hillard switch from himself to the nanny as quickly as he does at a couple of points in the movie? Then there is the film's "sitcom shininess," as Janet Maslin referred to the domestic squabbles in the *New York Times.*

Kids might dismiss those criticisms. Williams's performance as the governess in the bodysuit and latex face is the only real reason for this movie, which is adapted from the novel *Alias Madame Doubtfire* by Anne Fine. He is a spectacle to behold.

True, there's a lot of other stuff to sort out, which kids will do according to their experiences, if any, with the breaking up of a family. Columbus is an everyman's director without a great deal of subtlety, and his film lays out the family crisis as if it were a box of cereal on the breakfast table. Daniel and Miranda split openly and painfully in front of their three children, two of them adolescents and one a small child. The children's roles are handled nicely, but the kids in this film are there only as victims of their parents' mess.

Daniel, an actor, is a free spirit and loose cannon (a child really) while Miranda is a play-it-by-the-book interior decorator and domestic neatnik. Daniel takes the separation hard, and with Williams there is always the danger of slopping into mawkish excess. Daniel gets sticky but keeps control, if just barely. A custody hearing is a little strong on pathos, as is his leave-taking from his children gathered on the stoop of the picturesque family, or ex-family, homestead.

Harry Potter notwithstanding, Columbus has made some hugely profitable, straight-ahead, middle-American movies. Steven Spielberg brought him to Hollywood to make *Gremlins* in 1984, and later he made the two *Home Alone* films. On the *Doubtfire* DVD, he delivers rapid-fire, direct comments about why he did what he did with the film. He says he was urged to speed up the marital breakup to get to the comedy faster but resisted because he needed the separation in all its detail to set up the comedy.

As Mrs. Doubtfire, Williams takes off as if at the crack of a starter's pistol. One of Columbus's problems, and not necessarily the worst problem to have, was Williams's prolific extemporizing. By film's end, he had tried two hundred voices and generated countless variations in most every scene. Looking for special nuggets, Columbus shot most of them. Sometimes they replaced what had been written, but at other times they were too salacious, over the top, or otherwise out of sync with the tenor of the film.

Needing a nanny, Miranda advertises, opening the improvisatory floodgates for Williams to respond on the telephone as a gangster, Marilyn Monroe, any number of people. Then Daniel decides to get serious. He calls as the quintessential British nanny and plays the role straight. Miranda asks him her name and he glances at a newspaper with a story about the police doubting a fire was accidental. "Doubt-fire, dear," Daniel replies.

Some of the movie's best moments follow when Daniel's gay brother (Harvey Fierstein), a makeup artist, gets to work creating just the right appearance for the redoubtable new nanny. Williams experimented with several looks. A Barbra Streisand approach left him looking like a Shakespearean Laurence Olivier. As a voice, Margaret Thatcher wasn't right, nor was Julia Child. The sixty-something English woman finally ushered into the Hillard household is a work of art. Eight overlaying patches of latex mask were applied to Williams's face every day in a three- to four-hour process. Only when his son spots Doubtfire urinating standing up is his identity revealed.

Internally, too, there is a makeover. To bring off the transformation, Daniel must act the part, which is to say responsibly and with discipline. No more of Dad's irrepressible nonsense for these kids. Now it's homework and bedtimes and a little spit and polish around Miranda's cutesy designer living room. The new routine calms Daniel down and, since he can use his insider's knowledge to ask some loaded questions, he starts to recognize some truths.

First, the marriage is better off over and done with. "I didn't like who I was when I was with him," Miranda tells Mrs. Doubtfire. (Who she is without him isn't much of an improvement.) Second, the end of the marriage doesn't mean the annihilation of the family. Daniel remains a father, if on different terms, which will make sense to children in this situation.

At its best, Columbus's movie uses Daniel and Mrs. Doubtfire's dual identity effectively and almost eerily. For example, it is never stated as such, but when Mrs. Doubtfire's cover is finally blown, Miranda and the kids miss her more than they miss Daniel. Unfortunately, the film drags in its last stages, with a second court scene that covers more or less the same ground as the first. But the aftermath is a good one. When Miranda sees that Daniel accepts the divorce, she is able to accept him as an important continuing presence in the lives of the kids.

Some Williams improvisations are sexual, and while Columbus kept them in the movie, they had much to do with the PG-13 rating. At one point, Mrs. Doubtfire tells Miranda's suitor (Pierce Brosnan) that when she uses a sex toy "the lights dim like in a prison movie." Young children may well miss the meaning of such remarks and they don't happen often, but they are a factor to consider. And, of course, the movie gets right down to cases on every aspect of divorce, which could be either upsetting or instructive. In any event, about age nine and up seems right.

65. THE MUSIC MAN

Robert Preston, Shirley Jones, Buddy Hackett, Hermione Gingold, Paul Ford, Ron Howard, Pert Kelton

DIRECTED BY MORTON DACOSTA

1962. 151 minutes. No rating

This is one of those musicals that practically grabs kids by the lapels (or the equivalent) and tosses them in the middle of resounding, astonishingly accomplished production numbers. Older kids could bolt, but for younger ones Morton DaCosta's film is one of a half-dozen musts of the genre. The reasons go beyond the music. There are the moral questions surrounding the slickster "Professor" Harold Hill (Robert Preston), who would flimflam the folks of River City and remains such an ethical question mark that one wonders how the movie will extract him in the end. Then there is the film as pure Americana with its vibrant slice of Iowa at the turn of the twentieth century.

Preston established the role on Broadway, where *The Music Man* beat *West Side Story* for the Tony Award in 1958. The show and subsequent film made Preston's career. He also won a Tony, then starred in the movie before dropping from view in lesser parts. His face has a certain corporate look, which could be out of place in a musical if it weren't for his freshness and quick, liquid grace. Hill is a natty dresser, but everybody in River City dresses neatly and formally so staying spruce befits a traveling hustler working the heartland, "wherever the people are as green as the money," as he puts it.

River City is modeled after Mason City, where Meredith Willson, the show's composer, grew up in the 1930s. A fine expositional number, called "Iowa Stubborn," explains how life works in the hay and sarsaparilla belt. Iowans can be dry. Arriving in River City, Hill asks for a good hotel. Try the Palmer House in Chicago, he's told. They are matter-of-fact and parsimonious. Anything they don't have they can do without, or so they proclaim, but that isn't entirely true, as we see when the Wells Fargo wagon arrives carrying coveted mail-order goods. Iowans are temperate but also gullible, which is not to say stupid but initially trusting.

In "Rock Island," a taut, syncopated number on a swaying railroad car, a dozen traveling salesmen worry about the threat that a bounder like Hill poses to them all. Hill's scam is punctuated in several places by "76 Trombones." What River City needs, he contends, is a marching band made up of the town's youth. He'll supply the uniforms and instruments. All he requires is cash up front. His exit, or so he plans, will be timed right down to the brakeman's last wave on the last train out of town.

His problem is that River City doesn't see the immediate need for a band, especially since the kids can't play music. But a reason soon materializes at the Pleez-all Billiard Parlor: a pool table. Pool isn't billiards. Ya got trouble, Hill famously tells the town, springing up on the nearest lamppost to regale a crowd. Organizing a band will deter kids from pool's degradations. They don't need to be able to read the notes; they will play by merely thinking about the music. "A meeting of two minds—Beethoven's and yours," Hill tells band members at their first rehearsal.

Soon the movie is selling us its own bill of goods. Certainly Hill is out to pick the pockets of River City, but he goes about his con with such panache and uplift that he's more than worth the money the good folks stand to lose. Or that's more or less the reasoning employed by Marian Paroo (Shirley Jones), the town's lovely and virtuous librarian, who falls in love with Hill. A music teacher herself, Marian surely recognizes a charlatan, but she also sees a well-camouflaged beneficence in the vitality and life Hill pumps into the hidebound community.

Children will sense the same spirit in the fellow, although it will take them a while. On the verge of a good tar-and-feathering, Hill doesn't seem convinced himself. He does know that he's tired of dodging and running. So he stands by while Marian placates the town. As if in salute to Hill's teaching methods, the band even manages a wheezing march or two before more practiced legions take over and strut off in the perfectly orchestrated finale.

Big production numbers each got three weeks of rehearsal and they show it. Warner Brothers wanted Frank Sinatra for the Hill role, but Willson told them that if he couldn't have Preston there would be no movie. Onna White, the film's choreographer, says that the remarkable thing about Preston was that he could generate such freshness and spontaneity after playing Hill for so long on Broadway. "What I expected from someone who knew the role that well was that he would come on the set and say you can't do that because we did it this way," she says on the DVD. "It was as though he was creating the role all over again." Preston, she added, brought the Broadway trait of consistency, or the ability to perform a take or scene exactly the same way over and over. "Which doesn't mean boring," she says.

Jones's Broadway experience went back to *Oklahoma!* and *Carousel* in the '50s, but prior to *The Music Man*, she won an Oscar for portraying a prostitute in *Elmer Gantry*. She had the movie star looks for the screen Marian, which she managed to maintain while being pregnant. The pregnancy was a well-guarded secret. Jones says Preston was thunderstruck when he got kicked by the baby during Marian and Hill's first kiss.

Alert the kids to the great character actors in smaller roles, notably Paul Ford as the mayor, the English actress Hermione Gingold as his wife, and Pert Kelton as Marian's mother. Kids will especially appreciate the little redhead who plays Marian's kid brother, Winthrop—Ron Howard. We know Howard as the director of *Apollo 13* (see page 10) and *A Beautiful Mind*, but back then eight-year-old Ronny already had appeared on *The Andy Griffith Show*. Later he would gain fame as Richie Cunningham on *Happy Days*.

The Music Man lost the best picture Oscar to *Lawrence of Arabia*, but it was appreciated in Mason City. One hundred marching bands turned out for the opening, and so did Arthur Godfrey.

The townsfolk promise to get nasty with Hill, but thanks to Marian nothing comes of it. The only sex, much decried by the puritanical mayor's wife and her followers, lies in the books of Balzac and Chaucer at the library. Obscenity would also be out of place in River City. All told we have good clean viewing for kids of any age.

66. MY FAIR LADY

Audrey Hepburn, Rex Harrison, Stanley Holloway, Wilfrid Hyde-White

DIRECTED BY GEORGE CUKOR

1964. 170 minutes. No rating

It rines in Spine, of course, and in 'artford, 'ereford, and 'ampshire 'urricanes 'ardly ever 'appen. Programming the cockney out of poor Eliza Doolittle (Audrey Hepburn) has the blustery Professor Henry Higgins (Rex Harrison) beside himself with frustration. "Look, put your tongue forward until it squeezes the top of your lower teeth," he orders. Around them in the professor's lavish, wood-paneled language lab, Edwardian gizmos gauge every nuance of spoken sound. Breathe properly and make the flame pop up. Higgins has Eliza put six marbles in her mouth. Now then, repeat after him: "With blackest moss, the flowerpots were thick-crusted one and all." Eliza swallows a marble but is told not to worry. He has more. After all, chides the professor, Demosthenes learned to speak like this.

Every generation knows this story, adapted from George Bernard Shaw's *Pygmalion,* itself an adaptation of Greek myth. Higgins makes a wager with his friend Col. Hugh Pickering (Wilfrid Hyde-White) that he can turn this ragamuffin of a flower girl into a perfectly spoken creature high society will mistake as one of its own. Harrison plays Higgins with a combination of polished arrogance and ebullient enthusiasm. He and Hepburn got on well together, though they both preferred their left profiles and occasionally got into what is described on the DVD as "the battle of the faces."

Kids will love their big, lively performances, the music, and the film's opulent look. A pleasingly kitschy documentary on the DVD gushes about the custom-made wallpaper for the ornate Higgins household and the "rarest of furs and richest of fabrics" for the costumes.

Cecil Beaton, the English costume and scenery designer, got particularly lavish for Eliza's first foray among the swells at the Ascot races and at the grand ball, where a snotty fop who specializes in spotting social impostors identifies her as Hungarian nobility. A Beaton hat could be three feet across and not fit into a phone booth. The studio chief Jack Warner produced this film himself, and though he never was one to throw money out the window, he realized the desired effect demanded a hefty outlay. One scene could require 250 costumes. There were seventeen wardrobe people (including one who tended nothing but white gloves), twenty-six makeup men, thirty-five hairstylists. Dressing areas looked like factory floors. On occasion there were two thousand female and fifteen hundred male makeup jobs a day. Wigs, beards, and mustaches were arrayed by the score in rows and on pegs, disquietingly suggesting a collection of small animal carcasses.

A big part of the story was Hepburn's own transformation, which went more or less in the opposite direction of Eliza's. Hepburn, in fact, played a princess in *Roman Holiday* (1953), a role that won her an Oscar, and went from princessly to spritely in *Sabrina* (1954), which got her another Oscar nomination, to *Funny Face* (1957). By the time she reached *My Fair Lady,* her image had undergone directional changes in such films as *The Nun's Story* (1959), in which she won a third Oscar nomination as a nun in the Belgian Congo, and

Breakfast at Tiffany's (1961), which let her gambol as the frisky New York sophisticate Holly Golightly.

As Eliza Doolittle she starts out smudge-faced and scrappy with "Wouldn't It Be Loverly," the first of the movie's songs by Alan Jay Lerner and Frederick Loewe. Critics complained that Hepburn was more convincing moving among the high-born than she was roaming in the streets. Some said that Wendy Hiller was more natural at the lower end of the social ladder in *Pygmalion* (1938), but it's hard to fault Hepburn's exuberance and intensity.

Shaw wrote parts of the *Pygmalion* adaptation and was given the Oscar for the screenplay, but that film wasn't a musical. *My Fair Lady* opened on Broadway in 1956 with Julie Andrews as Eliza in one of the most spectacular debuts ever. Shaw's estate insisted that the lyrics match the text of the play, which drove away Rodgers and Hammerstein. Lerner stepped in with the likes of "Why Can't the English?," "Just You Wait, 'enry 'iggins," "I Could Have Danced All Night," and "Get Me to the Church on Time." Married eight times and something of an eccentric, Lerner was also a chronic nail biter who prowled the set wearing white gloves to prevent himself from chewing off his fingertips.

Hepburn's problem was that she wasn't a singer, which isn't to say that she couldn't sing at all. On the DVD, we have some examples of her screechingly giving her all to a couple of numbers, and in fact some of her singing was left in the movie. She certainly had the heart and soul. But the vocal range approached light opera and, as everybody knows, the singer Marni Nixon was brought in to dub the big numbers. Dubbing had been common knowledge since Nixon stood in for Deborah Kerr in *The King and I* (1956, see page 139), but to avoid shocking Hepburn's public, Nixon got no credit and was sworn to secrecy.

It was an awkward situation. Many thought Hepburn should have won the Oscar, which was given that year to Julie Andrews for her performance in *Mary Poppins*. And many held that Andrews got the Oscar as a consolation for not getting the film role of Eliza Doolittle, which was denied her because she wasn't yet a major star. Nixon obviously never had to do any dubbing for Andrews, but as a reward for being the voice behind the stars, she did play a nun in *The*

Sound of Music. On the *My Fair Lady* DVD, Nixon describes Andrews as direct and spontaneous (read brusque). Hepburn, in Nixon's view, was sensitive, considerate, thoughtful.

The director George Cukor came to the film after Hepburn was cast. "I was delighted with her and the way she played it," he says in *Who the Devil Made It,* Peter Bogdanovich's book of interviews with prominent directors. Cukor won the Oscar for *My Fair Lady,* and he could well have won for other films, including *A Star Is Born* (1954), starring Judy Garland, the first *Little Women* (1933), and *The Philadelphia Story* (1940), the last two with Katharine Hepburn. Cukor was considered a particularly adept director of women, from Jean Harlow and Joan Crawford to Jane Fonda and Anna Magnani. But he was fine with men. In Bogdanovich's book he says that Harrison tended to fade after five or six takes of a scene. "He *played* it just as well, but it didn't have that fine edge," Cukor said. "Audrey Hepburn, on the other hand, the more often she did it, the better she was."

Kids from about the age of eight, perhaps younger, will be enthralled with the film. Hepburn's Eliza is a strong character for kids to identify with, and Higgins is a sight to behold. It is also a movie of the utmost gentility. Many situations that would erupt in wild screen brawls today only result in measured responses and even a tip of the hat from potential combatants.

67. NATIONAL VELVET

Elizabeth Taylor, Mickey Rooney, Donald Crisp, Anne Revere

DIRECTED BY CLARENCE BROWN

1944. 125 minutes. No rating

Take it from the critic Pauline Kael about this film: "One of the most likable movies of all time." First there is the setting, a glorious swatch of rolling emerald English down by a vividly blue sea. Clarence Brown was noted for his pictorial sense, and nearly sixty years after the film was made, the vibrancy of sea and sky and land still leap out. Such a countryside needs a village that won't let it down, and the film comes through with shopkeepers who wear ties and wrap meat in butcher paper, ivied churches, and cozy, worn domiciles with comfy seating, crackling fires, and the family savings hidden away in cookie jars. All this and one corker of a horse race coming up.

Just looking at this scene provided a lift to a world at war, and the aesthetics are no less pleasing today. Out in those fields is a horse. "Sixteen hands, a nice mover, all right," says Mi Taylor, a former jockey portrayed by Mickey Rooney. A rebellious roan gelding, the animal pleases Velvet Brown, played by twelve-year-old Elizabeth Taylor, who is so infatuated with horses that she gallops around half the day pretending she is one.

Five years later, Taylor, then seventeen, would be dating Howard Hughes, but that's another story. In addition to his fine visual sensibilities, Brown was known for handling difficult actresses on the set, notably Greta Garbo. There was no need in this case. As Velvet, Taylor is a young girl with a dream and a faith she clings to with a starry-eyed tenacity. (And, Lord, those eyes. In this film they shine so intensely, they seem to come right off her head, which at times gives off a whiff of horror film and can be a bit alarming. Little kids won't notice this, however, so it's not an issue.)

Velvet is fresh, innocent, wise, steely in her resolve, and over-whelmingly sweet in her manner. That horse out there—she names him the Pi—will be hers, and the movie works hard to get it for her. An unruly critter, the Pi is raffled off by its owner. The wildly enthusiastic Velvet is so sure she'll win, she falls ill when she doesn't. But when a technicality necessitates another drawing, she wins. Here the film feeds the fantasy, quite realistically douses it, and then feeds it again. We see this same sort of tempering later in the film, proving that the improbable and reality can exist side by side in a movie.

How does Velvet's father like a horse around the house? Mr. Brown (Donald Crisp) is the village butcher, but the Pi, snorting and rearing, will have none of pulling a delivery cart. Out in the fields the horse clears high bushes in graceful bounds. One day, after measuring carefully, the astonished Mi Taylor determines that the Pi has cleared the equivalent of the most challenging leap at the Grand National Steeplechase held each year at Aintree.

As far as Velvet is concerned, the next step is obvious. She determines to enter the Pi and to win. Her mother (Anne Revere) favors the quest. "Everyone should have a chance at a breathtaking piece of folly once in his life," she tells Velvet. Revere won the Oscar as supporting actress for her portrayal of the poker-faced, all-wise Mrs. Brown. The character makes a fine fit with Mr. Brown. Crisp (General Grant in D. W. Griffith's *Birth of a Nation* in 1915) is very solid as a man of stern rules and high principles who isn't above breaking his own ban on feeding the dog scraps under the table.

Such a man can be relied upon to support Velvet's dreams and modulate her intensity. Add Velvet's two sisters (one played by Angela Lansbury) and brother, all with their own sometimes skeptical views of Velvet's obsession, and the film has a fine, healthy family dynamic kids will relate to. The strongest is Mrs. Brown, who lived her own dream once by becoming the first woman to swim the English Channel. That took perseverance, and it is with a faint flicker of a smile across her otherwise noncommittal countenance that she encourages Velvet.

And what of Mi Taylor? When he appeared in *National Velvet*, Rooney, twenty-four, had already been divorced from Ava Gardner (the first of eight wives). At five feet three inches, he was fine jockey material and in 1979 played an older version of Mi Taylor in *The*

Black Stallion (see page 36). Having left the racing game after the death of a friend, Mi has become a vagabond. Velvet simply can't do without him as a trainer and Mr. Brown warily gives him a bed out in the barn with the Pi. With an eye to hitting the road, Mi quickly cleans out the family cookie jar, but faced with the Browns' kindness he returns the money and stays to build a close working relationship with Velvet. He professes not to share her dream. Who is he kidding?

Children will be enthralled by Velvet and her quest, her family and its support, the growing trust between her and Mi Taylor—and we haven't even come to the race. It is a thrilling affair indeed, with no surprise at the finish. Then a very nice thing happens. Instead of the inevitable and usually improbable boffo triumph, there is a quieter victory, more a sense of satisfaction. Velvet and the Pi are disqualified, but it doesn't matter. She has achieved what she wanted. As her mother told her earlier, it's "how you take it that counts, that and letting it go and moving on to the next."

This is a film for all ages, beginning perhaps at five or six and running on until whatever point kids begin to scoff at such family fare, which in this case may well be never. The race is a red-blooded affair, with riders thrown and horses crashing, but all is from afar and appears not that serious. There is no sex or profanity.

68. NEVER CRY WOLF

Charles Martin Smith, Zachary Ittimangnaq, Samson Jorah, Brian Dennehy

DIRECTED BY CARROLL BALLARD
1983. 105 minutes. PG

Alone and shivering in the Arctic wilderness, a researcher named Tyler (Charles Martin Smith) spots his first wolf. It's a large white one, which is quite rare, and appears also to be by itself at a remove of several hundred yards. Seized by excitement, Tyler calms himself and summons what little he knows about wolf-watching: choose an observation post downwind and watch without revealing his presence. That's the last he sees of the animal. With other tactics called for, Tyler tries the opposite of stealth and goes marching around the area, loudly vocalizing, rattling tin cans, and making a general commotion.

It doesn't happen immediately, but one day as Tyler sits reading in his tent, he hears a scuffling directly outside. The wolf not only has come into camp, he's about five feet from Tyler and peering in at him around the tent flaps. The bespectacled Tyler gives the wolf a tenderfoot's look of scholarly wonder and incredulity. This is truly a don't-even-breathe moment. But the wolf is as uncertain as Tyler, and after the two nervously regard each other for a while, the animal retreats. After this initial contact, a two-way observation between man and wolf is joined from a respectful distance. Man and animal are equally curious about each other, though the wolf always maintains a mysterious detachment. As the film teaches, one learns only so much about the wolves.

Carroll Ballard has two other entries in this book, *The Black Stallion* and *Fly Away Home,* which may seem a disproportionate number for a director whose total oeuvre since 1967 consists of five films. His extraordinary gift for cinematography and endless patience with animals result in fine films for children. "Endless" is an operative word for Ballard, however, and endlessness never sits well with studio accountants. *Never Cry Wolf* took three and a half years to make and came in at more than twice the projected budget.

Wolves and other creatures—humans, mice, and caribou—ate up 750,000 feet of film, leaving Ballard to winnow at such length that Disney threatened to take the picture away from him. Adapted from an autobiography by Farley Mowat, the movie follows a young biologist sent to study wolves by the Canadian Wildlife Service. *Canis lupus,* the biggest of the dog family, stands accused of wiping out most of the Arctic's caribou population, which used to number in the millions. Is this true, or are the wolves unjustly accused?

Caribou can't be rushed. Ballard rented five hundred of them from "reindeer barons" near Nome, Alaska. He insisted on shooting after the snow melted in early June, but that gave him only two weeks before the barons needed the caribou back to cut off their antlers, which are valued in Asia as an aphrodisiac. Then Ballard's caribou ran off during a storm and it took several days to round them up. Other delays further reduced the shoot. The project moved on to year two.

Smith, a familiar face after his role in *American Graffiti,* makes a sturdy, resilient geek of Tyler, who gets unceremoniously dumped with a pile of crates full of weird supplies (including lightbulbs and countless tins of asparagus) on a frozen lake by a bull-necked bush pilot named Rosie (Brian Dennehy). Ballard fired the first actor chosen to play Tyler, William Katt, because he was too handsome, which could have been a distraction. But Tyler's academic airs and helpless ineptitude are a distraction themselves in early scenes that somewhat incongruously (and a little too cutely) abandon a neophyte in a wilderness that could well kill him.

This is spring, however, and though the movie playfully hints at doom, Tyler is likely to survive. At least he knows what to do with a canoe the Canadian government has given him. After spending a chilly night in a crate, he hears howls and spies big, dark shapes loping toward him across the ice. Crawling under the canoe, he hangs on tight as the animals snuffle and growl. Then he sees a man's feet. The wolves, it turns out, are sled dogs belonging to Ootek (Zachary Ittimangnaq), an Inuit elder.

At first Ootek is contemptuous of this misfit and leaves him, but when Tyler passes out running after his sled Ootek doubles back and packs the poor wolf researcher and his supplies off to a little hut in the woods. From here Tyler watches his big white wolf friend and later a white female, who is the mother of several cubs.

Despite their eerie detachment, wolves among themselves are warm, social animals. Ballard used about thirty of them. Not to deglamorize, but most came from Animal Actors of Hollywood and Lloyd Beebe's Animal Farm near Seattle. Some wolves were called on to hang around hotel lobbies waiting for scenes. As a supplement, seven big German shepherds, attack dogs all, were brought along. Ballard says they were the crazy ones and had to be watched constantly.

Wolves actually ate only a small number of sick or disabled caribou, which strengthened the herds rather than depleting them. In the spring, wolves live almost entirely on mice. Tyler has determined to live like the wolves, and to prove that a large mammal can flourish solely on mice, he decides to eat nothing but. Ootek reappears with his son, Mike (Samson Jorah), and they offer Tyler some fish, but he declines. Tyler eats only mice (really chopped beef with tails of linguini): mice grilled, broiled, in a sandwich with the tails sliding into his mouth as into a snake's maw.

Months in the wild turn Tyler into an intellectual outdoor man. Early on in his effort to live like the wolves, he establishes his territory in the big white alpha male way. Ballard needed fifty-seven takes to get the wolf from California to urinate flawlessly on the spot that establishes his territory. After watching the wolf, Tyler consumes a bootful of alcohol and goes around urinating all over while singing Gilbert and Sullivan. From then on, man and animal observe each other's boundaries.

Caribou appear finally for their big scene, and Tyler runs among them. They have surprised him after a swim in an icy pond. Waking from a warming nap in the sun, he has no clothes on. Wolves trail the herd, looking for an easy mark. The naked Tyler runs among the caribou and watches the wolves size up their prey. Ootek's son Mike also has been appraising the wolves. He sports a toothless grin and a vaguely menacing manner. Mike hunts wolves for a living, and in a quiet, earnest conversation with Tyler he makes his case for doing so.

Mike wouldn't shoot Tyler's subjects, would he? He says not, but admits he'd like to. Toward the end of the film, watch for a clue that tells whether he keeps his word. By now, Tyler has defied Rosie, who has flown in with developers who talk of bottling the area's hot springs. When we last see Tyler, he has moved beyond such matters. The first snow is flying and he is tramping out with Ootek. We are left with a snatch of Inuit song: "All the vital things I had to get and to reach, and yet there is only one great thing, the only thing, to live to see the great day that dawns and the light that fills the world."

This film is fine from about age six. Mouse consumption will bring exclamations of disgust. In a dream sequence, the wolves chase Tyler and drag him down, but we quickly see this didn't actually happen. The wolves fell a caribou, but the scene quickly drops from sight. There is no sex in the bush. A little profanity might be excused in trying moments, but none is uttered.

69. NORTH BY NORTHWEST

Cary Grant, Eva Marie Saint, James Mason, Leo G. Carroll, Martin Landau

DIRECTED BY ALFRED HITCHCOCK

1959. 136 minutes. No rating

For kids this is the perfect Alfred Hitchcock film. "His genius was tapping in to the most basic human emotion: fear," says Eva Marie Saint, the femme fatale of the movie, in an interview on the DVD. That's true enough, but there's nothing too fearsome in *North by Northwest*. The film plays as a jaunty riddle with plenty of humorous bits. At least one of them is unintended, which is a rarity for the fastidious Hitchcock, who micromanaged every scene down to its tiniest detail.

Late in the movie, Eve Kendall (Saint) appears to shoot Roger Thornhill (Cary Grant) in the crowded cafeteria at Mount Rushmore. In the group of extras posing as tourists, a little boy can be seen ducking and covering his ears in expectation of the shot before it goes off. No one noticed this until later, and in the days before digital manipulation, so it stood. No one would be foolish enough to fiddle with it now.

Every child needs an introduction to Hitchcock, whom they will encounter as teenagers in shockers like *Psycho* and *The Birds*. Hitchcock had a playful side. As everybody knows, he fleetingly appears in all his films. In *North by Northwest*, he can be spotted approaching a bus only to have the door shut in his face. A year or so before he made the film, MGM assigned him and the screenwriter Ernest

Lehman, a regular Hitchcock collaborator, to make *The Wreck of the Mary Deare*. A seafaring yarn being of zero interest to either of them, Hitchcock decided to substitute a project he had long thought about.

He told Lehman he had always wanted to make a movie with a chase across the presidential visages on Mount Rushmore. And he had always wanted to make one with a scene at the United Nations in which a speaker declares, "I refuse to continue until the delegate from Peru wakes up."

The Peruvian is dead, of course. By now in the film the debonair Thornhill has been through a bewildering identity mix-up and his own kidnapping. An international cloak-and-dagger saga unfolds, with Thornhill framed for murder and on the run from he knows not who. On a train he encounters the beautiful Kendall, who helps him. Or does she? Children may have trouble sorting out the plot, but probably no more so than their parents will. In an interview, Saint advised not to try too hard, Hitchcock was fooling around. "It was just a spoof," she said. "We all jumped in with both feet."

The point, she added, is that cast and crew had a load of fun making the film, and that included Hitchcock. Saint was Hitchcock's surprise choice for the groomed, ladylike vamp secretly in the employ of Thornhill's enemies. "His eyes always followed beautiful women," Patricia Hitchcock, his daughter, says on the DVD. He liked white gloves and beige clothes, and Saint wore both to an introductory lunch. Later he took her shopping at Bergdorf's for everything she wore in the film.

The DVD documentary says that he never called actors cattle, as is claimed—only that they should be treated like cattle. Whatever the case, there was some friction between Grant and Hitchcock. The documentary calls this little more than natural tension between two dominant talents at the tops of their games. In the interview Saint said the director couldn't have been more gracious and accommodating. The trick with Hitchcock was getting chosen in the first place. "You got the sense that you were the only one who could do it because you were there," she said. "Once he had you on the set he had the utmost respect for you."

The movie generally stays breezy and loose, which children will appreciate. They will love Grant as the dashing but beleaguered advertising man slipping and sliding around a spoofy world of international intrigue that constantly double-crosses him. The action gets all the way to Siberia, but there are two scenes no one forgets. One is on a road through cornfields where the terrified, sprinting Thornhill is pursued and strafed by a crop duster. The other is at Mount Rushmore.

Hitchcock originally planned to shoot directly on the face of the monument, but there was a cry of protest and refusal by the Interior Department. So they re-created the presidential faces in Hollywood. In one mock-up, Hitchcock's was among them.

People are shot and punched, but by today's standards the violence is restrained. Some scenes are moderately intense, but again, there is nothing that should seriously upset children from about eight up, depending on maturity. Most parents are familiar with the film and will judge accordingly. Some sex is intimated between Thornhill and Kendall, but the movie is so pristine and proper in this regard they are barely in the mood (to resurrect a '50s term) before the scene disappears entirely into a train tunnel. And there is no profanity.

70. PETER PAN

With the voices of Bobby Driscoll, Kathryn Beaumont, Hans Conreid, H. Bill Thompson

DIRECTED BY HAMILTON LUSKE, CLYDE GERONIMI, WILFRED JACKSON
1953. 77 minutes. No rating

Walt Disney had James Barrie's story on his mind since the 1930s. To survive succeeding generations of children, Disney films needed a timeless feel and ageless philosophies. Barrie's tale about a boy with such youthful spirit that he would never grow up seemed deathless enough, but it took Disney years to become convinced of its audience appeal. With a Cinderella, say, one feels emotions of the heart, but he worried that one never really gets close to Peter Pan.

Other story elements finally carried the day, not the least of them the adventure of soaring off into the stars for an encounter with Captain Hook. *Peter Pan* isn't the greatest of the older Disney animated feature films, but it stays the freshest from era to era. "Our notions of *Peter Pan* have changed considerably since 1953," the critic Stephen Holden wrote in the *New York Times* in 2002. "In the 1970s the Peter Pan syndrome became a cliché of psychobabble applied to male baby boomers perceived as reluctant to grow up and settle down. And Michael Jackson, in professing to portray Peter on the big screen, tainted the image by confusing the character with his own weirdness and emotional regression." As beloved as they all are, Snow White, Cinderella, or the edgier Pinocchio don't have Peter Pan's coattails.

Having decided to do the film, Disney got rolling with it in 1950. The postwar years were a difficult time at the studio, which had a hard time regaining its form with animated features. *Cinderella,* released in 1950, ranks with Disney's best, but observers say that Disney had become aloof and preoccupied with the studio's first efforts in television. But on a DVD of *Peter Pan,* old Disney hands report otherwise. "Walt was a great story man," says an artist who worked on the film. "*Peter Pan* or *Pinocchio,* it didn't matter. He'd get up and act it out and you'd think, 'Is it going to be as good as this man is doing?'"

It was also a great time for vocal talent. Disney liked radio actors, still plentiful in that era, because they could create characters with their voices alone. They were also good at playing off one another. Character and effects animators worked with sculpted and live models, and this was one of the most interesting parts of the process. Before it became animated, *Peter Pan* was a live action feature of sorts with actors filmed playing out the action on stripped-down soundstages so that the animators could get a feel for characters and movements. "If you were walking through a forest, there would be some sticks and some tape on the ground," says Kathryn Beaumont, the voice of Wendy, the most famous of the children who fly off with Peter to Never Land.

Animators watched these films repeatedly. Performers who could supply voices that did characters justice were particularly prized. Hans Conreid, a fine character actor (from Nazis to eccentric professors) and proficient in many dialects, was the voice of Hook and gave animators a model to work with. "Usually they had pantomimists and/or dancers, but they felt I could play the part," he says in Leonard Maltin's book about Disney. "I was in costume, and they had an elemental set, and I would go through the business making my physical action coincide with the soundtrack, which was already finished. Usually, in dubbing, which I've done a lot of for foreign actors, you have to make your sound coincident with his latent action, but here you make your physical action coincident with the soundtrack. That was lots of fun."

The film is a rather straightforward retelling of Barrie's story. Unlike big Disney animated features of the '80s and '90s—*The Little Mermaid,* for example, or *Beauty and the Beast*—music doesn't drive the action. In fact, Peter's big song, "Never Smile at a Crocodile," was initially cut from the film and didn't become well known until later. Another song, "What Makes the Red Man Red," carries if not blatantly racist then stereotypically insensitive overtones today. Some would view the film as sexist. At the time Walt Disney was accused of using Marilyn Monroe as a model for the curvaceous Tinkerbelle, which he denied.

Barrie's perceptions are picked up in the film. The eternal child, Peter Pan carries a certain nobility, saves people's lives, and rallies the Lost Boys who serve as Hook's pirate crew. The regal-appearing Hook, on the other hand, is a willful, selfish child. "The film asks us to look at how adults and children behave and make an assessment of who's really a grown-up," says John Canemaker, an authority on animated film and a commentator on the DVD.

The pirate captain, of course, has an even darker side in Steven Spielberg's live action *Hook,* with a superb performance by Dustin Hoffman in the title role but with much of the fun squeezed dry. *Return to Never Land,* the 2002 animated Disney sequel, places the story in London during the blitz. This time, Wendy's daughter flies off with Peter and turns the crocodile who ate Hook's hand into an octopus. Kids will love what digital imaging and other technology do for the newer film, but they will take to the original as well. Watching Hook try to stay out of the jaws of that crocodile is one of the great sights in all of animation.

There is a sword fight but really nothing too upsetting for kids from about the age of four. Issues of race and sexism are more subjects of discussion than causes for avoidance.

71. PINOCCHIO

With the voices of Dickie Jones, Cliff Edwards, Christian Rub

DIRECTED BY HAMILTON LUSKE AND BEN SHARPSTEEN
1940. 88 minutes. No rating

Introduce kids to *Pinocchio* around the same time you present them with *Snow White*. Together they are the one-two punch of the earliest feature animation, but *Pinocchio* breaks out in terms of narrative and execution. By now Disney had learned to make full use of the multiplane camera, a multiple-platform affair about the height of two bunk beds that enabled camera movements akin to live action.

Nice visual gags jump out of early Disney films. In *Snow White and the Seven Dwarfs*, Sneezy's beard was tied around his nose to stifle a nasal eruption. In *Pinocchio* smoke pours from the blowhole of a whale as it speeds along the surface. In its belly, Pinocchio and Gepetto toss scores of tuna fish onto a fire to induce a sneeze that will blow them out of the beast. The difference in the two sequences—the first a snippet, the second a full-blown action scenario worthy of a wild ride at a water park—represents Walt Disney's big leap from his first animated feature, *Snow White*, to his second.

Disney was famous for his attention to detail. To prepare he first filmed his stories live, sometimes using name actors, to give his animators a feel for how people moved. Scale models were made of every character, even every object. In Leonard Maltin's book *The Disney Films,* a reporter from the era noted evidence of "meticulous caution" with every drawing. "The labor involved is staggering even to think about," he wrote. This absorption with minutiae led to superbly produced films, but when added to Disney's Middle American views and emphasis on the upbeat and sentimental, it also inspired criticism that dogged Disney to the day he died in 1966.

Where were the darker, more complicated issues of life? Leonard Maltin quotes Thomas Burton writing about *Pinocchio* and Disney in *The Saturday Review*: "His art is all good-natured curves. Disney has discarded the straight line as bad for animation and the pure joy he sees in life. Both his technical limitations and his background have kept him from being another Rowlandson, Daumier, Leech, Gavarini, or Hogarth. He cannot, like them, be casually cruel or see with their cold artistic lassitude. This gives him all his talents to be put into surface entertainment. There is no place for social bite."

Snow White had drawn the same kind of criticism. But Disney, Maltin points out, felt no need for social bite or the artistic grand manner. As far as he was concerned, he was telling his stories for people like himself and within those parameters his standards were the highest. Displeased with *Pinocchio* at first, he threw out five months of finished film. One of his problems was the extreme length of his source material. Disney adapted the story from Carlo Collodi's book, which in the nineteenth century had been written for magazine serialization and, with Collodi being paid by the word, grew accordingly. Disney's reduction seems a little rushed, leaving a somewhat episodic feel to the transitions. Otherwise, the film is a full-blown feature with a sophistication and completeness that advances it far ahead of *Snow White* in terms of developed story line and execution.

With its belly of the whale and a few other troubling scenes, *Pinocchio* was called Disney's most frightening film for small children. It's hard to imagine that holding true for kids today. Gepetto's beloved wooden puppet brought to life by a universal fairy godmother is promised transformation into a real little boy if he is judged to be brave, truthful, and unselfish. Then he is immediately provided with a full complement of foibles to prevent that from happening (and without which there would be no story).

Pinocchio is vulnerable to being led astray by the conniving fox J. Worthington Foulfellow, who calls himself Honest John, and his greedy but simpleminded sidekick, Gideon the cat. Foulfellow dangles the promise of fame on the stage: Pinocchio is to be the world's first stringless singing and dancing marionette. When that doesn't work out, the puppet is shanghaied with a lot of other impressionable lads and shipped off to Pleasure Island, where a life of debauched revelry supposedly awaits. A rowdy named Lampwick has the puppet smoking cigars and shooting pool, but the truth is that all of them are to be turned into donkeys and clapped into slavery.

Since a wooden carving so precipitously dumped into temptation is unlikely to find his own way onto the straight and narrow, guidance is provided by Jiminy Cricket, a cheerful footloose hobo of a bug who happens to be taking shelter in Gepetto's workshop when the puppet comes to life. In Collodi's story, the bug gets squashed, but here he becomes the first in a line of secondary characters Disney used to serve as mentors and voices of reason for challenged central figures with moral mountains to climb.

Most makers of major animated films have had some connection with Disney in their careers and that influence shows up in various ways. Well-developed sidekick characters like Jiminy Cricket are everywhere—for example, the garrulous donkey who is counselor and naysayer to the big green ogre in *Shrek* (see page 243). Most provide a comic element to lighten the load at scary moments. In *Pinocchio* the main frights come when the slave donkeys are lashed with whips and when Pinocchio goes to the rescue of Gepetto in the belly of the whale. The cricket was there to question the puppet's gullibility and lack of steadfastness when he took off with Foulfellow, and he's loyally on hand at sea, a good fellow in a crunch.

Note the scary parts above. They should be weathered easily by the very young, but there is one troubling spot that might be discussed. On Pleasure Island one of the greatest treats offered rioting adolescents is smashing and destroying objects like stained-glass windows and the

Mona Lisa. *Kids like to wreck things, but this has a particularly nasty, creepy feel. One wonders why such objects are singled out. The Nazis were up to the same kind of violence at the time. Such destruction leaps out in a children's film.*

72. THE PRINCESS BRIDE

Cary Elwes, Robin Wright, Chris Sarandon, Andre Rousimof, Christopher Guest, Mandy Patinkin, Wallace Shawn, Peter Falk

DIRECTED BY ROB REINER
1987. 98 minutes. PG

At the start of Rob Reiner's film an old man (Peter Falk) starts to read his grandson a story. He says the tale is from back in the days when television was called books. The kid is skeptical. Grandfather tells him to relax. This one has everything: fighting, torture, revenge, fencing, giants, monsters, chases, true love, miracles. His grandson agrees to give it a try.

The Princess Bride did fairly well in movie theaters, but like many smaller movies released without a whole lot of promotional ballyhoo, it caught fire later on home video. Rob Reiner says the studio, 20th Century Fox, never knew how to market the movie. Was it a romance, a comedy, an adventure? On the DVD, William Goldman, who wrote the book and the film, describes his story: "She gets kidnapped. He gets killed. But it all turns out okay." He and Reiner were aiming to make a movie that would appeal to both kids and parents. Goldman, a novelist as well as a screenwriter, writes of more adult things in films like *Marathon Man* (also adapted from his book) and *All the President's Men,* but he can get shaggily playful, as we see in his screenplay for *Butch Cassidy and the Sundance Kid* (see page 51).

He wrote this book at the request of his two young daughters.

The Princess Bride
(Used by permission of MGM Home Entertainment)

One wanted a story about a bride, the other a story about a princess. On the disc, Goldman states emphatically that he loves traditional fairy tales. If the film is a spoof, it's done with fondness and respect for the story form. As a foundation we certainly have a traditional plot: noble boy overcomes bad people and dangerous situations to win lovely girl of snow-driven purity. Through the Goldman prism, however, the movie quickly turns quirky and not a little tongue-in-cheek.

Our hero is Wesley (Cary Elwes), farm boy and nascent swashbuckler. Our princess and bride is Buttercup (Robin Wright), blond and gorgeous. For villains we have the preening Prince Humperdinck (Chris Sarandon) and a six-fingered man (Christopher Guest). For the bouncing gaggle of lesser lights who fill out any fairy tale, we have a kindly eight-foot giant (Andre Rousimof), a slightly buffoonish swordsman named Inigo Montoya (Mandy Patinkin), and a self-styled murderous wit (Wallace Shawn), who does himself in with his own cleverness.

Goldman gives them some catchy lines. "When his head is in view, hit it with a rock." Or, "You're trying to kidnap what I've rightly stolen." Montoya is continually practicing a line he will deliver to the six-fingered man when he finally catches him: "My name is Inigo Montoya. You killed my father. Now prepare to die." Montoya repeats that line a lot during the movie. Reiner says that he had dinner in New York one night at a restaurant frequented by the mobster John Gotti. When he left, he encountered one of Gotti's wiseguys leaning against a limousine. "You killed my father. Now prepare to die," the gangster called out to him. How's that for a little recognition?

The film's perilous places include the "fire swamp," where jets of flame suddenly erupt, and the Cliffs of Insanity, a sheer slab of rock on the Irish coast. Wesley, now masked in pirate garb, climbs it in hot pursuit of Buttercup, who is in the clutches of the giant. In the book there is the Zoo of Death, which for budgetary purposes is sized down to the Pit of Despair in the movie but still has a good torture device powered by a waterwheel.

Shrieking eels nearly consume Buttercup, as does a Goldman creation called the rous, or rodent of unusual size. A rous is a rat about the size of a golf cart played by two "little people" in quite lifelike rat suits. The two of them attack Wesley in the fire swamp and it's a frightening sight. Reiner says it's the one place in the movie that could disturb small children. It is a little weird, all right, a stopper in a film that otherwise is a delight from start to finish.

The giant runs the Brute Squad, but he's a sweetheart. Rousimof, a professional wrestler called Andre the Giant, weighed 550 pounds and had a very bad back. Required to catch people and throw them around in the film, he was in such pain he could hardly pick up a teaspoon. Harness and ramps were fashioned to lighten the load. Goldman says that he used to watch Andre wrestle in Madison Square Garden and wrote the book with him in mind.

Reiner says that the movie is perfectly cast, and that's hard to dispute. For Wesley he was looking for a hip young swashbuckler in the Douglas Fairbanks Jr. mold. Elwes does well with slightly overdone satirical flourishes and has a comic sensibility. "Beautiful, athletic, and funny," Goldman says. "Those guys are hard to find." Wright is great to look at and manages a fair English accent for someone born in Texas and raised in the San Fernando Valley. She made a mark in *Forrest Gump* and a number of films associated with her husband, Sean Penn. Goldman says that she would have become a major star but didn't want to. Offered a big role in a big film, she preferred to have a baby. "Barbra Streisand wouldn't do that," Goldman says.

Sarandon and Guest are excellent as bad guys with a smirk. Billy Crystal gets caked in makeup for a short shtick as a specialist in miraculous recoveries. Late in the film he is called on to revive the apparently dead Wesley. "Don't rush me or it's a rotten miracle," he says.

Goldman wrote the book in 1973 and tried to get it made into a movie for the next fourteen years. Four studios optioned the property at one time or another, but key executives kept leaving or getting fired before green-lighting. Finally the television producer Norman Lear put up $16 million to make the picture. That was a tight budget, and many elements from the book were cut. Goldman says that he never reads or watches what he writes, but he read and watched *The Princess Bride* and he liked it. Coming from him, that sounds authentic.

He particularly liked its pace and efficiency. "We shot what we wrote," he says on the DVD. There are no chunks on the cutting room floor, and today there is no second-guessing about why they did this or didn't do that. "One good thing is that it's short," he adds. "If you can't do it in an hour-fifty, you had better be David Lean."

Blood is spilled in a couple of swordfights, but minimally. The one scene that causes concern is the rous attack in the fire swamp. Wesley gets bloodied and one of the big rats is scorched and run through with a sword. "There was a big discussion," Goldman says. "You're going for a certain tone. This is not a bloodbath movie. You could have made it a lot gorier." Sure, but it's scary and creepy nevertheless. Before and after, though, it's clear sailing in a wonderful movie for kids from about age six and their parents. There is no sex or profanity.

73. RAIDERS OF THE LOST ARK

Harrison Ford, Karen Allen, Paul Freeman, Ronald Lacey, John Rhys-Davies, Denholm Elliott

DIRECTED BY STEVEN SPIELBERG
1981. 115 minutes. PG

"To get to the point immediately," wrote the *New York Times* film critic Vincent Canby, "*Raiders of the Lost Ark* is one of the most deliriously funny, ingenious, and stylish American movies ever made." How outright funny this film is could be argued, but some delirium was the order of the day in 1981. The country was looking for broad escapist adventure after a decade of realism in films like *Serpico, All the President's Men, The French Connection,* and *Dirty Harry.* What we needed was some wild fantasy, and any moviegoer around then will recall the big blast of fresh air *Raiders* brought to the screen.

In fact, there was little new about this film aside from the impact it had on the media and on audiences accustomed to more sober stuff. Ready for retro, the country was rediscovering what it had loved in the '30s and '40s when craggy heroes raced through serials on Saturday afternoons and crazy, schlocky B flicks poured out of studio back lots. *Raiders* was a throwback, an idea whose neoconservative time had come along with the former B star and new president Ronald Reagan.

The director and producer George Lucas passed along the idea to Steven Spielberg in 1977, the year Lucas's *Star Wars* (see page 262) set a precedent for escapist action fare. But *Raiders* was a different breed. Lucas wanted a rousing, serial-style feature. It would have an archaeological theme, archaeology and related "ologies" having served as breeding grounds for fedora-hatted adventurers in the deserts and jungles of serials past.

In the film the year is 1936, the perfect time for serials in Lucas's estimation. Harrison Ford wears a leather jacket and carries a bull whip to go along with a fedora in the role of Indiana Jones, the professor and fistfighter who sprints and battles his way from Nepal to North Africa on a quest to find the Ark of the Covenant before a team of Nazis can grab it for Hitler.

In facial expression alone, no action figure expresses peril and stress with more sheer desperation than Harrison Ford. By 1981 the country knew him as the seat-of-the-pants space jockey Han Solo in Lucas's *Star Wars*. Now in his sixties, Ford has long since moved into moderately varying roles in films like *The Mosquito Coast* (1986), *Frantic* (1988), *Working Girl* (also 1988 and his first comedy), *Presumed Innocent* (1990), *Regarding Henry* (1991), and *Sabrina* (1995). But he will be best remembered wild-eyed and embattled in *The Fugitive* (1993), as the ex-CIA agent Jack Ryan in *Patriot Games* and the two sequels adapted from Tom Clancy novels, even as the Russian submarine commander in *K-19: The Widow Maker* (2002).

Ford plays Indy in two *Raiders* sequels, *Indiana Jones and the Temple of Doom* (1984) and *Indiana Jones and the Last Crusade* (1989). Try the last two with the kids if you like, but both films veer off into what parents might consider unacceptable for young children in terms of violence and language. Not that *Raiders* is *Gidget Goes Hawaiian*. Booby traps cocked and ready for two thousand years graphically impale intruders seeking prizes in ancient caverns. Snakes slither out of eyeholes in skeletons' skulls. Indy hates snakes. Six thousand of them—cobras, pythons, boa constrictors—guard the ark. One cobra, a twelve-footer, had its own trainer.

Indy battles a large German military contingent racing him for the ark. (Remember that World War II hasn't broken out yet so it's Yanks vs. the Germans on an unofficial basis.) At one point he shoots an Arab antagonist point-blank and rather cavalierly since he really doesn't have to. Back at his teaching job in front of a class of enthralled coeds, Indy is shy and tweedy. Out in the desert he isn't the nicest guy you could run into.

Personality aside, this is one of the great action films of all time, a trendsetter, and it should be a part of a kid's movie education. Children accustomed to action in the new millennium will find plenty in a twenty-year-old thriller to make their eyes pop and maybe scare the daylights out of them in places. The chases are absolutely lunatic in their intensity. The Germans may outnumber Indy and his tough, sassy lady friend, Marion (Karen Allen), but they get their just deserts from a vengeful spiritual power emanating from the ark.

The ark and other objects are important for Spielberg, who was interested in the Nazis as a subject a dozen years before *Schindler's List* (1993). *Raiders* plays on Hitler's interest in the occult and the notion that the ark would bring triumph to those who bore it into battle. In his book *The Films of Steven Spielberg*, Douglas Brode wrote, "The Indy we encounter at film's end will have realized through terrifying contact with the ark that there is magic, even metaphysics, in the cosmos."

The film came at a difficult time in Spielberg's career. *Jaws* (1975) and *Close Encounters of the Third Kind* (1977, see page 66) helped establish him, but the extravagant period comedy *1941* (1979) got too big and unfunny for the critics and it sank at the box office. Lucas thought *Raiders* would make a nice point of recovery for his friend, and since he had no interest in directing it himself he turned the project over.

Spielberg shot the film in just seventy-three days on sets in France, Tunisia, England, and Hawaii at a cost of $20 million, which was high at the time. As with all Spielberg films, it is a sumptuous piece of work and won Oscars for art direction, sound, editing, and visual effects. You have to wonder how such a complicated far-flung project could have been completed so quickly. As a matter of fact, it was finished twelve days early.

As discussed, the film is plenty violent and probably not the best idea for small children. About eight might be fine, but parents will know the right age. There is no sex and little profanity.

74. REAR WINDOW

James Stewart, Grace Kelly, Thelma Ritter, Wendell Corey, Raymond Burr

DIRECTED BY ALFRED HITCHCOCK

1954. 112 minutes. PG

For kids the nice thing about Alfred Hitchcock is that he has such fun with dark subjects. Children needn't be exposed to murder (and in this case possibly dismemberment), but it would be a shame to deprive them of Hitchcock. More violent Hitchcocks like *Psycho* and *The Birds* can come later, along with many other of the more sophisticated Hitchcocks. Not lacking their own complexities, films like *Rear Window* and *North by Northwest* (see page 210) openly expose elements of great filmmaking that even young children can grasp. Some film guides go as young as age eight for *Rear Window*. That may be a little young, but maybe not.

This is a murder mystery with a sprightly attitude, tongue-in-cheek, to be sure, but sassy in a way that promises some fun. Hitchcock figuratively rolls an eye at the foibles of the world, but there's no reason to be grim about it. The film's title sequence is accompanied by a frisky, jazzy theme more suggestive of a Disney family epic than a movie that asks the question, Did Lars Thorwald (Raymond Burr) dispose of his wife's body in a steamer trunk?

We get to that matter in due course. If there's anything off-putting for kids, it may be the slow early pace while the situation and characters are established. Struck by a race car while on assignment, the globe-trotting magazine photographer L. B. Jeffries (James Stewart), called Jeff, sits immobilized in a waist-to-toe plaster cast in his Greenwich Village apartment. It's summer and in the nineties, but Jeff stays as cool as possible in pressed pajamas and is rubbed down daily with chilly alcohol by Stella (Thelma Ritter), an insurance company nurse sent to make sure his recuperation stays on track.

The other coolant in those days before widespread air-conditioning arrives every evening in the person of Lisa Carol Fremont (Grace Kelly). The classic composed Hitchcock blonde, Lisa dwells on Park Avenue or the movie equivalent, dines accordingly (a picnic supper at Jeff's is catered by the restaurant 21), and edits the chic *Harper's Bazaar*.

A favorite of Hitchcock's, Kelly had more or less the same role in *To Catch a Thief* (1955), another good if less substantial Hitchcock film for kids. There a woman of wealth falls for a reformed cat burglar (Cary Grant). In *Rear Window* the Hitchcock blonde is again madly in love with an opposite. Jeff feels somewhat the same about Lisa, but is strongly skeptical that people of such different backgrounds and lifestyles could remain compatible for long.

The pair provides one half of a typically Hitchcockian two-pronged story: the troubled romance. The other half of a thriller falls outside that, but in this case the action is restricted to claustrophobic proportions by Jeff's immobility. Hitchcock opens this up cleverly and famously with the view out Jeff's window and into the apartments of tenants across the courtyard: Miss Torso, the struggling dancer; Miss Lonelyheart, desperate for companionship; the couple who sleep on the fire escape in the heat and lower their little dog in a basket; the composer with writer's block; the newlyweds; the burly man with the nagging invalid wife. The name on the mailbox is Thorwald.

Hitchcock sets up Jeff's neighbors' lives as if on separate cinema screens embedded in the brick wall of the building opposite. With little else to do all day, Jeff watches them out his window. What better person for this than a renowned photographer with keen intuition and a gigantic telephoto lens that brings details close? Nearly fifty years later the people we meet seem dated but not critically so. The most fascinating one is Jeff, or, more properly, Stewart as Jeff, who is as fresh and alive as if this were yesterday.

In an interview before his death in 1980, Hitchcock explained his subjective filmmaking to the writer and director Peter Bogdanovich: "You can have a man look. You can have him see something. You can make him react to it. Without him speaking, you can show his mind." Jeff sits and watches the little personal dramas across the way. He does or says nothing, but his expressions—amusement, resignation, sympathy—illuminate the little triumphs and tragedies beyond. Stewart went on to make *Vertigo* with Hitchcock, but it's hard to rate any Stewart performance over this one.

On the DVD, the director Curtis Hanson mentions Hitchcock's technical brilliance, his way with humor, voyeurism, guilt, sexuality, and relationships. Hitchcock could also tell a story, even from a wheelchair. At first, Jeff's alarm at the disappearance of Thorwald's wife from the window across the courtyard is regarded as paranoid. For kids the film takes off when his suspicion that Thorwald has disposed of her is finally shared by Lisa and Stella. From that point, the story takes on thrillerish form, with much excited conjecture and leads both promising and disproved. Lisa submits to physical peril as Jeff's stand-in, and at last there is an assault by the suspect, which proves that if you can look into other lives through the window they can also look into yours.

At the conclusion, kids will appreciate a marvel of complicated, highly detailed filmmaking fitted together with the utmost precision. And they'll have some fun and chills in the bargain. Years from now they can ruminate about Hitchcock: the bit of Everyman in all his characters, even villains; the male-female incompatibility in his films (no great hope is held out for a lasting relationship between Jeff and Lisa); his concern with isolation. They can dive into piles of Hitchcock books and studies. The director himself wondered at all the theorizing. On the DVD of *To Catch a Thief*, Hitchcock's granddaughter, Mary Stone, recalls asking him to help her analyze his *Shadow of a Doubt* (1943) for a school paper. They got a C.

Jeff theorizes that Thorwald disassembled his wife for removal from their apartment, and the fellow is seen with knives and a saw in support of that idea. But this comes with a Hitchcockian wink, more as a kind of shivery notion. Thorwald hangs Jeff out his own window, cast and all, but again there is something vaguely comic about the attack, which is tame by today's standards and shouldn't faze young viewers. One scene will definitely upset many children and parents, however. Late in the film the dog in the basket is found strangled in the courtyard, which leads to a loud lamentation about the cruel impersonality of city people. The scantily clad Miss Torso and the newlyweds present plenty of sexual suggestion, but nothing is viewed. (Remember that we are still in production code days.) And there is no obscenity.

75. ROCKY

Sylvester Stallone, Talia Shire, Burgess Meredith, Carl Weathers, Burt Young

DIRECTED BY JOHN AVILDSEN
1976. 119 minutes. PG

If Americans love underdogs, this is America's movie. In this corner: Rocky Balboa (Sylvester Stallone), part-time fighter, forgiving collector for a Philadelphia loan shark, good guy around the neighborhood; in the opposite corner, Apollo Creed (Carl Weathers), heavyweight champion of the world, celebrity, businessman.

Las Vegas says Balboa won't last three rounds against the champ. Stallone himself faced long odds when he made the film. *Rocky* was his idea. At the time he was a struggling actor so broke that he had to sell his dog because he couldn't afford to feed it. These days his image is tarnished by a succession of very bad movies from the '90s aimed with increasing desperation at restoring his fading stature as an action star. *Rocky* happened when he and the concept were young and fresh. He wrote the movie himself in three days in an eight-by-nine room. The script ran ninety pages, about 10 percent of which made it into the final film.

Shortly thereafter Stallone auditioned for another film with the director John Avildsen and the producer Irwin Winkler. He didn't get the part, but he said that he had written this screenplay. "What we loved the most was that he lost the fight," Avildsen says in a DVD commentary. "If he had won maybe we wouldn't have taken it."

They showed the script to the studios. Gradually the bidding rose to $260,000, a staggering prospect for an out-of-work actor riding the bus after his $40 car blew up. MGM took the film, but as is usually the case at the studios, they had trouble with an unknown in the title role. Ryan O'Neal, maybe, Burt Reynolds, Robert Redford.

Stallone survived along with his movie. The idea jelled fully when a super-underdog of a boxer named Chuck Wepner knocked down Muhammad Ali during a heavyweight title fight. Wepner lost to Ali, but to Stallone it was a metaphor for life: We can't all be champs, but we can make the most of our opportunities. Carpe diem is a much-used notion in movies before and since, but for Stallone it was a catalyst. Rocky would have his moment, but to take advantage of it, he would have to commit himself.

Avildsen says the film is about living up to commitment. That isn't easy for Rocky. A tough old gym owner named Mickey (Burgess Meredith) screams that Rocky could have been a good fighter but he has wasted his ability because he has no focus. That's true, but Rocky has other concerns. Stallone says that the film is as much about misperception as it is about commitment. Rocky may look like a big, tough street palooka, but as a collector for a Philadelphia loan shark he can't bring himself to break the thumbs of a deadbeat who is behind on his payments. Around the neighborhood Rocky is the one who tries to keep a young girl out of trouble with the wrong crowd. So under that hulking physical presence we have a good guy, a Samaritan.

A simple man, he reacts openly and occasionally awkwardly, but he's hardly a fool. He's also reflective. Stallone says that Rocky has nothing to do, so he moves slowly and observes people and happenings more closely than most people. For example, only Rocky detects an inner beauty in Adrian (Talia Shire), a clerk in a pet store and the sister of Rocky's friend Paulie (Burt Young). Soul mates from the start despite her shyness, they fall in love.

Rocky is also a realist. When a ranked opponent drops out of a fight, the promotion-minded Creed announces that in the great American tradition of giving everybody a chance, he will allow an unknown to challenge him for the title. When he's chosen, Rocky shows no elation or much reaction at all. He knows he is regarded as harmless fodder. What's important to him is that he has been provided a moment.

Stallone himself had to train hard for the movie. Avildsen notes that the actor was hardly the chiseled specimen he became in the *Rambo* movies. The movie opens with a view of Jesus Christ on the wall of the Resurrection Gym in East Los Angeles. But the movie is about a Philadelphia fighter, so Rocky (and Stallone) trained there. Like many American cities in the '70s, Philly was a falling-down, trash-clogged mess. In the film, Rocky runs in the streets at dawn. It was winter and freezing and the camera crew had a hard time with congealing equipment. People threw fruit at Stallone, which was all right. Rocky and Stallone were good-natured about that kind of stuff.

Before the fight Rocky tells Adrian that all he wants to do is last fifteen rounds. After a wild brawl, both fighters are left barely standing. Modeled after Ali, Creed is a showman and not a bad guy. He does tell Rocky that there will be no rematch. Rocky says he doesn't want one.

Stallone "is amazing to watch," Pauline Kael wrote in *The New Yorker*. "There's a bull-necked energy in him, smoldering, and in his deep caveman's voice he gives the most surprising sharp, fresh shadings to his lines. The picture is poorly made, yet its naive, emotional shamelessness is funny and engaging."

The movie won an Oscar as best film. Avildsen was best director. Stallone, Shire, Young, and Meredith were nominated. Like Rocky, the movie accomplished what it wanted, and it did so on budget. On the set economies were often ingenious. For example, on their first date Adrian and Rocky go skating at a city rink. But that would have required hundreds of extras so rethinking was in order. The pair go to the rink after it has closed, Rocky pays the attendant $10, and the couple shuffle around the ice by themselves.

Later he and Creed fight in a big-time arena, requiring a crowd of thousands, another impossibility. To impart the feeling, Rocky visits the arena alone for a look around the huge hall. For the fight scene as many people as possible were put in the seats. One group from a nursing home ended up in the wrong seats and couldn't be moved easily because they were so elderly. "When you look at the place, it's practically empty," says Avildsen.

For a Thanksgiving scene the production could afford one turkey. Paulie gets so angry at Adrian that he takes the bird she is preparing and throws it out the window. Several takes were required so a crew member was stationed outside in the alley to catch the turkey each time and take it back to Paulie.

The fight is violent and little ones could be upset. They could also be disturbed by the turkey episode and fairly heavy domestic violence at Paulie's. As for sex, Rocky and Adrian sink to the floor in an embrace, but they are clothed and that is that. There is some rough talk but little real profanity.

76. THE ROOKIE

Dennis Quaid, Rachel Griffiths, Jay Hernandez, Angus T. Jones, Brian Cox, Beth Grant

DIRECTED BY JOHN LEE HANCOCK
2002. 129 minutes. G

One night on a West Texas road, Jim Morris (Dennis Quaid) stops his pickup truck in front of a speed-detector sign, fingers a baseball, exhales sharply, and throws it as hard as he can. The detector reads seventy-six miles per hour, which is a distinct disappointment to a man who regularly threw eighty-eight miles per hour before four arm surgeries ended a pitching career that might have gone on to the majors but ended in the Milwaukee Brewers farm system. But as he trudges into the darkness to retrieve the ball, we learn something he won't realize until quite a while later at a tryout with the Tampa Bay Devil Rays. The sign was malfunctioning. Morris really threw ninety-six miles per hour.

Few men in the game throw that hard. Injuries or no injuries, a high school science teacher in his late thirties is suddenly performing better than he did fifteen years earlier. Yes, a miracle has occurred, but the most miraculous thing about John Lee Hancock's movie is that with the schmaltz potential precariously high, the story, which is a true one, manages inspirational uplift without smothering under the globs of overwrought sentimentality that kill off many a similar tale.

We can thank Quaid, who "lets his face register the pained doubts of a careworn man chewing over major life decisions," as the critic Stephen Holden described him in the *New York Times*. "Now and then that face breaks into a radiant dimpled grin (a Quaid specialty), and the boy inside the man beams out reassuringly." For the most part, kids watching the movie will appreciate a down-to-earth fellow who goes about his duty as he sees it, which is to provide loving care for his wife (Rachel Griffiths) and three children, explain neutrons and protons to his students, and coach the school's underachieving baseball team.

The scene is Big Springs, a dusty, browned-out town on the Texas plains. Morris's father (Brian Cox) landed here as a navy recruiter, dragging along a son who was a top-notch pitcher in school but never could stay in one town long enough to taste a championship before the navy reassigned his father again. Later there was junior college and a shot at the big time, but when that didn't work out, Jimmy gravitated back to Big Springs the way men from towns like this tend to. As Jim will tell his high school players, most of them will work the oil rigs or for Bo's Tire Barn, have families, and retire, and there's nothing wrong with that. That's what he's doing. But if they want something special to remember in their lives, it will happen out there on the ball field this season.

In West Texas, football gets the glory, the money, the grass seed, and the water to grow it. One of Morris's players says that if baseball were football, the diamond would look like Tiger Woods's backyard. In Big Springs they play baseball on dirt. The game got its roots here back in the '20s when two nuns scratched out a dirt diamond so the oil workers could play some ball. These days Morris and a school groundskeeper work at coaxing Bermuda hybrid No. 5 out of the baked earth, but what few blades emerge are munched by the deer.

Morris tells the team that if they keep playing as badly as they have been, baseball will vanish from the town altogether. His players wonder what their motivation might be. None will get college scholarships. Morris says it's not about college, it's about having dreams and wanting something in life. Suddenly, though, he finds the tables turned. He's been throwing some batting practice and the boys have witnessed his new fastball. "You're the one who should be wanting more," his catcher tells him. So they make a deal. If the team reaches the regional championship, Morris will again try for the big leagues.

Quaid is very fine as a coach and a father to his doting eight-year-old son, Hunter (Angus T. Jones), who follows him everywhere, but mostly he succeeds as a man who recognizes reality and tries to make responsible decisions. When the Devil Rays hold a tryout in San Angelo, it's Jim's day to watch the kids so he takes all three of them to the ball field. In one of the film's best scenes he leads them across a diamond full of aspirants virtually half his age. A scout from the old days recognizes him and thinks he's bringing one of his players to the tryout. "I'm here for me," Morris tells him.

When he's called to the mound for his tryout, he's changing his baby's diapers. During the tryout, he throws hard over and over. "I call the office and tell them I got a guy here almost twice these kids' age and I'm going to get laughed at," the scout tells him. "I don't call in a ninety-eight-mile-per-hour fastball and I'll be fired." But a comeback doesn't come easily. A much better teaching and coaching opportunity arises in Fort Worth. Morris would be smart to take it. He and his wife work out the pros and cons and it's painful. But, as she finally points out, what would he tell an eight-year-old if he turned his back on one last chance?

Weeks in the minors leave him lonely for his family and reconsidering the Fort Worth option. The film does a very good job with the profession of playing baseball, which can be pure drudgery. Morris pitches well in minor league ball, but it's strictly routine. Then comes the call. The Devil Rays are playing in The Ballpark at Arlington, home of the Texas Rangers.

No boy who walks into a major league stadium for the first time will ever forget its emerald brilliance, and so it is for the Big Springs players who turn out for Morris's first major league game, along with his family and half the town. Hancock's movie catches their gut-grabbing wonderment as well as it catches everything else. The film's "stately pace and appreciation of the austere grandeur of the Texas landscape and the eerie beauty of night baseball contribute mightily to its aura of modern American folk tale," Holden wrote.

The real Jim Morris pitched two years in the majors and went home to Texas. Quaid was forty-seven when he made this film. A realistic-looking pitcher, he needed to ice his arm after each day of shooting. On the DVD Hancock says the film crew had to put dirt over a grass field to re-create the diamond in Big Springs. Realism was always the goal. When a crew member drew a picture to look as if it were by a two-year-old, Quaid found a child in a crowd of onlookers and had her draw one herself.

It's hard if not impossible to come up with any reservation whatever for a movie that is fine for any child old enough to understand what is happening. There is no violence, sex, or profanity.

77. THE SECRET GARDEN

Kate Maberly, Heydon Prowse, Andrew Knott, Maggie Smith, John Lynch

DIRECTED BY AGNIESZKA HOLLAND
1993. 103 minutes. G

When ten-year-old Mary Lennox (Kate Maberly) disembarks all by herself on a gloomy day in Southampton, other orphans with her on the ship from India mockingly recite, "Mary, Mary, quite contrary." That's not the nicest farewell for a little girl whose mother and father, like the parents of her shipmates, have been killed in an earthquake, but to be honest the truculent, dismissive Mary hasn't worked that hard at making friends on the voyage. Though no one in England has yet to experience her abrasive disposition, it seems more or less in keeping that she is the last of the children to be collected at the pier by relatives and taken off to new lives.

Actually she is met, finally, not by a relative but a relative's servant, Mrs. Medlock (Maggie Smith), who is as rude and dismissive as Mary herself. Mary is to go live with her uncle, Lord Craven (John Lynch), master of the hundred-room Misselthwaite Manor that looms in the North Yorkshire mists. Craven himself is nowhere in evidence, nor is he likely to appear and welcome Mary anytime soon, according to Medlock, who hustles the child into a baronial bedroom as a jailer escorts a prisoner.

Once again we are launched in a highly stylized adaptation of a classic story by the English children's author Frances Hodgson Burnett. As in Alfonso Cuaron's wonderfully fantastical treatment of Burnett's *A Little Princess* (see page 167), the tale begins in colonial India with British children of privilege uprooted and shipped off. In the Cuaron film the princess is sent to boarding school in New York while her father goes off to fight in World War I. She is a beautiful, magical child. Mary Lennox, by contrast, is all edges.

Mary is the very different movie daughter of Agnieszka Holland, the Polish director noted for such unchildlike fare as *Europa, Europa,* about a young German Jew who survives the Nazis by joining Hitler Youth, and *Olivier, Olivier,* the story of a French country couple who lose their son only to find him years later as a Paris street hustler. Holland has some fun in her films, but heroines are unlikely to be precious little girls in sweet scenarios.

Mary, in fact, is a haughty nineteenth-century child reared in India by servants of parents too preoccupied with their own social and professional agendas to pay their daughter even the slightest bit of attention. On top of this, as noted disdainfully by Medlock on the pier, Mary is no attractive little bundle of sunshine, though behind that stormy little countenance we immediately sense the humor and spirit that haven't been stamped out of her. But neglect amounting to abandonment has soured Mary, turning her belligerent and aggressively entitled as a defensive reflex.

"Her tight little face and wary eyes repel the easy affection we want to feel for children and force us to take the moral struggle of her character as seriously as we would that of any adult," wrote Richard Alleva in the English journal *Commonweal* in 1993.

As in many children's films (and many in this book), the adults fail. At Misselthwaite Manor, the children soldier on. In fact, in the face of utter incompetence, they brush adults aside. Mary's perfect ally in this is the very haughty Colin Craven (Heydon Prowse), also ten, the supposedly stricken son of the master of the house. Advertised as virtually crippled and deathly prone to germs and even light and air itself, the boy is kept sequestered in a sealed lair deep within the mammoth house, where he is tended to by Medlock and fawning servants in surgical masks. No wonder he is given to hysterical tirades. Only Mary can reach him.

Lynch's Lord Craven is a most unlikely looking fellow. Holland gives him flowing locks and the look of either a rock star on a very bad trip or a pirate on the run. Craven is just the word for him. Shattered by his wife's death, he cowers like a wounded animal in his own hideaway in the huge pile, fleeing house and country for long periods at the slightest sign of any development that might force him from his shell. That leaves Medlock, something of a hysteric herself in her rigidity, and a flock of kowtowing servants.

"As in many of Holland's films, the camera homes in unerringly on the gulf between the worlds of children and adults, on the violence that abyss engenders and on emotions of jealousy and rage," Roger Cohen wrote in the *New York Times*. "There is a constant struggle, as in the director's own experience, between life and death."

Driven inward, Mary and Colin eventually break free and connect with each other. "Maybe, after fifteen years of trying to analyze human stupidity, I turned to children for a kind of hope," Holland told Cohen in 1993 before the film was released. "I don't believe children are innocent, but they are more innocent. You can always hope that, by being provocative, you might make them more curious and imaginative."

Left isolated without a friend or anything to do, the curious Mary encounters Dickon (Andrew Knott), a ruddy-faced boy on a white horse, who points out that actually there is much to do in the natural world of the moors if she'll only look about her. For Mary the clouds begin to lift, the hint of a smile breaking up her black look. Her salvation lies in the gnarled tangle of a ruined garden she discovers close to the manor. A robin leads her there. Because his wife, Colin's mother, died in the garden, Lord Craven has locked it and forbidden entry.

"To call *The Secret Garden* D. H. Lawrence for kids would be smart-alecky but not inaccurate," Alleva wrote in *Commonweal*. "Mrs. Burnett shared with Lawrence certain beliefs: the restorative powers of nature, the essential goodness of instinct, the need to fight the deformations of a biologically parched society. Holland responds to this and everything else in the book."

She is certainly capable of magic. It may not be similar to Cuaron's in terms of colorful flight, but it is richly mystical and flamboyant. After years of solitary communion with the flora and fauna, Dickon has become a creature of the wind and a master of the soil. He instructs Mary, who then liberates Colin from the servants' ridiculous ministrations and sends him blinking and colt-legged into a bright, blossoming world. Some critics noted that such profuse horticulture was a tall order for three children, which is a point of sorts. The Holland production's gardeners reportedly employed 17,200 pots of annuals and grasses, 1,200 perennials, and 4,000 wild geraniums.

Garden is metaphor, or, as Alleva put it in *Commonweal,* "the near animism of the garden cure." Even the elder Craven warms and opens at the sight of it. Holland allows herself a happy ending, but she works with what Burnett gave her and, after all, this is a group that could use a little happiness.

The film is fine for children from about age seven. In an unusual twist, parental death isn't as much of an upset as usual because the loss of her mother and father doesn't seem to bother Mary one jot. What does upset her, and will disturb many young viewers, is that her parents virtually abandoned her as a little girl, which is depicted in a garden dream sequence in which Mary's mother (Irène Jabob) gaily runs off leaving little Mary, about age two, crying by herself. There is no sex or profanity.

78. THE SECRET OF ROAN INISH

Jeni Courtney, Mick Lally, Eileen Colgan, Richard Sheridan

DIRECTED BY JOHN SAYLES
1994. 103 minutes. PG

"Neither chains of steel nor chains of love can keep her from the sea," says an old man who is relating a bit of Coneelly family history on the bleak speck of island called Roan Inish off the northwest coast of Ireland. Hand a Hollywood production a line like that, and bows would fairly saw through violin strings in a rush of loud, tacky sentiment. Thankfully this is a John Sayles movie, which is to say that intense feelings are in no way lessened but refined in a relatively small and closely observed study of how life works in such a setting. Sayles calls it an edge of reality.

Kids will love the heroine, a wise, highly observant little girl (Jeni Courtney) who in the way of many good children's films takes the adults in hand and steers them in the right direction. And she does it quietly. "There are no apocalyptic resonances; the heavens don't open," Stephen Holden wrote in the *New York Times*. "One of Mr. Sayles's artistic strengths (and commercial liabilities) is his refusal to make movies that knock you over the head with larger-than-life characters and emotions."

Arguably this country's preeminent independent filmmaker, Sayles stays sharply focused and gets the most out of his resources. His subjects range all over the cultural map, from baseball (*Eight Men Out*) to the labor movement (*Matewan*) to a woman's recovery from traumatic injury (*Passion Fish*). In *Roan Inish*, kids get a wonderfully told and deeply touching story of family roots as seen through the eyes of ten-year-old Fiona (Courtney) who is sent to live with her grandparents in the Irish isles shortly after World War II.

There she becomes involved in the legend of the selkie, a seal who sheds her skin to become a woman and marry a Coneelly on Roan Inish. She bears many children, then dons her sealskin again and returns forever to the sea. Sayles says that in one version of the myth the selkie's children try to follow her and drown. In his film, adapted from the book *The Secret of the Ron Mor Skerry* by Rosalie K. Fry, the one Coneelly child claimed by the ocean is the baby Jamie, Fiona's brother, who floats off in a cradle left by the water's edge.

At the time, the Coneellys were evacuating Roan Inish to move to less harsh conditions, as did many families after the war when the fishing industry failed and cities and other lands beckoned. But Roan Inish, her brother, and her roots are deep in Fiona's heart, and Sayles lets a pensive little girl explore these inclinations while drawing her family back to its heritage.

Some young viewers will find the film slow, but parents should encourage their patience. Saylesian pace and tone are catching after a while, even for kids. Sayles's companion, the producer Maggie Renzi, had loved Fry's book as a child, found a copy of it for twenty-five cents, and presented it to Sayles. He calls it his most inexpensive source material to date but notes that he still had to invest some of his own money in the production. The movie cost $3 million, a comparative pittance by Hollywood standards, and was shot in coastal County Donegal. Sayles and his colleagues looked at more than two thousand little girls before he found Courtney, who was from Northern Ireland. One of the things Sayles liked about her was that she instinctively knew what to do and did it. Or as he puts it, "She had her own through-line going on in her head."

Fiona is a riveting central figure for kids, winsomely good-looking, gentle, and strong. Susceptible to dreams and fantasy, she remains the level-headed core of the film. Her grandparents (Eileen Colgan and Mick Lally) fill her with stories of the old days and provide the warmth and support the child will need to accomplish her dream of reunion with her brother and reconnection with Coneelly roots on the island they abandoned.

Sayles says it was important that Fiona come across as a child who had no exposure to the media, as she would have been in that time and region. She learned orally or from books. The entire production has a feeling of removal from worldly concerns. Special effects were limited to the simplest devices. "It's nice to make special effects work in a film that has the feel of a children's book," Sayles says in the DVD commentary.

He talks a lot about working with animals, which, one surmises, isn't exactly his favorite thing to do. Seals populate the film from the start, affecting and guiding Fiona spiritually and physically. That meant training a few of them, and a couple of animatronic specimens were devised for trickier moments. Courtney spent a lot of time around the real seals, which made them all a little more comfortable. Virtually no progress was made with a supposedly trained seagull, which insisted on walking when it was supposed to be soaring and vice versa.

It was hard to get humans and animals in the same frame in a movie that used no computerized assists as does, say, *Jurassic Park*. Like armies, seals and gulls performed according to their stomachs. Bits of food produced the desired behavior until they were full, whereupon filming them stopped for the day. Sayles takes some degree of satisfaction in noting that a meal could be quickly snatched from the gull's throat, keeping him hungry and thus good for another take or two.

The crucial factor was the weather, which changed six or seven times a day. Sayles says he couldn't afford to wait more than twenty minutes for the right sky or light or amount of precipitation so he always had three scenes ready to roll at any one moment during the shooting day. "Everybody had to triple prepare," he says. The cinematographer, Haskell Wexler, was a genius with light. That far north, the days were long and sometimes the best time to shoot was between 10 and 11 P.M. The magic hour, Sayles calls it.

Some mildly scary scenes on the water could upset the very young. Parentless children are common in movies set among the Irish, who have never had an easy time, and that could be mildly disturbing here. But Fiona's quest is a thrilling one for kids from about the age of eight, maybe younger. This is also another of those rare family films that appeal to parents as much as children.

79. SHANE

Alan Ladd, Brandon De Wilde, Van Heflin, Jean Arthur, Jack Palance

DIRECTED BY GEORGE STEVENS

1953. 118 minutes. PG

Many films these days are made for fourteen-year-old boys of all ages, which, as any moviegoer can attest, often results in trashy action. What makes *Shane* so intriguing is that a film originally for adults and generally ranked among the best ever, also works so well for children. In this case, fifty-year-old sensibilities and techniques yield a classical, forthright simplicity that puts characters and values into high relief. Kids can grab hold of *Shane* because it's larger than life.

Critics are forever lionizing this film for its look, its flow, and its artistry. All of this is true enough, but with any great old movie being spoon-fed to children by Mom and Dad, too much buildup can lead to skepticism. Some explanation of the film is warranted. *Shane* is great because it handles a complicated dynamic in a most accessible way. Here is a civilization where, as one character puts it, "there ain't a marshal within a hundred-mile ride." Without authority, people have only themselves to rely upon. For example, during a brawl that is wrecking his establishment, a shopkeeper can only stand in the middle of the melee and shout, "Stop, you men." There is something poignant about that.

For children, it's fascinating to see how this world works. Representing them is little Joey Starrett, played by the ten-year-old Brandon De Wilde. The son of homesteaders (Van Heflin and Jean Arthur), he watches with apprehension and curiosity as his parents are threatened by cattlemen who would drive them from their land. Into this scene, gorgeously set in the Grand Tetons, rides one of the most famous figures in movie history. Shane (Alan Ladd) is the reformed gunfighter determined to keep the six-shooters hung up (though he still packs a couple of them among his belongings). How many times has this character been emulated in the American western, most lately perhaps by Clint Eastwood in *Unforgiven* (1992)? Shane is trying to move on, to what he isn't sure, and he recommends the same to cattle barons who still think they own the country. The only difference between them, he tells a cattleman, is that he realizes it's over.

This leaves Shane at loose ends, the outsider who can never fully belong. He realizes this, too, and his wistfulness gives the film much of its strength. At the Starrett homestead he pitches in with chores and is the good citizen, all the while looking longingly at family life. But always there is Shane's duality. In town, where he purposely doesn't react when humiliated by the cattleman's lackey, there is something in his look and manner that is unmistakably lethal. The cowboy who humiliated him sees it as clearly as anyone. For all his reticence, Shane is instant death.

At the core of the film is his relationship with little Joey. The boy is fascinated by an adventurous and mysterious figure, but at the same time he studies Shane and how he fits into his new surroundings, and especially how he affects his father and mother. Joey looks to Shane so intensely for clues as to what is right and wrong and important and worthwhile in life that he almost visibly aches. Unfortunately, brilliantly, Shane can't stay to partake of any of it. Naturally he has to strap on his six-shooter.

On *The Ed Sullivan Show* in the '50s, Jack Palance, who plays Wilson, the killer brought in to intimidate the homesteaders into vacating their spreads, strode onstage wearing his renowned viperish grin and complaining that he hasn't killed anybody since lunch. In the '90s he won an Oscar playing the Wilsonish Curly in *City Slickers*.

In *Shane*, Wilson is easily dispatched, a straw man blown away and left under a pile of beer barrels. To lend him menace, George Stevens, the director, gave Palance a small horse, which was supposed to make him look bigger. A New York stage actor, Palance had never ridden or handled a gun, but he worked hard at both. In one scene he backs his mount out of the homesteader's yard as if the horse were a pickup truck in a parking lot.

One of this country's great filmmakers, Stevens (*Diary of Anne Frank, A Place in the Sun, Giant, The Talk of the Town*) was a craftsman and a perfectionist. A shot of homesteaders leaving in a wagon required 119 takes. When the film was finished, the studio didn't think it had much—just another Alan Ladd movie.

Stevens fought in World War II and he was bothered by Hollywood westerns, many with John Wayne, that blasted away offhandedly as if nobody really got hurt when shot. He had seen what guns really do to people, and he wanted Shane *to deglamorize the six-shooter. But shootings in* Shane *are tame compared to today's films. There are a couple of brawls, with faces bloodied, but there is honesty and purpose to the violence that children will recognize.* Shane *and the homesteader's wife are attracted to each other, but there is nothing improper. Nor is there profanity. Mature eight-year-olds can watch this film. A little older might be better.*

80. SHREK

With the voices of Mike Myers, Eddie Murphy, Cameron Diaz, John Lithgow

DIRECTED BY ANDREW ADAMSON AND VICKY JENSON
2001. 89 minutes. PG

Shrek never would have made it with the old Disney. For one thing, he takes an eyeball in his martini. Recent Disney characters have livened up considerably, but the traditional mystical-magical ones weren't too hip or pop cultural. Know that Shrek has 180 digital animation controls in his face. The big, green ogre lifted from William Steig's children's book comes from a computer-animated land far removed from a drawing board of the '30s and '40s. Shrek's creators, from a division of DreamWorks called Pacific Data Images, talk about 836 "shapers" in his body's "deformation system." Can't say that about Pinocchio.

Nevertheless, *Shrek,* winner of the first Oscar in the new animated film category, does a particularly good job of bringing traditional values into the here and now for a young audience. At a time when physical looks and cultural profiling assume new significance, the film's approach to the beauty-and-the-beast theme is especially apt.

A scuzzy, fearsome-looking character with a hygiene deficiency, Shrek drives others in the opposite direction. The fact is that while he may never be the gregarious type he is a fellow of gentle and noble instincts. Trapped in the ogre stereotype, he is more or less obliged to put on a gruff defensiveness that isn't the real Shrek at all. Misconceptions mire him in disastrous relations and his own displeasure with himself. It's a perfect case of shooting oneself in the foot. The movie is very good with this. We feel his pain.

Shrek has a good deal to say about self-image and personal frustration; however, perhaps the most important lesson is that sometimes things aren't what they appear or what they are made out to be. That's true for the movie's sleeping beauty, a princess named Fiona, and here the film makes a neat switch on age-old fairy tale expectations. In the most inaccessible reaches of a castle guarded by the fire-breathing dragon from every fairy tale ever told, Fiona is awakened by a kiss from what she expects to be a princely hunk with a flawless curriculum vitae and a ton of money. True, there have been some slip-ups in that scenario in fairy tales past, but isn't that basically her traditional right? She is not thrilled to learn that she's been smooched, and reluctantly, by an ogre.

But it develops that Fiona also is not what she appears. She has the same image and identity problems as Shrek. The film spoofs her as a Snow White look-alike before whisking her off for a riotously effective transformation. *Shrek* has fun with all the classic fairy-tale folk. At the start, many of them are banished to the ogre's swamp by a runty despot named Lord Farquaad. Much to Shrek's disgust, his mudhole becomes an internment camp, overrun by the three blind mice and a horde of other displaced Disneyites.

Back at Farquaad's towering fortress, the vaunted mirror from *Snow White* is consulted. Just what, Farquaad asks the glass, will it take to make him king? Marry a princess, the mirror tells him, and the throne is his. But which princess? Here the film takes a new young audience on one of its spirited jaunts into pop culture. To pick a princess, Farquaad sets up a competition resembling television's *Dating Game*. As on the show, there are three competitors. "She likes sushi and hot-tubbing. She's Cinderella!" exclaims the announcer.

Farquaad's choice is Fiona, who likes piña coladas and getting caught in the rain. Later a jousting tournament turns into a World Wrestling Federation–style brawl, another example of the movie transporting the medieval into the present. High-profile voices of the characters raise the immediacy, and none more recognizably than Eddie Murphy's as a jivey donkey who accompanies Shrek on his mission to free Fiona and save his swamp. Lithgow makes an imperiously conniving Farquaad. As the voice of Fiona, Cameron Diaz reportedly went into a kung fu routine in front of the microphone when the princess flattens a band of Robin Hood's not-so-merry men with Hong Kong efficiency. Fiona belches well, too, a must in a kids' movie.

Characters get right down to cases, stand by values and friends, and persevere when all looks bleakest. Mike Myers, the voice of Shrek, has said the film's message is that beauty comes in all shapes and sizes: we should all strive to be who we are and not disguise our true selves to live up to some ideal. Spoken like a standard fairy tale, but *Shrek* is a hip, funny piece of contemporary entertainment.

Does that make it better than a Disney oldie? Kids will like it better, but not because they have anything against older values that make as much sense to them as they do to their elders. It's just that *Shrek* is so completely now. Of course, the technology helps make it so. Few crow more about their accomplishments than the makers of digital animated feature films. If Shrek's face has 180 controls, Farquaad's, given the five o'clock shadow on his almost photo-realistic human features, must have at least that many running up and down a head many times too big for his body.

Shrek animators say they could have traced human movements in live action films and transferred them to Shrek, Fiona, and the others.

But that would be too real. It wouldn't have looked like animation. "We had to dial her back," one animator said. Just not back to *Snow White*.

There is some violence as Farquaad's soldiers get rough with the peasantry and combatants get banged about in the jousting pits and so forth, but no one stays hurt in cartoon strife. As for sex, some wisecracking about Farquaad's size could have connotations and there are other faint allusions. Without reservation, however, this is fine entertainment for children of all ages.

81. SINGIN' IN THE RAIN

Gene Kelly, Donald O'Connor, Debbie Reynolds, Jean Hagen, Millard Mitchell, Douglas Fowley, Cyd Charisse, Rita Moreno

DIRECTED BY GENE KELLY AND STANLEY DONEN
1952. 103 minutes. No rating

On-screen a big-toothed man draws so close we are practically against the tip of his nose. "Notice how my lips and the sound issuing from them are synchronized in perfect unison," he says with good enunciation and a slightly nasty leer. The arrival of the talkies distresses many. At Monumental Studios storm flags are flying. The screechy silent star and studio mainstay Lina Lamont (Jean Hagen) can't keep her mouth shut forever. Even the cocksure desert heart-throb Don Lockwood (Gene Kelly), Monumental's answer to Rudolph Valentino, allows that he's feeling shaky at the prospect of having to speak. "The new Don Lockwood," dryly remarks his friend Cosmo Brown (Donald O'Connor).

In its own reaction to the talkies, Kelly and Stanley Donen's "greatest musical ever" is especially fine for children. Kids tend to run from silent movies (until they get caught up in one), and here, in a movie within a movie, they encounter a sea change in American entertainment and culture. Loud and colorful and supremely fine, *Singin' in the Rain* slides down like ice cream. It also goes behind the scenes to show how pictures are made. In the principal story line Lockwood (a down-to-earth guy, actually), Cosmo, and the pert young song-and-dance gal and love interest Kathy Selden (Debbie Reynolds) try to resuscitate *The Dueling Cavalier*, an archetypical overblown silent costume epic starring Don and the voluptuous Lina. When he views the first talkie, *The Jazz Singer*, Monumental chief R. F. Simpson (Millard Mitchell) labels it a flash in the pan. Then he takes a look at the box office tallies. From now on, R. F. declares, all Monumental projects will be talkies.

Lockwood goes along with the changeover, and he has an idea. They'll make *The Dueling Cavalier* into a musical, *The Dancing Cavalier*. But what to do with Lina? Kids will love a scene in a garden with Don and Lina in full *Cavalier* regalia grappling with unfamiliar recording equipment. A mike planted in the bushes doesn't work because Lina keeps emoting in the opposite direction. "Talk to the bush," screams the director, clad in jodhpurs in the silent style. The mike is then planted between Lina's ample breasts. "What's that, a thunderstorm?" a technician asks. Actually it's Lina's pearl necklace rubbing together.

In movies set at the end of the silent era, audiences dressed formally and roared and hooted, which is exactly the reaction at the *Cavalier* premiere when voices are not only out of synchronization but Don's voice emerges from Lina and vice versa. It is decided that the thrush-toned Kathy will dub every sound Lina utters, a fictional precursor to Marni Nixon singing for Audrey Hepburn in *My Fair Lady* (see page 200) and all the other dubbing through the years.

Singin' in the Rain rides on its astonishingly athletic song and dance numbers: O'Connor walking up a wall; Kelly and O'Connor in unbelievably swift, precise tandem (O'Connor says they both naturally turned the same way); Cyd Charisse's legs flowing forever;

Reynolds hoofing her heart out; Kelly's immortal solo in a downpour. The story of how all of this came together is in step with the film itself, so much in character that it almost makes a movie within the movie within the movie.

At MGM (as at Monumental) they were churning out a movie a week when the renowned studio lyricist and producer Arthur Freed, father of the '40s and '50s Hollywood musical, summoned the writers Betty Comden and Adolph Green and told them to create a musical with all his songs in it. Freed's career began in the silent era, but by 1929, the dawn of sound, he had been hired by Irving Thalberg, MGM's artistic director, and was churning out songs for shows like *The Broadway Melody,* a source for several numbers adapted by Comden and Green, and *The Hollywood Revue,* which had a number called "Singin' in the Rain."

Given the material they were to work with, Comden and Green decided to set the movie at the time and in the environment that spawned Freed: right in the seam between silent and talking films. Kelly was Freed's choice. In a portrait of Kelly for the American Masters series on PBS, his daughter says her father was the only adult she knew who was happy with himself. Green says that Kelly, who died in 1996, combined a boyish ingenuousness with a hard worldly quality that sprang from a tough, scrambling boyhood. If Fred Astaire was the aristocracy of dance on-screen, Gene Kelly was the proletariat. A muscular young performer who revolutionized the musical in the '40s with his restless, explosive style, Kelly made dance masculine. Whereas Astaire danced high, Kelly moved low to the ground. He was often described as outspoken, brash, and rude. As a choreographer and movie director, he was a taskmaster. He and Donen made three musicals together, beginning with *On the Town* in 1949. One observer called Donen the chutzpah and Kelly the charisma.

On the *Singin' in the Rain* DVD, Charisse says she was black and blue after rehearsals. Kelly was especially good at driving inexperienced performers. Reynolds was a feisty nineteen-year-old when shooting began. The studio wanted Judy Garland or Jane Powell, but Freed, Kelly, and Donen demanded Reynolds, for reasons she says she doesn't quite understand even today. No one was sorry, though there were moments of stress. "She thought she knew more than she

did," Donen says dryly. "It was hard to convince her." Kelly drove
Reynolds until her feet bled. "You did it Gene's way, Gene's steps,
Gene's style," she says. "I was in tears a lot." She adds that Kelly
taught her well enough to last fifty-two years in show business.

At 9 A.M. on July 17, 1951, Kelly and crew began shooting one of
the most famous scenes in American movie history. In Los Angeles
water pressure had dropped because of lawn watering. Kelly was
unsure about what moves he would make. "It'll be raining and I'll be
singing" was all he could say about it.

*Fine viewing for everybody from the age of six or so, with really nothing
untoward to worry about in the way of sex, violence, or language.*

82. SNOW WHITE
AND THE SEVEN DWARFS

With the voices of Adriana Caselotti,
Lucille La Verne, Moroni Olsen, many others

DIRECTED BY DAVID HAND
1937. 83 minutes. No rating

In 1934 the ground shook at Walt Disney's studio. Summoning his
key people back to work after dinner, Disney told them that he was
planning a new film based on a story from 1812 called *Sneewitchen*
by the brothers Jacob and Wilhelm Grimm. By the 1930s, Snow
White had already been the subject of at least five silent shorts,
including a 1910 version called *The Little Snow Drop*, a 1916 six-
reeler that Disney saw as a boy, and a 1933 Paramount animated
short directed by Dave Fleischer and starring Betty Boop. But
Disney's new project would be the first animated feature. It would
employ three hundred animators and include songs. The film's title
notwithstanding, dwarfs would be referred to as "little people."

Almost six decades later, *Snow White and the Seven Dwarfs* stands as a seminal event in the history of filmmaking. Via a two-disc DVD special edition, kids will be present at the creation, so to speak. Conditioned by the lifelike computer-generated images in Disney films like *Toy Story* and *Monsters, Inc.,* they might not absolutely adore the quaint *Snow White,* but they will have a good time nevertheless. The little people are cute, as is the menagerie of cuddly creatures relied on in Disney films to rally around lead characters and help audiences through upsetting developments.

The Grimms' story didn't make it easy on Disney. The Grimms' queen (Disney's wicked stepmother) is a cannibal, dining on what she thinks is Snow White's heart like some gothic Hannibal Lecter. Disney by contrast keeps the organ—actually belonging to a pig—in a pretty little box. The movie pares down the queen's attempts to kill Snow White from three, as the Grimms had it, to one. The wicked stepmother's death is assigned to the forces of nature when a lightning bolt shears off a piece of cliff and she neatly and quickly disappears into the ocean. In the Grimms' story, the otherwise joyous wedding party doesn't make it that easy for the queen: "But iron slippers had already been put upon the fire, and they were brought in with tongs and set before her. Then she was forced to put on the red-hot shoes and dance until she dropped down dead."

To skirt darker elements, Disney elevated the dwarfs and downplayed the queen. No Grumpy, Sleepy, Bashful, or Dopey for the Grimms, who didn't name their dwarfs. But Disney's alterations can't be viewed purely in terms of censorship. He wanted to present the story in a way that he thought Americans would relate to and appreciate, and no one ever accused Disney of being out of tune with American sensibilities. In the beleaguered 1930s, film turned from fantasy toward forthright statements of faith in democracy and similar high-minded subjects. Disney perceived other needs. In his book *The Disney Version,* the critic Richard Schickel writes that his success was in part "because his visions appealed to the longings for the vanished past that were universally present in the national psyche."

Disney decided to position the film as a fairy tale rather than a prince-and-princess love story. He chose "Snow White" for its nostalgic potential. Schickel writes, "Its use of the sleeping beauty theme automatically makes it a work that caters to nostalgia, for all of us would like to go to sleep, as Snow White does, and then awaken to find the world unchanged, indeed improved, since it is her lover's kiss that awakens her. Moreover, as a nursery story, first heard in childhood, it is bound to stir the sweetest memories when it is revisited in adulthood, especially with one's offspring in tow."

Schickel points out that Disney's passion for a simplistic if brilliantly animated realism derived from the illustrators of nineteenth-century children's books, which perfectly describes the look of the film. Many illustrators scoffed. The caricaturist Al Hirschfeld called the film's major characters "badly drawn attempts at realism: they imitate pantographically the actions of their counterparts in factual photography. . . . To imitate an animated photograph except as satire is in poor taste."

But Disney wasn't concerned with gibes from the artistic and intellectual establishments. Schickel writes that his approach to illustration is in step with the cultural conservatism typically found in small-town, middle-class Americans. Disney was from such a background. An intuitive genius at ground level, he was defined by a narrow mind-set and the literal rigors of the struggle to succeed. Critics call the film a major cinematic achievement, but in a curious way. In avoiding the Grimms' plunge into blacker issues, Disney in effect makes the film's myriad small details, superbly animated for the period, its true subject. "In the end, they disarm all criticism in much the same casual way Disney brushed aside the dark mists that enveloped the basic legend," Schickel writes. "It does not matter that there is an occasional lapse into overly broad humor or sentiment. There is a genuine sunniness of outlook here, a sense that one sometimes gathers from works in the higher arts, of the artist breaking through to a new level of vision and technical proficiency and running joyously."

Young kids need little more from the movie than its lessons of loyalty, love, and perseverance. Since *Snow White and the Seven Dwarfs* is a multigenerational cultural phenomenon that still reaches into the lives of children today, parents might try to enlarge the perspective. In appropriating folk literature, Schickel writes, Disney was unable or unwilling to see it as "the primer picture-language of the soul," as

Joseph Campbell described it. True, Disney didn't regard that as his mission, and wouldn't have been equipped to respond if he had.

"Perhaps if Disney's psyche had been a little less the product of a petit bourgeois striving," Schickel continues, "perhaps if he had a little less education of the wrong kind—had been more truly a primitive—he might have found the inner spirit to comprehend the power of the material he was going to depend upon." That he didn't, Schickel concludes, kept Disney from greatness.

In 1937 the film was criticized for its violence and frightening situations. It's hard to imagine little ones being too put off today, but parents should be aware that the wicked stepmother carries on menacingly, the huntsman raises his dagger as if to strike, and other developments could be fleetingly disturbing. In the Grimms' story, the queen hankers after the prince, raising the romantic ante, but there is none of this or anything remotely sexual with Disney.

83. SOME LIKE IT HOT

Jack Lemmon, Tony Curtis, Marilyn Monroe, Joe E. Brown, George Raft

DIRECTED BY BILLY WILDER
1959. 119 minutes. No rating

"They told me, 'Billy Wilder wants to talk to you,'" Tony Curtis said in a recent interview. When Wilder beckoned in 1958, Curtis had earned an Oscar nomination as an escaped convict in *The Defiant Ones,* but he was still uncomfortable around big names in Hollywood. "I was intimidated by him, by all those guys," he said. But Wilder, by then the director of *Sunset Boulevard, Double Indemnity, Lost Weekend, Stalag 17, Witness for the Prosecution,* and other acclaimed films, didn't bite him. He had an idea for a movie. "Two musicians see a murder so they have to dress as women," he told Curtis.

Cross-dressing is everywhere in the movies (see *Mrs. Doubtfire*, page 194). Treatments can be stupid and trashy, but when done intelligently the subject has a lot to teach children about gender and role reversal. No movie does it better than this one. It's 1929 and Jerry (Jack Lemmon) and Joe (Curtis) witness the 1929 St. Valentine's Day gangland massacre in Chicago. To escape the mob they dress as women (Daphne and Josephine, respectively) and join an all-female band headed for Florida. On the train both are smitten by the band's voluptuous singer, Sugar (Marilyn Monroe), who is on the lookout for a rich husband.

One reason the film works so well is that Daphne and Josephine are so spontaneous. Curtis and Lemmon had to be themselves. Wilder was on a tight schedule. A female impersonator was brought over from Europe to consult but gave up immediately. "We had no time to break into it, so there was no difference between reality and the movie," Curtis said. Daphne and Josephine clop around in high heels, clambering in and out of upper berths on the train, constantly almost blowing their cover with Sugar, and narrowly escaping detection by others in the band. This is superbly paced physical comedy, and kids will love it.

Behind the frolics, though, are some elements that will need a little explaining. For example, after becoming women both men begin to appreciate how men typically treat women. Sugar gives Josephine an earful about life as a perceived bimbo, information she never would have shared with a man. Joe, something of a womanizer, sees what it's like to be hit on all the time. Daphne decides it's actually fun being a woman and is so good at it that she attracts a rich and ardent suitor (Joe E. Brown). When he proposes, she accepts and seems quite moved at the prospect.

Wilder keeps the film from looping off into mannered excess. Lemmon had a great time fooling around with his costumes; Curtis was more reserved. Wilder played it right down the middle. "He didn't want to denigrate guys being girls, and he didn't want to elevate it either," Curtis said. "We didn't flaunt it, there was no double meaning."

Some Like It Hot (Used by permission of MGM Home Entertainment)

There's no rush to introduce kids to Monroe, an American institution, but the film is as good an opportunity as any. Wilder had directed her in *The Seven Year Itch* (1955), but here he had his hands full. Notoriously troubled and late on the set, Monroe didn't show up at all on occasion. Wilder was patient. "He had to wait to get it from Marilyn," Curtis said. Wilder told him and Lemmon to be at their best for every take because he never knew when Monroe would be on or off. "He'd say, 'If she gets it right, that's the one I print,'" Curtis said. Nevertheless, Monroe is sensational as Sugar.

Wilder was a taskmaster, but he was also patient with Curtis and Lemmon. The calm Joe and the flighty Jerry were an odd couple. "We understood from the first day that we had to balance each other," Curtis said. Wilder let them do little variations on each take, shift emphasis, try something new. Curtis was a poor kid from the Bronx, a pretty boy who talked funny, as in, most famously, "Yonda lies the castle of my fadda." At one point in this film he stops being Josephine and becomes a yachtsman in blazer and cap. Wilder let him choose the accent, and Curtis does a very passable Cary Grant imitation. "I've never understood all this heaviness about my accent," he said. "I came out from New York. My accent was no more pronounced than John Wayne's."

Age ten and up is about right, though some younger children might be ready. In the role of Spats Columbo, George Raft gives a good-natured parody of himself while supervising the mowing down of unfortunate rivals in a parking garage on St. Valentine's Day. Sugar is sexual all movie long and downright steamy with Curtis's yachtsman, though they remain clothed. On balance, there is much sexual spoofing and innuendo, but not so much that it will offend most family viewers. There is no profanity.

84. THE SOUND OF MUSIC

Julie Andrews, Christopher Plummer, Eleanor Parker, Richard Haydn, Peggy Wood, Charmian Carr, Heather Menzies, Nicolas Hammond

DIRECTED BY ROBERT WISE
1965. 174 minutes. G

When he heard "Climb Every Mountain" sung on Broadway, Robert Wise was overwhelmed and not favorably when the mother abbess came right up to the footlights and tried to blow the house away. "I felt like crawling under my seat," Wise says in his commentary on the DVD. In the film, Peggy Wood plays the abbess. Wood was seventy-two and couldn't sing at all, which didn't much matter because the song could be dubbed (as many songs were in all the great movie musicals). Wise cast her for her dramatic abilities (she was nominated for an Oscar as best supporting actress). But he says he toned down the scene visually as well, putting Wood at a slight distance, sometimes in profile and silhouette.

The Sound of Music ran four years in movie theaters and has been a video and television staple seemingly forever. Who doesn't know this film, its songs by Richard Rodgers and Oscar Hammerstein, and the story of the von Trapp family? On DVD it's interesting to hear what thoughts occurred as it was being made. Wise and his two principal stars, Julie Andrews and Christopher Plummer, all say they were worried about the sweetsie-schmaltzy factor.

"Whom could this operetta offend?" wrote the critic Pauline Kael. "Only those of us who loathe being manipulated in this way and are aware of how cheap and ready-made are the responses we are made to feel. We may become even more aware of the way we have been turned into emotional and aesthetic imbeciles when we hear ourselves humming the sickly, goody-goody songs."

Kael wasn't hooked, but kids will love the film as they always have. Andrews gives Maria an "air of radiant vigor" and "plain-Jane wholesomeness," as Bosley Crowther put it in the *New York Times*. The classic opening number in the mountain field, "The Hills Are Alive," was one of the last scenes shot. Prop wash from the helicopter zooming in for the take knocked her flat several times, and the scene required eight or nine takes.

A stage and television star, Andrews had just begun a screen career in a nanny role in *Mary Poppins* (see page 185). She wasn't sure she wanted another one as nanny to the seven von Trapp children. A couple of years earlier she and Carol Burnett had spoofed the Broadway *Sound of Music* on Burnett's television show. On the DVD, she says she asked Wise what could be done about the sugar buildup: the seven kids matched up and down the age scale, all singing and dancing; the sweet nuns; the glorious scenery in Salzburg and the mountains.

Wise says that he sought to de-prettify any chance he got. Facades of buildings were imposing but deliberately kept simple. Plummer brought a dark edge to the role of Baron von Trapp, the naval officer who resists the Nazis and flees with his children and his new wife, Maria. "Looking as handsome and phony as a store-window Alpine guide, Mr. Plummer acts the hard-jawed, stiff-backed fellow with equal artificiality," wrote Crowther. But while the baron lends stern authority to the children's upbringing, he softens and bends when he has to.

These days Plummer is a superb character actor (as a psychiatrist in *A Beautiful Mind*, for instance). He consented to play the baron when the role was made larger than it was on Broadway. On the DVD he talks about the experience self-deprecatingly. Wise says that Plummer asked to record his songs after the filming was done. Though he took voice lessons and practiced hard, he wasn't vocally up to the climactic love scene with Andrews. The screenwriter Ernest Lehman comments that this particular moment required a great voice, not just a good one.

The play and movie made big adjustments to the von Trapps' real-life story, but what movie doesn't? Aside from the entertainment factor, kids get a lesson, albeit a softened one, about intractable situations necessitating a change in life choices. On-screen, the baron and Maria are married shortly before the Nazi takeover in 1938, whereas the real baron and Maria were married in 1927 and had a child of their own. As a show of support for his motherland, the real baron deposited all his money in the bank of Austria, which then went broke, impoverishing the family.

Shortly thereafter, Maria organized the Trapp Family Singers. It is true, as depicted in the picture, that the baron resisted the Nazis and was headed for major problems if he stayed in Austria. But when the family fled into Italy, they were on a train leaving on tour and not pressed into a mildly thrillerish quasi–car chase and grand hike into the hills, as is depicted in the movie.

The musical ran for three and a half years on Broadway. When it opened the critics were lukewarm. Though the general truth of the von Trapp story couldn't be disputed, the mixture of Nazis and operetta raised questions of manipulated pop entertainment. "Yeah, but it happened," says James Hammerstein, son of Oscar, on the disc. The song "Edelweiss" in the show was the last his father wrote before his death in 1960. He and Rodgers collaborated on a dozen big movie musicals beginning with *State Fair* in 1944 and including *Oklahoma!, Carousel, The King and I* (see page 139), and *South Pacific*. Wise thought that three songs in the staged *Sound of Music* served no dramatic purpose in the film and Rodgers agreed to have them cut. A couple of songs were added.

Wise came to the project through the back door, so to speak. It was a horrendous time for 20th Century Fox, which had nearly driven itself into bankruptcy making *Cleopatra*. Darryl F. Zanuck had just resumed control and was looking for another moneymaker to add to *The Longest Day* (see page 173), a big war film that was providing Fox some lift at the box office. On the disc, Richard Zanuck, Darryl's son, recalls that Fox had always wanted to make *The Sound of Music*. The studio wanted William Wyler to direct, but he wasn't too enthusiastic. Later he was suspected of harboring plans to turn the picture into a war movie. Hearing that, Lehman quickly finished the script along prescribed musical lines, whereupon Wyler left the project altogether.

A superb film editor, Wise directed some horror in the '40s (*The Curse of the Cat People*) and by the early '60s had made a wide assortment of movies: *The Day the Earth Stood Still* (see page 69), *Executive Suite, Somebody Up There Likes Me,* and, most important to this project, *West Side Story* (see page 293).

When Wise was approached about *The Sound of Music,* he was about to make *The Sand Pebbles* in Taipei. Rains delayed that film so he took this one. On the disc he continually mentions his lifelong friendships with others on the film, including Andrews. The movie won the Oscar as best picture. Wise was named best director, but he wasn't around to collect. By then the weather had improved in Taipei, and he had moved on to *The Sand Pebbles.*

Very young children could be upset by the Nazi threat, but this element is kept relatively toothless. Otherwise there are few if any problems for anyone over six.

85. SPIRITED AWAY

With the voices of Daveigh Chase, Suzanne Pleshette, Jason Marsden

DIRECTED BY HAYAO MIYAZAKI
2002. 125 minutes. PG

Amid the flood of American animation these days it's refreshing for children and the rest of us to experience a different consciousness and voice and see where these can lead the spirit and imagination. Anime, a style of Japanese animation, has been a cult favorite in this country for twenty years or so, frequently but not exclusively in films involving much sex and violence. Here, in the hands of the great Japanese animation director Hayao Miyazaki, the form takes a wonderful fantastical turn into mystical areas of thoughts and dreams where all kids dwell.

The film broke attendance records in Japan, where Miyazaki is so revered that he has a museum devoted entirely to his eight animated feature films and many television shows. American audiences have had a taste of his work in *My Neighbor Totoro,* about two sisters' discovery of a forest spirit, and *Princess Mononoke,* a complicated if intriguing epic about power and competing personal values set in the fourteenth century. *Spirited Away* is something else, "a masterpiece, pure and simple, a film that can stand with the Disney classics of the '30s and '40s in the range of its imagination and the quality of its execution," the critic Dave Kehr wrote in the *New York Times.*

Kids will relate to a film about separation and the discovery of identity. "Like Disney in his early features, Mr. Miyazaki deals with the deepest kind of childhood trauma—the loss of a parent, the resentment of a sibling, the difficulty of belonging to a family and the difficulty of separating from it," Kehr writes. Yet no one will mistake this for a Disney film. As the story begins, young Chihiro is distressed at having to leave friends and familiar surroundings to move to another city with her parents. On their drive to their new home they come across a large and mysterious settlement resembling an amusement park. The place appears to be deserted, but as they wander the streets they come across a food stand heaped with steaming dishes that have obviously just been prepared. With no attendant in sight, Chihiro's famished parents decide to partake, but something deters the little girl, who will have none of it.

Instead she wanders off into the park and into a world of dreams where she encounters strange and forbidding sights and apparitions. One of them is in the form of a boy, named Haku, who warns her that she and her parents must vacate the place by dark. Returning to the food stand, she discovers that displeased Shinto spirits have turned her gluttonous mother and father into hogs. Miyazaki describes her as "a very angry little girl," but she seems more determined, and not a little frightened, as she plunges headlong and forthrightly into the unknown to find help.

In this dreamworld there are no easy answers or ready helpers, aside from the boy she encountered and now even he appears suspect. "Mr. Miyazaki's specialty is taking a primal wish for kids, transporting them to a fantasyland and then marooning them there," the critic Elvis Mitchell wrote in the *Times.* "No one else conjures the phantasmagoric and shifting morality of dreams—that fascinating and frightening aspect of having something that seems to represent good become evil—in the way this master Japanese animator does."

Chihiro finds herself in a strangely contradictory world. Black phantoms and indeterminate dark shapes materialize, but there are pockets of cozy warmth with great heaps of food passing by on conveyor belts. It appears that the place is some kind of spa. Humans are unwelcome, but one denizen, a menacing, greedy matron named Yubaba, sees a use for Chihiro and puts her to work stoking the furnace that provides steam for a bathhouse of the gods.

Chihiro learns that the only way to make progress is to quit complaining, buckle down, and work hard. She becomes a heroine of sorts when she saves the bathhouse from inundation by a huge, melting pile of filth called the Stink God. But the act earns her no particular satisfaction or accolade as it would in many American scenarios. Furthermore, Yubaba tells her if she doesn't hide her human identity she will lose it forever. Yet all these threatening creatures and situations never cause Chihiro any actual harm. Of course, she doesn't realize this as it is happening, and Miyazaki keeps her guessing. This is a world where little if anything is as it seems, which is what distinguishes Miyazaki from Disney or most other American animators. By not defining creatures as good or bad, he makes them unintentionally treacherous.

Yes, there is a "happy" ending when the parents are restored to human form. But they remember nothing, merely declaring that it is time to go and wondering where Chihiro has been all this time. The little girl, somewhat thunderstruck, is left to contemplate the inexplicability of it all.

Miyazaki pays great attention to light and texture. "The beauty of the animation, a skillful blend of hand-painted foreground and well-placed computer background, works to generate the storytelling," Mitchell wrote. Artistically speaking, anime is a mix of Japanese pictorial tradition, with its silk painting and woodblock prints, and American-style stories and characters. In Japan the form is intended for low-budget television and thus uses fewer drawings per second than American movie animation. Since the Japanese are used to manga, the comic books published for both adults and children, a certain flip-book quality to animation doesn't matter.

"Where Western animators struggle to create a convincing illusion of life, Japanese animators are more interested in capturing single expressive gestures, or in evoking a particular mood through the careful use of color," Kehr wrote in the *Times*. "Unlike Hollywood animation, anime does not aspire to the condition of live-action cinema; it remains its own stubborn self."

That said, the average American viewer finds nothing to trip over visually in Miyazaki's films. Thematically they are eminently thought-provoking affairs, even for kids. *My Neighbor Totoro*, with its laughing, spirited young sisters, is especially suitable for children as young as four or so. And by all means try *Princess Mononoke*, though its length and theme make it a better choice for older children. Within an unspoiled forest is an elaborate moral universe fought over by the forces of nature and humankind, as represented by an industrialized group of weapons makers, no less. But this is Miyazaki, so expect some surprises and no winners or losers.

According to reports from parents, children as old as eight have been frightened by the threatening apparitions, gruff personalities, and dicey situations but worked through all that to really love the film. It certainly is well worth it.

86. STAR WARS

Mark Hamill, Harrison Ford, Carrie Fisher, Alec Guinness

DIRECTED BY GEORGE LUCAS
1977. 121 minutes. PG

For kids watching what parents know as *Star Wars*, it's important to place the movie in the six-part series represented most recently by *Star Wars: Episode I—The Phantom Menace* (1999) and *Star Wars:*

Episode II—Attack of the Clones (2002). George Lucas, director of some of them and creator of them all, is responsible for the convolutions, as is his privilege. In 1977, Lucas's original *Star Wars* was a phenomenal stand-alone; now it has been redubbed *Episode IV—A New Hope* and will fall in line after *Star Wars: Episode III,* to come in 2005 and before the final episodes of the set, *The Empire Strikes Back* (1980) and *Return of the Jedi* (1983).

In other words, the first three movies will now be the last three in theaters and in the DVD boxed set sure to come along in 2006 or so. Critics titter about the unwieldiness of it all, but no matter the synergy of Lucas's grand scheme, the bellwether remains the film that will always be referred to as *Star Wars.* Lucas's plot can, in the much-quoted words of Vincent Canby in the *New York Times,* "be written on the head of a pin and still leave room for the Bible." Rescue the princess—a tough, smart one named Leia (Carrie Fisher)—help rebel forces to defeat the evil empire, for the moment at least.

In 1968, Stanley Kubrick's *2001: A Space Odyssey* had given us a taste of startling intergalactic special effects, but in 1977 the *Star Wars* opening scene with the underbelly of a gigantic spaceship passing over our heads, surround sound rumbling on all sides, literally plastered us deep in our seats. The famous initial blasts of John Williams's score still open the newer *Star Wars* films, as do the caption panels sliding by, but in 1977 the novel beginning so rattled the Directors Guild that it demanded Lucas start with the standard credits. He refused and quit the group.

Unlike Kubrick's chilly voyage to another dimension, *Star Wars* is a sleeves-rolled-up sprawler and brawler. Back then Lucas had his gigantic series fully in mind so it was perfectly natural to jump-start *Star Wars* right in the middle of the action with the two droids, the prissy C-3PO and his little trash can of a sidekick, R2-D2, trying to escape a chase party from the giant Death Star commanded by Darth Vader. Lucas added digital touch-ups when the film was rereleased in theaters in 1997, but the original effects, electrifying for their time, still do fine.

"The juggernaut grows with each generation," the critic A. O. Scott wrote in the *New York Times* in 2002. "Unlike virtually everything else in this irony-saturated, ready-to-recycle cosmos of postmodern pop culture, stories of this kind don't seem to date. Yes, the hairstyles in the original *Star Wars* are a little shaggy, and the FX are a little rickety by current standards, but ten-year-olds watching it today experience the same freshness and sublimity their parents discovered in the '70s."

Star Wars was the first true blockbuster. The film reshaped Hollywood finances, but its real lift was to the spirit. Coming in the midst of national doldrums following Vietnam and Watergate, *Star Wars* cheered us up, so to speak. Lucas was as American as the West Coast adolescents in his film *American Graffiti* (1973). A student of the mythologist Joseph Campbell, he developed a universal story that is basically allegorical in its quest for roots and answers, heroes and colorful places, its discovery of truths. Then he added touches from the American past. Scott wrote in the *Times,* "Turning his back on the dark, dystopian visions of the era's science fiction, which extrapolated a stark future from the confusion of the present, Mr. Lucas situated his epic in an ancient, distant world intended to recapture the gee-whiz spirit of Buck Rogers and the 1939 World's Fair."

Before developing his original concoction, Lucas envisioned resurrecting Flash Gordon, but there were expensive rights problems. So he threw another genre into the pot. *Star Wars* has the look and feel of a western, with space guns slung low on hips like six-shooters and the brash space cowboy Han Solo (Harrison Ford) wrestling the controls of his beat-up space wagon as if at the reins of a runaway stagecoach. When the young Luke Skywalker (Mark Hamill) and friends arrive at a remote space port—a "wretched hive of scum and villainy," in the words of Obi-Wan Kenobi (Alec Guinness)—it's like trail bosses coming to town to round up hands for a cattle drive. In perhaps the most famous bar scene ever, Solo and Chewbacca, his seven-foot "walking rug" of a sidekick, are recruited in an establishment full of mutant galoots spoiling for a through-and-through western showdown at the drop of an insult.

But there are many influences at work: opera, soap opera, the comic books, pirate tales, war movies, *The Wizard of Oz.* Confined to his uncle's farm, young Luke wants to escape as Dorothy longed to leave Kansas, and, like Dorothy, leave he must for his odyssey and passage to begin. Add a quasi-religious element with the Force, that mighty spiritual hand available to Jedi knights. Darth Vader, in fact, calls the force "their religion." Lucas even borrowed from Akira Kurosawa's *Hidden Fortress* (1958), about a princess rescued by a band of misfits.

The most recent *Star Wars* films get tangled in intergalactic political complications, and the technology is so digitally slick and cold it seems almost a detriment. Back in 1977, after a wild ride in Solo's all-purpose rattletrap of a space cruiser with its World War II gun turrets, you felt like hosing it down and sweeping it out. Ford is spectacular in the film, and the others are earnest and competent, their "clunky enthusiasm polished at the Ricky Nelson school of acting," in the words of the critic Pauline Kael. But for young audiences, Kael added, the film is "like getting a box of Cracker Jacks that is all prizes."

Star Wars is suitable from about the age of six, with perhaps some mildly scary moments but none that will upset the youngest too severely. A competition over Leia begins to form between Solo and Skywalker, but there is nothing approaching a smooch, let alone sex. Who needs profanity?

87. STEAMBOAT BILL, JR.

Buster Keaton, Ernest Torrence, Marion Byron, Tom Lewis, Tom McGuire

DIRECTED BY CHARLES F. REISNER
1928. 71 minutes. Black and white. No rating

At one point the diminutive William Canfield Jr. (Buster Keaton) tries to spring his father, Steamboat Bill (Ernest Torrence), out of the local hoosegow by hiding pliers, a screwdriver, and other implements in a loaf of bread he says he has baked for his old man. Naturally everything spills out on the floor in front of the sheriff. "Must have

Steamboat Bill, Jr. (Used by permission of Kino International)

happened when the dough fell in the tool chest," reads the title card, a pretty good line that shouldn't escape little ones even if it has to be read and explained to them. Just about everything else in this supremely physical film should be evident, and any misgiving kids might have about a silent black-and-white movie should disappear as quickly as it takes Bill Jr. to walk into a wall or fall off a porch.

Keaton reputedly broke his neck at one point in his career, though he didn't realize it until he was being examined for another injury quite a while later. Born Joseph Keaton in Piqua, Kansas, in 1895, he was given the nickname Buster at the age of six months by none other than the magician Harry Houdini, who was impressed when the infant emerged unharmed from a fall down a flight of stairs. Keaton's parents were medicine show performers, and in a skit called "The Human Mop" they literally wiped up the stage with Buster. Bad falls and near drownings dogged him during his years in vaudeville and on-screen in scores of shorts, many made with another knockabout artist, Fatty Arbuckle, and his own feature films.

Keaton also had that stone face, locked perpetually in deadpan but never so immobile that it couldn't flicker with consternation and incredulity. A handsome man, Keaton used his eyes to tell of his hurt and frustration. Small of stature, he played restrained and sensitive young men trying to cling to dignity in ignoble conditions. In *Steamboat Bill, Jr.* he honors his mother's wish and goes to seek out his father, a crusty lout of a riverboat captain who hasn't seen him since birth.

Bill Jr. has just graduated from college in Boston, which puts him at as far a remove as possible from his crude and cranky wharf rat of a father. This also sets up the classic conflict befalling Keaton, or Charlie Chaplin, who often found himself similarly misplaced in the style of the silent comic. Bill Jr. arrives in town wearing a beret and a little mustache, having alerted Bill Sr. by letter that he'll be the one with a white carnation. Of course, when the big day comes, everybody has a carnation, but that's only one feature of a whimsical and finely paced farcical search that ends when each comes to the horrible realization that indeed they are Bill senior and junior.

A polite and gentle soul, young Bill can only stand in deference to his father's authority, despite the fact that the son is grown and the father has paid him no heed since birth. The pathos of it is that Bill Jr. actually harbors a loyalty to his father, which in a perfect bit of Keaton characterization only heightens the effect of the riotous struggle Bill Jr. will put up in defense of what's good and right. Big Bill, on the other hand, can't abide this effete little fellow who stands before him. The beret and mustache have to go, the latter with two quick strokes with a straight razor at the barbershop. At the haberdashery, Bill Sr. rejects at least a dozen replacement hats to clap on his son.

The sartorial question is settled finally by Marion (Marion Byron), a petite young woman who is also home from college in Boston, where she was a schoolmate of Bill Jr. Marion is attracted to Bill for reasons having nothing to do with riverboating or anything else within a million miles of this place. Bill is a gentleman, and she decides he would look well in a double-breasted blue serge captain's uniform.

Marion happens to be the daughter of J. J. King, the magnate of the town and owner of a spanking new steamboat that will drive Bill Sr.'s battered old craft off the river. A battle is joined between the haves and the have-nots with the young couple caught in between. Buster and others, including the high-and-mighty King, are soon cartwheeling over the side into the silty waters, sent flying as one vessel rams the other, and conducting various assaults.

Keaton, who was given complete artistic freedom with his feature films, was adept at gags and superb at timing, which always seemed exquisitely right. He also took interest in the technical aspects of filmmaking, which often heightened the special effects. At the climax, all hell breaks loose during a cyclone that literally sends the midlands town and citizens flying. Keaton and other silent stars, Chaplin for one (see *The Gold Rush,* page 105), liked to be flattened by great winds, and here twenty-three airplane propellers break up the town like kindling, lay Buster parallel to the ground, and sink both riverboats. As the storm rages buildings fly apart, one of them around Keaton's head. After careful measurements beforehand, it was figured that if he stood in one exact spot, an open window would pass over him. They were right, by about two inches on all sides.

Tell children that Keaton was as popular in his time as Tom Hanks or Leonardo DiCaprio are today. More so, in fact. Between 1923 and 1928, Keaton made ten independent feature films. Kids will also like *The General* and *The Navigator.* Later he signed a contract with MGM, lost autonomy, and went into a general decline. His father was an alcoholic, and Buster's own problems with drink undermined him. So did the talkies, which weren't kind to Keaton. Television helped rejuvenate his career, and when he died in 1966 he was generally recognized as one of the greatest early film artists. But life had been unpredictable, and to be on the safe side, no chances were taken at his burial. Depending on where he was sent, one hand held a rosary, the other a deck of cards.

Children from about six will have no trouble understanding and loving this film. That said, the collapsing buildings and spectacular damage could trouble some.

88. SULLIVAN'S TRAVELS

Joel McCrae, Veronica Lake, Robert Warwick, William Demarest, Robert Greig, Eric Blore

DIRECTED BY PRESTON STURGES

1941. 90 minutes. Black and white. No rating

Early on in Preston Sturges's film, kids of all ages are treated to a slapstick scene that rivals anything from Chaplin or Keaton. Hitting the road to find out what it's like to be poor, the big-time Hollywood director John L. Sullivan (Joel McCrae) accepts a ride from an underage driver (eleven at most) in a homemade hot rod. It's wartime and the boy is playing tank. Sullivan is trying to shake a busload of press and publicity people following him to record his excursion into the heartland to examine poverty. The flivver hits seventy or so, and he tells the kid to floor it and hang the first left.

Buses don't handle well through sharp turns and over rutted side roads and the Hollywood flaks and the cook in the galley go flying as if in a tossed salad. Even stonefaces will have trouble stifling mirth through this sequence. Kids should realize, though, that in addition to big physical comedy there's also plenty of relatively serious business ahead as Sullivan explores life in hobo camps and homeless shelters. That said, children can enjoy a highly accessible movie for whatever they get out of it.

One of the great studio directors of the '40s, Sturges brought wonderfully sophisticated sensibilities to films like *The Great McGinty, Hail the Conquering Hero, The Lady Eve,* and *The Miracle of Morgan's Creek.* He was brought up in Europe by his mother, a cosmetics executive and traveling companion of Isadora Duncan, so he was worldly and erudite by his teenage years. But he was also close to his stepfather, a Chicago businessman, who helped make him a fond and keen observer of the American scene.

His movies inspire reams of analysis, but they are broad enough to let children onboard. Authors of family film guides differ somewhat about what age kids will begin to get the most from *Sullivan's Travels*. Some say ten, others twelve. Bright ten-year-olds should begin to get the message here, if not every nuance, and the comic elements let them have fun in the bargain. Simply put, Sturges is telling us that whatever we do has some value if we do it honestly. So stick with what you do best and, unlike Sullivan, recognize and avoid things that don't suit you.

Even more simply put, be yourself. Though he never would be confused with Sturges, Sullivan is intended as somewhat of a counterpart. A highly successful director of comedies and potboilers, Sullivan, like Sturges to a degree, feels a stab of dissatisfaction that he isn't doing serious films in a time of depression and war and burns to get out there among the poverty-stricken. He'll make a Steinbeckian epic about being down and out. He'll call it *O, Brother, Where Art Thou?* (a title the Coen brothers caught up with in 2000).

His studio bosses, a comic lot of stogie puffers in double-breasted suits, are horrified. Their meal ticket has lost his senses. Sullivan's butler tells him, "The poor know about poverty. Only the morbid rich would find the subject glamorous." Another servant notes, "You can try tennis, you can't try starvation."

Sullivan is a tall, good-looking fellow with an earthy manner. Critics note that McCrae, a staple in westerns, was a good choice for the role because he wasn't a big star and could project vulnerability. Sullivan may have studied the Depression in prep school, but he's ready to go learn in the field, even though he has no real conception of what he is getting into. On his first foray in hobo rags (from studio wardrobe), he encounters a smashing blonde (Veronica Lake), called simply the Girl, in a diner.

Lake was famous for her long hair over one eye. Women working in wartime factories emulated the look and ended up getting their own hair caught in the machinery, so Lake cut hers short and urged others to follow. The Girl, a failed wannabe starlet on her way home back east, has a big heart and empathy for the downtrodden. In the diner, she buys the artfully penniless Sullivan a plate of ham and eggs. Kids will appreciate a terrific knockabout comedic pair. A little scuffed up and suffering from a fever after his first brush with poverty, Sullivan is bused back to his mansion for a little rehab. The Girl goes with him and after a bit of escalating slapstick, everybody, butlers included, gets tossed into the swimming pool.

For their next outing with the poor, Sullivan and Girl are delivered to a rail yard in a limousine. Some great physical comedy follows as they scramble on and off freight trains and try to fit in among the ragged masses in teeming mess halls and homeless shelters. Sturges has a fine way with irony, never shying from comedy in hard situations. As kids well know, films these days treat poverty much more harshly and realistically. At one point Sullivan arrogantly, if well meaningly, hands out sheaves of five-dollar bills to his fellow sufferers, as if that has any real effect or meaning.

The money only gets him accused of murder and thrown on a chain gang. In the end he decides to go back to comedies because it's what he knows how to do and there is nothing wrong with making people laugh. He begins to rediscover this one night when he and his fellow prisoners are shown a cartoon with Mickey Mouse and Pluto. Sullivan watches amazed as the miserable convicts crack up at the antics. Finally, even he can't stifle a guffaw. "Did I laugh?" he exclaims.

Age eleven or twelve is best for the full effect of the film, but younger children will be quickly caught up in the frequent fast action and physical comedy. Slapstick mixes with serious issues, and there is a fair amount of violence. Muggings occur and Sullivan slugs the railroad guard who coldcocked him, landing himself on the chain gang. There is no profanity. As for sex, there is none of that either in the days of the Hayes Code, which cleansed the movies of such activities. Natural or not, here we have two attractive people in continual close physical proximity without it leading to sex as it often would today.

89. SUPERMAN

Christopher Reeve, Margot Kidder, Gene Hackman, Marlon Brando, Glenn Ford, Phyllis Thaxter, Ned Beatty, Valerie Perrine, Marc McClure

DIRECTED BY RICHARD DONNER

1978. 143 minutes. PG

Richard Donner was watching his movie while making a director's commentary for the DVD. On the screen Jor-El (Marlon Brando), ruler of the doomed planet Krypton, regards his infant son, whom he is about to send rocketing off to Earth to become DC Comics' man of steel and all-American icon. "The kid's diapers are worth a fortune," Donner said. "Brando's dialogue is on them."

Brando, of course, is famous for not memorizing lines, which through the decades has inspired ingenious postings on cue cards and other objects all over movie sets. Here, moments before Jor-El is destroyed in the film's otherworldly first scene, his last words to the infant set up family viewers for what quickly becomes a whimsical and good-humored action fantasy.

We next meet Krypton's sole survivor by the side of the road in Kansas, where his space capsule has bored a smoldering crater in the earth. Peering in wonder, a farmer and his wife, Ma and Pa Kent (Phyllis Thaxter and Glenn Ford), behold the newcomer. Kent's truck has a flat tire, and the baby lifts the vehicle one-handed. Adopting the foundling, the Kents begin one of the movies' nicer family relationships.

Ford is superb as a simple, caring man who entrusts himself with raising a lad who can kick a football a half-mile and outrun an express train. Such a boy, named Clark and grown into Christopher Reeve, is best advised to wear his talents loosely. Pa Kent is quietly there to remind him of this when adolescent slights and pressures tempt displays of powers that must not be revealed. Then one day Pa feels pain and clutches his left arm. "Oh, my," he says softly as he collapses. Care of the boy wonder is now the sole responsibility of Ma Kent, and it's a poignant parting when Clark leaves home for Metropolis on his mission to serve humankind.

Reeve's Superman is a fine figure for young children. Reeve must play two characters: the bumbling, mild-mannered newspaper reporter Clark Kent and the figure in blue tights who leaps tall buildings in a single bound. He does this with a singular grace and humor. Reeve, himself a famous figure now in a wheelchair, felt a responsibility. "I was temporary custodian of a past that was an essential piece of American mythology," he says. Exuding that same modesty, the caped Boy Scout who makes the earth spin backward musters plenty of credibility even in this cynical day and age.

He certainly wows Lois Lane, played with fine sass and intelligence by Margot Kidder. Casting is one of this film's great strengths. Big names were needed to attract financial backing. Brando helped, obviously, as did Gene Hackman, who is absolutely first rate as the wickedly comedic Lex Luthor, the suave, deadly, and uproarious Superman nemesis and bad boy of the Metropolis underground. Robert Redford was among those mentioned for Superman, but a problem arose with a big name in the title role. Superman has to fly. Robert Redford flying in tights with an *S* on his chest? Everyone dreaded making a ridiculous-looking movie.

Doubters wondered if any kind of polished product could come from a comic book. Flying was the ultimate challenge. The answer was Reeve, a tall, black-haired impossibly handsome unknown who somehow looked good aloft. One of the tests of this film today—and all the more so with a young audience—is how well the special effects hold up in an era when digital manipulation can accomplish anything. In the '70s there were no such aids. Everything was done by hand. Like people aloft in movies before him (and now in martial arts extravaganzas like *The Matrix Reloaded* and *Crouching Tiger, Hidden Dragon*) Superman had to fly on a wire, sometimes with a thirty-five-pound camera pack strapped to his chest. Before Reeve, everybody had looked silly, but his takeoffs and landings, essentially stepping off the ground and alighting on it, were athletic and natural.

This is a fine film for parents to watch with children, if for no other reason than to get their reaction to the special effects. As Donner puts it, verisimilitude was also a star of this film. The sets, assembled on three continents by some of the people who had worked on *Star Wars,* are works of genius. One of the most memorable is Lex Luthor's watery lair in a flooded Grand Central Station, complete with speedboats and towering library to fit the Luthor intellect. The library was an opportunity for some fine Buster Keatonish rides around the shelves on a ladder pushed by Otis (Ned Beatty), the slavish Luthor flunky.

Effects are accomplished with miniatures, models, hydraulics, glass plates, and layers of film combined by optical printer. The Golden Gate Bridge, from which Superman catches a falling school bus, was seventy feet long; *Air Force One* was four feet across. Algae, taken from the ocean around Bermuda, was lighted a certain way to resemble pieces of the exploding Krypton.

Ultimately, it's the goodness of the people, from Kent to Jimmy Olson (Marc McClure), and clean, simple values and emotions that make this film. The sequels were all right, but they seem slicker somehow, a little used. This is the one. "It was Americana," Donner says. "Our moment in history."

There is some stylized violence as Superman takes on evil forces, but nothing too upsetting for children over the age of, say, six and perhaps younger. There is no sex, but attraction between the sexes is nicely acknowledged. Nor is there profanity. Children from six to ten are ideal here, though the littlest ones will have fun (and with video there's plenty of opportunity for parental explanation), and older ones may enjoy what may seem like an entertaining relic.

90. SWISS FAMILY ROBINSON

John Mills, Dorothy McGuire, James MacArthur, Tommy Kirk, Kevin Corcoran, Janet Munro, Sessue Hayakawa

DIRECTED BY KEN ANNAKIN

1960. 126 minutes. No rating

Ten versions of Johann Wyss's novel have been produced, beginning with Edward Ludwig's somewhat dark adaptation in 1940, and including a Japanese film and two television productions. There's nothing dark about Ken Annakin's film. Pure lavish fantasy, it may have dated a bit, but has enough good looks and rousing adventure to captivate everybody from age five on up. Walt Disney sent Annakin and a large retinue off for six months of well-funded shooting on the island of Tobago, next to Trinidad off the coast of South America. It was a substantial production. On the DVD Annakin says there were eight taxicabs on the fourteen-mile-long island when they started and sixty-seven when they finished. The film is lush and elaborate, the cast handsome and blond. Stiff-upper-lip positivism prevails among the Robinsons, and why not when every hardship is cushioned and every battle rigged? The designer tree housing could come from a glossy shelter magazine, the animals from an Abercrombie & Kent safari.

Call the film a catered shipwreck. But an artfully tattered fantasyland in no way damages the entertaining story of Mother and Father Robinson (Dorothy McGuire and John Mills) and their three sons who find themselves stranded on their way to a new life in New Guinea. What they all eat on the deserted island is never made clear. One quashes thoughts that they might well have started with the flock of domesticated animals left awash when the ship that brought them swamps and blows onto some rocks. The production's shipbuilders anchored the hulk on posts drilled deep into the sea bottom.

Splashing in the hold are pigs, cows, horses, chickens, geese, and two huge rambunctious dogs that become the family's fast friends and allies. Needing to get themselves and some livestock ashore, the Robinsons instantly whip up a substantial and highly picturesque raft and go poling off into high seas.

Onshore the production's wildlife formed a moviemaking zoo. Annakin brought one hundred animals, and their trainers, with him from Hollywood. Not all were of the barnyard variety. In the film, Ernst Robinson (Tommy Kirk), the bookish middle son, theorizes that an ancient land bridge must have been responsible for the tiger, elephant, ostriches, zebras, hyenas, and python they find ashore. Soon the youngest Robinson, eight-year-old Francis (Kevin Corcoran), has tangled with the tiger and trapped the elephant, which immediately becomes a useful beast of burden. Kids will love all of this. Who wouldn't? Annakin says that the trainers came to him each day and asked, "What do you want from my animal today?" From the sharks he wanted more animation. Several of them attack a flotilla of farm animals, buoyed by barrels, paddling laboriously from the wreck toward shore. The sharks got no trip to Tobago and had to labor in a tank in Los Angeles. Annakin says that Caribbean sharks were too placid. Anyway, the L.A. stand-ins needed prodding with sticks to show much interest.

The film was made in the days before disclaimers about mistreatment of animals on the set. Annakin says they were well treated. Walt Disney himself insisted that the dogs fight the tiger, which they did apparently without damage. In the movie's most bizarre animal scene, and one that could disturb little ones, hyenas try to grab a quick bite or two out of a zebra mired in a mudhole. The zebra was given a mild electric shock to make him kick harder. Annakin says he gave himself the shock first to make sure it wouldn't be too painful. At another point, the oldest son, Fritz (James MacArthur), and some stunt doubles battle a python. That too will frighten young children, but assure them no one got hurt in a scene managed by the movies' greatest stunt coordinator, Yakima Canutt.

The wreck serves as a furniture warehouse. The Robinsons retrieve a pipe organ and fine sideboards to hold their best china. Clearly the raft isn't big enough to accommodate the organ, and the film doesn't show us how they wrestled it ashore. Father admits it got a little wet, but it sounds fine and looks grand on Christmas Eve in the largest of several stunning tree houses he and the boys instantly construct to please gentle, cultured Mother. Rock Resorts couldn't have done it better.

There is some trouble in paradise, however, which is a good thing because it gives the Robinsons plenty of opportunity to keep their wits about them and act bravely, nobly, and warmly in just the way young viewers and their parents will appreciate. Sailing off in a dugout to see if they are on an island or a peninsula, Ernst and Fritz come upon pirates milling about on a beach. They are a strange band indeed, kind of a cross between Penzance and *Tora! Tora! Tora!*

At their head is Kuala, played by Sessue Hayakawa, so fine three years earlier as a prison camp commandant in *The Bridge on the River Kwai*. Here he growls and carries on dutifully, but he can't help looking faintly amused. On the DVD Annakin says that Hayakawa worked hard and pleasantly and otherwise stayed in the company of two women companions who always traveled with him.

The pirates have grabbed themselves an English admiral and captain of commerce and someone they are told is their prisoner's fourteen-year-old grandson. Actually it's the admiral's granddaughter, Roberta (Janet Munro), shorn of her long red hair. Sprung by the Robinson lads, Roberta escapes with them back to the tree encampment, arriving on the very same Christmas Eve singing the exact same carol Mother has been playing on her organ.

Ernst and Fritz fall in love with her and in conflict with each other. In the film's best scene their mutual jealousy spills over as they dance with her. Later the tension between them builds nicely. But rest assured, these are genteel folk who will do the right thing by each other. The real fight is with the pirates, who return for a pitched battle. Afterward the Robinsons decide to stay on the island. The admiral, who has come back to save his granddaughter, expansively notes that all this will be a new colony. Ah, development.

"There is no blood in this picture," someone proudly states in the commentary on the DVD. Perhaps not, but there is plenty of violence of the kind that is often overlooked or treated lightly in films of such spirited

---

good fun. When the pirates return at the end of the movie they storm the Robinsons, who defend themselves from the top of a hill. The castaways have devised many weapons, from grenades to accumulations of boulders and logs they roll down on the attackers. Annakin says they are made of light material, which is true, but they do a very realistic job of crushing people. Then the Robinsons open fire with muskets and ignite land mines of gunpowder. Here we have a glorious adventure for everybody from about age five, but nonviolent it isn't. There is no sex, however, or profanity.

91. THE THREE MUSKETEERS and THE FOUR MUSKETEERS

Michael York, Charlton Heston, Oliver Reed, Richard Chamberlain, Frank Finlay, Simon Ward, Geraldine Chaplin, Jean-Pierre Cassel, Faye Dunaway, Raquel Welch

DIRECTED BY RICHARD LESTER
1974 and 1975. 105 minutes and 108 minutes. Both rated PG

It's fun to know that movies so full of comic subterfuge were something of a subterfuge themselves, or so it struck the cast laboring on Richard Lester's films for twenty-four weeks in Spain in heat that sometimes approached 120 degrees. Oliver Reed, Richard Chamberlain, Frank Finlay, Michael York, Charlton Heston, Christopher Lee, Raquel Welch, Faye Dunaway, Geraldine Chaplin, and the rest were all under the impression that they were making one very long movie based on Alexandre Dumas's novel. "I had a script, *one* script, I hasten to add," says Lee, prominent today as the evil Saruman in *The Lord of the Rings* films.

In fact, they were making two movies. *The Three Musketeers* might have been released as one three-hour "road show," as it were, with an intermission. But with the release date fast approaching, there was too much movie to finish in one piece. The producer, Alexander Salkind, and 20th Century Fox chose to cut it into two movies and release them a year apart. For continuity's sake, the second film was named for the fourth musketeer, D'Artagnan (York), who got his promotion from vagabond swordsman to king's guard at the end of the first film and carries on flamboyantly as a central player in the shifting intrigues and wild forays of the second.

Having discovered the plan for a double bill well after filming had finished, much of the cast was miffed that they had been paid for one movie and not two. Some of them sued, but the matter was settled without too much complication. York notes that the producers took a big risk breaking it in two because if *The Three Musketeers* had flopped, there would be no future for the second film.

In any event, now we have both movies digitally restored in a set of DVDs, and they make a terrific family double bill. Dumas's story has been told so many times on-screen it's virtually its own little oeuvre. One thinks swashbuckler, of course, with Douglas Fairbanks playing D'Artagnan in the 1921 film and Gene Kelly in the role in a 1948 version, with Lana Turner in the Dunaway role as the treacherous Lady DeWinter. The latest rendition, in 1993, featured the likes of Charlie Sheen, Kiefer Sutherland, Chris O'Donnell, and Oliver Platt, and it's not bad at all, but Lester's films are definitely the standard and look as fresh as can be after almost thirty years.

In the seventeenth century, France is undermined by its own fool of a monarch, Lous XIII, portrayed by Jean-Pierre Cassel, and threatened with attack by the English led by the Duke of Buckingham, played by Simon Ward. "We could cast the movie literally perfectly," Ilya Salkind, Alexander's son, says on the DVD. Heston is superb as the scheming Cardinal Richelieu, a formidable and not altogether ignoble statesman. Lee is fine as Rochefort, the cardinal's one-eyed and archly hilarious hatchet man. Reed, Finlay, and Chamberlain are boisterous musketeers. No Fairbanks or Kelly, York is an engaging D'Artagnan, prone to boyish pratfalls and devastating with the ladies.

Welch plays Constance, hairdresser and confidante of the crass French queen, Anne of Austria (Geraldine Chaplin), who is having an affair with Buckingham and relies on Constance as messenger and savior in a pinch. On a career roll that could be called meteoric in its own way, Welch arrived on the set "overprotected by her representation," as one observer put it, but took Lester's advice to stop overacting, with the result that she was nominated for a Golden Globe Award. Chaplin is fine as the brattish Anne. Dunaway is spectacularly bountiful as DeWinter, who dispenses her favors as needed among such disparate interests as Rochefort, Buckingham, and D'Artagnan.

The two films could confuse kids who try too hard to sort out Dumas's intrigues. Unlike earlier musketeer adventures, these two dive right into plot complexities. Reviewing Lester's *Four Musketeers* in the *New York Times,* Vincent Canby wrote, "Even the crisscrossing of loyalties seems funnier in this second film, perhaps because one doesn't spend too much time worrying about who is doing what to whom or why. It doesn't matter." Children should mark his words.

The New Yorker critic Pauline Kael, on the other hand, saw *The Three Musketeers* as something darker. "This Richard Lester version was produced in the counterculture period—a time when some of the most talked about films made corruption seem inevitable and hence something you learn to live with; Lester saw corruption as slapstick comedy, and he turned out an absurdist debauch on swashbuckler themes."

That could be said, perhaps, but for kids the films are visual delights, full of funny people in plumed hats crossing themselves up doing silly things. To avoid a pack of savage guard dogs, Constance is carried off on stilts. The well-researched games and gadgets are fascinating. Royal chess is played with dogs as pieces, with checkmate resulting in a good dog fight. Jousting and swordfighting contraptions, pinball machines, and a submarine are of ingenious invention. York credits the prop man Eddie Fowlie. "He'd put a thousand things in a truck and drive to a location," York says. "If you wanted a chandelier or a blunderbuss, he was there."

These are films of bright sunlight and shining spectacle. For the actors it was an intensely physical shoot and a draining one in the heat. The films were made near the end of the Franco era in Spain. On the DVD a crew member says that they could bribe everybody, which made Madrid a great place to work. The production was given the run of the city's palaces. Interiors are splendid, as are great squares, back streets, and countryside villages.

A mercurial talent, Lester shook up traditionalists with his use of multiple cameras and other adventurous departures. Ilya Salkind says Lester was chosen because of his rollicking take on London in his Beatles' film *A Hard Day's Night* (see page 118). On the discs *Musketeers* cast and crew rave about his direction. Someone says Lester favored editing but disliked shooting because he hated early mornings. Actors favored him because he would let them do anything. Later he just quit making movies—like Garbo, someone says on the DVD.

These are fine films from about the age of eight. With all the dashing folk about, there is much sexual intrigue and though none of the action is shown in full cry, there is ample evidence that much is transpiring on this front. Most parents won't find this offensive, however. There is quite a bit of bloodshed, with duelists run through and much brawling. A lot of this is comic, but violence is violence, if that is an issue. Obviously there is no profanity of the modern variety.

92. TO KILL A MOCKINGBIRD

Gregory Peck, Mary Badham, Phillip Alford, Brock Peters, Robert Duvall, Collin Wilcox, James Anderson

DIRECTED BY ROBERT MULLIGAN
1962. 129 minutes. Black and white. No rating

One of the best things about Robert Mulligan's adaptation of Harper Lee's novel is that the story is seen through the eyes of children. Many kids will read the book in adolescence if not before, but the movie's perspective lets even younger children in on a grown-up world that is "so well informed by reality and emotional experience," in the words of the playwright Horton Foote, who wrote the screenplay. Imagine that—kids treated intelligently. For them it will be instructive to see how an old movie stripped of hokey situations, maudlin emotions, and overdone effects can be so riveting.

At first Hollywood was stumped by *To Kill a Mockingbird*. The studios needed a genre to put it in. Also, here was a story with no romance and little action (no profanity either, by the way). "Even though the book was a big bestseller, money didn't come right away from the studios," Alan J. Pakula, the film's producer, said in an interview. He shopped the film all over, including Paramount, where he had an affiliation. "They said, 'What story do you plan to tell?' I said, 'Have you read the book?' They said, 'Yes.' I said, 'That's the story.'"

Harper Lee liked Mulligan's film but had declined to write the screenplay. Pakula chose Foote, another profound voice of the deep South. Gregory Peck loved the script so much that he immediately agreed to do it. "It really wasn't until he signed on that Universal agreed to the financing," Pakula said. "I must say the man and the character he played were not unalike."

Peck won his only Oscar as Atticus Finch, a lawyer and widower in Monroeville, Alabama, during the 1930s. Atticus, who is modeled after Lee's father, Amasa Coleman Lee, is raising a young daughter and son, Jean Louise, called Scout (Mary Badham), and Jem (Phillip Alford). He is a calm, gentle man of deep conviction and stern resolve. A strong streak of individuality jumps the bounds of convention. For example, his children call him Atticus. He is careful not to discipline them but to guide and instruct and let them decide.

That proves vexing during a scene at the town jail when a mob gathers to lynch Tom Robinson (Brock Peters), a black man accused of raping a white woman. Atticus, who defends Robinson in court, bars their way. When Scout and Jem work their way to the front of the crowd to see what is going on, Atticus orders them to go home. They refuse, and despite the threatening situation, Atticus doesn't insist.

It's good to see a competent male single parent left alone with the kids around the house. Atticus is an attractive man and there could well be another woman in the offing, but it's refreshing to watch a movie that doesn't bend itself out of shape trying to match him with the next mom for the kids. Jem and Scout might have no objections to one, but it's plain they're not feeling deprived of parenting.

Their life in Monroeville is full of kindly folks, front porches, swings, games, and adventures. Sometimes they like to sneak over to the Radley house to take a look at the crazy son, Boo Radley (Robert Duvall in his first film), chained to the bedpost. Lee was superb with the texture and rhythms of southern life, and so is the movie, even with Mulligan, an Irish boy from the Bronx. The film is excellent with face-to-face family life at the dinner table and on the porch before television distracted everybody. Monroeville had become a little too modernized by the time the film was made in the '60s, so a carefully detailed town was built on the Universal lot. The set designer, Henry Bumstead, won an Oscar, as did Foote for best adapted screenplay. The film and Mulligan were nominated but lost to *Lawrence of Arabia* (see page 146) and David Lean (no disgrace there).

Lee also knew the southern dark side, and here too the movie stays in step. "Strangeness was expected," Lee wrote. Not ordinarily pressured into doing things, Atticus feels obliged to go along with prevailing notions of manhood and shoots a mad dog in the street. The dog is ill and should be put down, but the act is upsetting. Atticus and his children will help young viewers recover as the story accelerates.

The dog is a harbinger of madness related to the rape case and racial hostility in the community. Atticus tells Jem and Scout, a tough, resilient kid always in the middle of everything, that he wishes he could shield them from this situation but he can't. In court they hang on every word as their father defends Robinson. Collin Wilcox gives a gripping performance as the spectacularly troubled young redneck woman who accuses Robinson, and so does James Anderson as her abusive, violent father. The one piece of violence occurs later when Scout, dressed like a roast ham for Halloween, is knocked down and banged around by an assailant in the woods. Boo Radley comes to her rescue. Later it is thought he has killed her attacker (off-screen), but he is exonerated. As Scout tells Atticus, it would be as much a sin to prosecute such a misunderstood creature as it would be to kill a mockingbird.

Mary Badham was nine when she performed in To Kill a Mockingbird. *Depending on their maturity, children can safely and rewardingly start watching the film at about age eight. Some scenes may be disturbing, but at heart the movie is for them as much as anybody.*

93. TOY STORY and TOY STORY 2

With the voices of Tom Hanks, Tim Allen, Joan Cusack, Kelsey Grammer, Don Rickles, Wallace Shawn, Jim Varney

DIRECTED BY JOHN LASSETER
1995 and 1999. 81 and 92 minutes. Both rated G

When Pixar, John Lasseter's digital animation studio, set out to make the first completely digital animated feature film in 1991, it knew that the story and characters would seem much more lifelike than they would with standard animation. Part of this is because of the extreme clarity. "You get all this detail: there's dirt on the walls, there's texture everywhere," a *Toy Story* modeling specialist told the film critic Michael Sragow in the *New York Times* before the movie opened in 1995.

Pixar needed four years to finish the film. Often it took a week to finish four or five seconds. The dog Buster has four million hairs. A powerful computer required twenty hours to render a single frame. A bowl of Cheerios is so lifelike—sharper than life, in fact—the only reason you wouldn't put a spoon in it is that it looks unnaturally real. Such photo-realist physicality (and beyond) calls for a leavening ambience, and the best thing about both these movies is that they get it so right. When toy soldiers belonging to the boy Andy march off to do some spying for the toy cowboy Woody, they pause by the bottom of a door that is so naturally and realistically scuffed up, we know this movie is made by people who have kids constantly kicking and banging through doors like this one.

Tom Hanks, who is the voice of Woody in both movies, calls the films classic pieces of American folklore. Both are wonderfully relaxed and knowing about life in the suburban jumble. In a DVD special edition of both films, an animator says that Lasseter dwells on the secret lives of inanimate characters. As the world fully realizes by now, the two movies are set among the toys in Andy's room. With Andy present, they are lifeless objects with their set expressions. In his absence they become a volatile community with all its connivings, misunderstandings, fears, and aspirations.

Toys live to stay in good standing with their owners. Naturally Andy's older toys feel the heat every Christmas and birthday when the coolest new plaything might come along to displace them in their owner's affection. In 1991 when Lasseter and Pixar were developing the idea for *Toy Story* in league with Disney, the concept began as a road movie but changed to a buddy picture. For a main character, we have Woody, the cowboy figure. He's Andy's longtime favorite and a natural leader of dinosaurs, piggy banks, slinky dogs, toy soldiers, Little Bo Peep, and the others around Andy's room. For a "buddy" we have Buzz, the astronaut, who lands as a newcomer in the toy firmament.

Buzz at first sees Woody as a threat and reacts meanly, which puts him in disfavor with the other toys. For his part, the astronaut has grand visions of himself as a force for space exploration. "You're a toy. An action figure," Woody reminds him. Lasseter and company have a message: the best way to help yourself is to help others; true friends are those who give up something valuable for those they love. By the finish of both these films, plenty of that sentiment has taken hold, but everybody has to work at it.

First and foremost, these movies are about fear of rejection and abandonment, which any kid can relate to. In the first film, not only does Woody have space figures, the coveted new toy group, to contend with, he and the other toys have to worry about being left behind when Andy's family moves to a new house. In *Toy Story 2*, Woody again faces the prospect of losing his place in the family of Andy's toys.

Careful not to beat kids over the head with potential grimness, both films tackle these issues with savvy and wit. In *Toy Story*, Woody makes a huge problem for himself by jealously shunning Buzz and eventually nudging him out a window. Lasseter's movies carefully build a standard of ethics. His fellow toys love Woody, but believe he has gone too far. Whether they end up in the hands of the sadistic heavy-metal kid next door in *Toy Story*, or in the clammy grip of Big Al McWhiggin, the creepy money-crazed toy-store operator of *Toy Story 2*, Woody and Buzz swallow their pride and learn that in the spirit of the original *Toy Story* moral, it's best to help each other.

Again and again we are struck by the almost unnaturally real look of the films. The figures have computerized skeletons of amazing complexity, but their life comes from the animators who manipulate them and give them subtlety. "When I was looking for animators," Lasseter told Sragow in the *Times*, "I looked at guys who worked with clay, cel, sand, and pencils; no matter what the medium, I wanted to see if they were able to make us feel that it was breathing and thinking. You need to have an innate sense of time and motion to do that."

In the mid-'80s Lasseter and some other animation whiz kids from the California School of the Arts, founded by Walt Disney, began making digital shorts for Pixar. That led to a clash of animation cultures. Disney people tended to be older technicians who didn't mesh well with younger digital animators. "Disney at the time was interested in computers only to save costs, not explore the artistic edges of the medium," Lasseter told Sragow. "Back in 1984, we all understood that there had to be a synthesis of art and technology."

For a while *Toy Story* was caught in the animation culture gap. Then a new Disney screenwriter, Joss Whedon (the creator of *Buffy the Vampire Slayer* on television), got hold of the film and established a working relationship with the younger artists and animators. "We had the same kind of comic book, art school sensibility," he told Sragow. "We were raised on the same cartoons and toys."

Disney also wanted songs. Pixar resisted, but paid close attention to its speaking voices. Tim Allen is a fine Buzz, Don Rickles a prickly Mr. Potato Head, Wallace Shawn a good dinosaur. Best of all is

Hanks, whose delivery and timing is first rate. On the disc he says being Woody was very hard, "acting full-bore one hundred percent."

Transforming from a threatened and narrow-minded westerner, Woody becomes an enlightened leader. Still, the old habits die hard and at Christmastime he still dispatches soldiers to climb to the top of the tree to check out any new toys that may have arrived.

Very small children may be upset at various times and to varying degrees by the threat of abandonment that permeates both films. Otherwise they are fine viewing for the little ones, not to mention surprisingly seductive entertainment for their elders.

94. 20,000 LEAGUES UNDER THE SEA

James Mason, Kirk Douglas, Paul Lukas, Peter Lorre

DIRECTED BY RICHARD FLEISCHER
1954. 127 minutes. No rating

Underwater movies are spectacular these days, but in an odd, enduring kind of way so too is this one from fifty years ago. It would be fun to say that Richard Fleischer shot his film on a shoestring budget with miniature models on the bottom of a tidal pool on a public beach somewhere, but Disney was getting into live action during this period and laid out a then-astronomical $5 million for an eight-week shoot in the Bahamas and the construction of a gigantic tank on its lot in Burbank.

What the studio got for its money was an eighty-foot-long submarine that is mistaken for a sea serpent by South Seas mariners in the 1860s. Jules Verne conceived a submarine in his classic novel of 1870, and on-screen the art director, John Meehan, won an Oscar for a rivet-studded engine of war and science propelled by an unknown power source—electricity in Verne's era; nuclear power in the film—and outfitted with sumptuous quarters belowdecks, including a salon furnished with velvet chairs and couches and a pipe organ.

For kids (and the rest of us), it's a crazy-quilt craft that could seem ridiculous by today's special-effects standards but survives very nicely as a combination nuclear submarine and luxury liner. In an early scene, a half-dozen divers from the submarine, looking like astronauts in full, self-contained diving suits, bob about eerily on the ocean bottom as they conduct a funeral service, complete with casket, for a shipmate killed during a skirmish with a surface ship. The ocean is a milky white, shot through with sunlight from the surface, the bottom sandy. It is a striking scene to come upon and would be considered so in a film today.

The sub may look bizarre on the surface, but sliding deep underwater through coral-studded seas it is a lethal vessel that wouldn't be entirely out of place in *The Hunt for Red October*. The effects are outmoded by current standards, but odd-looking objects are often fascinating. Called the *Nautilus,* the ship is the brainchild of Captain Nemo (James Mason), one of the movies' great madmen. A genius of the deep, Nemo's vision and methods of harvesting and processing materials from the sea could spell salvation of a human race fast depleting its resources on dry land.

But Nemo hates and distrusts mankind, particularly nation-states always at war, to such an extent that he has withdrawn to the deep, where he plans to keep his innovations to himself. On the *Nautilus,* they smoke cigars made of seaweed and dine on sea snake. With the crew at battle stations, the *Nautilus* rams any craft it comes across, leaving only a few wild-eyed survivors to tell crazy tales of what they think attacked them.

Three of those thrown into the sea from a rammed frigate manage to get aboard the submarine and into Nemo's world. The most important of them—the only reason Nemo lets the others live—is Professor Pierre Aronnax (Paul Lukas). Nemo knows the professor's books and recognizes him as someone who will appreciate his underwater discoveries. Kids will prefer the ribald seaman and harpoonist

Ned Land (Kirk Douglas), a furiously energetic and combative sailor who knows a nut case when he sees one.

Kids will also appreciate the professor's assistant, Conseil (Peter Lorre), a perfect doubting Thomas of a sidekick who is always in peril. And they will love Nemo's pet seal, contentedly gulping laboratory specimens tossed him by Ned, who then quaffs the alcohol left in the jars.

New at live action, Disney had no talent under contract and had to look elsewhere. The urbane Mason is superb as Nemo, supremely competent but fatally conflicted. It is left to the professor to confront the captain. Nemo fears what the world would do with nuclear energy and destroys those who get near. He has undergone some brutal treatment in his own life, but is this an excuse for ramming ships and committing murder? The professor thinks not, nor does Ned Land, who hatches a plan to escape.

In the end, Nemo finds warships waiting for him at the island of Vulcania, the hidden and spectacularly picturesque island base where he has developed his undersea knowledge. In one of the best scenes, the mortally wounded Nemo maneuvers the craft through the jagged underwater peaks. Feeling betrayed once more, he destroys the island using the "power of the universe," which has driven his submarine and now produces a cloud that resembles a nuclear explosion.

Kids will understand the issues, which are simply and clearly presented. They will like the action. Land represents Everyman in an effort to stay out of the clutches of a demented genius who would destroy a world that doubts his vision. In the earlier stages of a prolific and varied career, Douglas seems to lift this film right off the ground with his lithe muscularity and sass. At one point, he rescues Nemo from a giant squid, which has attacked the submarine. Disney didn't stint on its sea monsters. This one had tentacles forty feet long and took twenty-eight men to operate. At first the scene was shot on a calm sea (really a calm tank), but the creature's mechanical parts were visible. So they whipped up a storm and tried again. This time it took a hundred people to handle the beast, but the winds and waves hid the grinding gears and made the squid look as good as it was going to get, which isn't bad at all.

Nemo asks Ned Land why he rescued him, and Land replies that he doesn't know. The hyperactive Land was always doing something around Nemo's "crazy iron skillet." Douglas even sings in this movie: "A Whale of a Tale."

Children from the age of seven or eight should have a grand time. The battle with the squid, ship sinkings, and the several explosions, especially the big one at the close, might distress some. Land is a lusty lad ashore with a woman on each arm in the streets of San Francisco, but there is nothing any more suggestive to contend with. And there is no cussing.

95. WALKABOUT

Jenny Agutter, Lucien John, David Gulpilil

DIRECTED BY NICOLAS ROEG
1971. 100 minutes. PG

To some parents this will seem an inappropriate film to recommend to ten- or eleven-year-olds. In other respects it is a natural for them, perhaps a classic. Running down the list of hazards many families go to lengths to avoid, we find full frontal nudity, strong if not extreme violence, killing of animals, awakening sexuality (though no sex is depicted), and several incidents that will startle if not shock. If you're concerned about profanity, rest easy. There is none. And the film is rated PG, remember, though a PG-13 is about right.

The favorable news is that kids will be absorbed by a strange and beautiful allegory about children from irreconcilably different cultures who come together in the Australian outback for one magical period that gets to the essence of life. That's a big bite, but if it suggests cranking up the Hollywood hype machine for another loud, splashy adventure building to an overblown crescendo, you have the wrong movie. Roeg, a British director known for curious, dark tales

(*The Man Who Fell to Earth*, *Don't Look Now*), tells this story (his first feature film) with much sensitivity but without a shred of sentimentality. He is also a cinematographer, and here we have a film of astonishing, almost pulsating physical beauty.

We begin in urban Australia with two gorgeous children of fourteen and six, called Sister (Jenny Agutter) and Brother (Lucien John, who is Roeg's six-year-old son), in the swimming pool of their high-rise apartment building by the sea. In a director's commentary on the DVD (disc is best for a film this breathtakingly scenic), Roeg starts right off contrasting the man-made and the natural by noting the unnaturalness of swimming in a pool with the ocean right beside them. Never mind that the ocean might not be suitable for swimming in that particular spot. In the movie's continual matching of man and nature, it's never any secret which is wanting in Roeg's estimation. This can become annoyingly heavy-handed in its correctness in places, but we are never turned off to the probable truth of it.

The children's parents are ciphers. Mother is tied to the kitchen; father is a geologist toiling mindlessly in a city office. Like all "civilized" adults in this film, he is totally overwhelmed by a desensitizing ennui. One day he takes Sister and Brother for a picnic in the desert, where he shoots at them with a pistol and then sets himself and his car on fire. There is no practical reason for this. Father is beyond reason. And so we have shocking incident number one. While it is certainly disturbing, keep in mind that it is symbolic, a severing of civilized deadness from the teeming life of the desert the children are about to enter.

Kids will need cautioning here, but they will relate to this. Father is a notion, not someone we care about personally. Having taken cover behind a pile of rocks, Sister and Brother carry on unaffected. Brother goes on playing with his toys and little boy's games. Sister, a lovely, long-legged teenager, seems mildly inconvenienced in the way a privileged Western adolescent might, but she gathers them both for the considerable trek ahead of them.

Off they go into the burning expanse, dressed primly in their private school uniforms, with Brother carrying his valise and Sister traipsing in her heeled shoes. Nature immediately intrudes, with bugs swarming and lizards and other creatures wryly noting the pair as they trudge past. Other than sunburn, there is no particular threat or danger. Those elements are replaced with wonderment and discovery as they are enveloped in the sands and plants and fruits and mud of a quick-drying water hole photographed so finely this could be a nature film, which in a way it is.

A couple of days out, they encounter an Aborigine boy (David Gulpilil) about Sister's age. He is on a "walkabout," a six-month test of skills that marks his passage into manhood. A tall youth like Sister, he lopes along with boomerang and spear, killing animals and tossing them on the fire to cook. He shows his citified new acquaintances how to tap a seemingly dry water hole by sticking a hollow stem deep into the mud and sucking as if on a straw. Later the three swim naked together in a desert pool, a strikingly beautiful and natural moment of play and, for the teenagers, blossoming sexual awareness.

Their idyll passes as if in a dream, but there is also a sad feeling of inevitability. Reality is about to intervene. The Aborigine blames himself that their worlds can never connect, which leads him to hang himself. Agutter, now in her thirties, says in the commentary that she and the rest of the cast never knew exactly what was going on in Roeg's mind. The film occasionally cuts away from the desert for flashes of the modern world, which the children are soon to rejoin. They have come to the end of an experience that they, like many children, can never repeat but will remember for the rest of their lives. At the close, the film quotes A. E. Housman's "Shropshire Lad": "Those happy highways where we went and cannot come again."

Most children will be transfixed by this film. "A child sees things rather beautifully," Roeg said. There is violence and other potentially upsetting acts ranging from the suicide (the act isn't shown) to white hunters in a truck slaughtering animals for pet food. All that said, mature kids from about age eleven should handle this movie well and come away with a rewarding experience.

96. WEST SIDE STORY

Natalie Wood, Richard Beymer, Rita Moreno, Russ Tamblyn, George Chakiris

DIRECTED BY ROBERT WISE AND JEROME ROBBINS
1961. 151 minutes. No rating

In 1949 when Jerome Robbins and his friend Leonard Bernstein began working with Robbins's plan to update Shakespeare's *Romeo and Juliet,* the story involved a Jewish girl falling in love with a Catholic boy from Greenwich Village and was called *East Side Story.* By 1955, however, when the show was being developed for Broadway, the action had switched to the west side of Central Park and the demographics to Puerto Rican on one side of the romance and Polish-American on the other.

Like Juliet, Maria, played by Natalie Wood, falls for the handsome leading blade of her people's enemy, the gang leader Tony, portrayed by Richard Beymer. Arthur Laurents, who wrote the book for the stage production, came up with the idea of warfare between the Anglo Jets and the Puerto Rican Sharks. More than fifty years later, one of the greatest and most original musicals retains a certain freshness and topicality, but now, as then, it sets up big tasks for itself. Three gang members die violently in *West Side Story,* a fact that young viewers have to deal with (about age nine or ten is fine), but it seems incongruous in the context of song and dance. A musical about race hate obviously is a difficult proposition, and in the city of Crown Heights and Amadou Diallo, rival gangs of dancing, singing kids can look a little silly. Indeed, it seemed so to some New York City kids, if not the rest of country, when the movie opened in 1961.

By then *West Side Story* had completed its Broadway run (1957–1959) and was pretty well engrained in the national consciousness. Ernest Lehman adapted the stage version for the screen. "I found it difficult reshaping the iconic stage musical into a movie," he writes in

West Side Story   (Used by permission of MGM Home Entertainment)

the notes with the DVD. "I wanted the film to flow with rising dramatic movement, with no intermission to break that tension." This isn't a Gene Kelly musical, with production numbers embellishing a narrative. Here the song and dance were the narrative, an extension of street life. But the movie couldn't ignore the stage, and for one very good reason. "The show was about theater," says Stephen Sondheim, who wrote the lyrics for Bernstein's score, "how you use music, lyric, and book combined in a new way . . . a musical about movement."

On-screen the story moves to dance. Even the dialogue has a syncopated rhythm. A grinding perfectionist, Robbins honed the movement and execution. Robert Wise, a superb tactician, turned it into a movie. Be sure to tell young viewers about the four-and-a-half-minute overture at the start lest they think something is wrong with the disc. After that the film moves to an aerial view of the city that could work beautifully in a film today, and from there we meet the Jets on a basketball court. It's here that the movie passes a crucial test. Will we accept the notion of tough street kids as dancers?

Wise and Robbins kept the movement slow at first, letting it build as we get used to the idea. "Watch how they do this, how they take this real world and introduce dance to it and make you buy it," said the director Michael Bay when he watched the movie for an article in the *New York Times* in 2001. "You know there's this moment really early on, while they're walking down the street and they start doing these pirouettes and you're thinking, 'This is weird.' But you buy it. They make you buy it."

One challenge for the movie was to merge New York street locations around West 61st Street (now the site of Lincoln Center) and sets in Hollywood, but the real task was transforming stage theatricality into screen immediacy. The movie is about youth under explosive pressure. Lehman says that he and Wise wandered around New York for a while talking to gangs and studying street life. Finally, Wise, the moviemaker, had enough. "Look, Ernie," he said, "we're not making a definitive study of juvenile delinquency; let's just go back to California and you write a screenplay."

Famous people made this movie. Tell the kids about Leonard Bernstein, who died in 1990. Some say his score is the finest ever composed for a musical. Robbins, who died in 1998, is remembered for many shows: *Call Me Madam, The King and I, Pajama Game, Peter Pan, Gypsy.* He was a tough man to work for. "He'd really get in people's faces," recalls Rita Moreno, who won an Oscar as Maria's fiery friend Anita. Critics might call one actor a little "femme" for a street kid, or another one too soft for a gang leader, but this is a young cast called on to do everything—act, sing, and dance. Robbins rehearsed them for three months and drove them through take after take until their feet bled.

The production fell behind schedule and ballooned over budget. Eventually the studio had had enough of Robbins's compulsion and fired him, leaving Wise to finish. But Robbins's name stayed on the picture, and he and Wise accepted their directorial Oscars together. Wise's cuts and use of many angles are vital. He may have saved the film, but if one talks to the surviving principals today—Sondheim, Laurents, Lehman, Moreno, Beymer, the actor Russ Tamblyn—they all credit Robbins, the fiery creator, and Wise, the masterful technician, about equally.

The movie won ten Oscars in all, including one for best picture. For a while, the *Harvard Lampoon* issued a Natalie Wood Award for the year's worst movie performance. In reality she began in movies at the age of five and did a perfectly competent job in films like *Miracle on 34th Street*, *Rebel Without a Cause* (as James Dean's girlfriend), *The Searchers*, *Splendor in the Grass*, and *Bob & Carol & Ted & Alice*.

Like other actresses in musicals—notably Audrey Hepburn in *My Fair Lady*—she wasn't vocally up to numbers like "I Feel Pretty" and the film turned to the ever-insertable Marni Nixon to provide the big voice. Wood's dancing was serviceable, and there was nothing wrong with her acting. Tony and Maria may fall in love at first glance, but Wood and Beymer weren't particularly fond of each other. Films today often founder because of a lack of chemistry between the romantic leads. No one can say that Wood and Beymer let that happen.

The climactic rumble results in two stabbings and a shooting that are reasonably tame by today's standards but could be upsetting to young children under nine or ten, especially in the emotional context of a musical. Passionate young people on steamy streets radiate a lot of sexuality, but there is no sex. And, shockingly for a gangland saga, no profanity.

97. WHO FRAMED ROGER RABBIT

Bob Hoskins, Christopher Lloyd, Joel Silver, Stubby Kaye, with the voices of Charles Fleischer, Mel Blanc, Amy Irving, Lou Hirsch, many others

DIRECTED BY ROBERT ZEMECKIS
1988. 103 minutes. PG

At the start of Robert Zemeckis's film the animated Roger Rabbit is acting in a '40s-style Baby Herman cartoon when the human director, Raoul Raoul (played by the Hollywood producer Joel Silver), yells cut. "The Rabbit keeps blowing his lines," Raoul howls. Suddenly we've jumped from a cartoon to a live set with technicians trotting around and an angry studio chief wondering why the latest Baby Herman epic is $25,000 over budget. "Moving out of cartoon into reality was the crucial scene in the movie," Zemeckis told Aljean Harmetz in the *New York Times*. "That shot had to work or everything would be over three minutes after it began."

Movies combining animated characters with live ones go back a long time. Gene Kelly danced with a mouse in *Anchors Aweigh* (1945). Penguin waiters serve Julie Andrews and Dick Van Dyke in *Mary Poppins* (1964, see page 185). In the 1940 cartoon *You Ought to Be in Pictures*, Porky Pig and Donald Duck barge into the real office of the head of Warner Brothers Animation to gripe about how they're being treated. But until *Who Framed Roger Rabbit*, Ms. Harmetz wrote, "no one has ever risked creating a movie which is breathtakingly complicated technically but can succeed artistically only if an animated drawing and a live man form a human bond."

In other words, the cartoon Roger has to get along with the live private eye Eddie Valiant (Bob Hoskins) in a film that is fifty-five minutes animated and forty-eight minutes live action. That's tough because humans generally have a problem with toons, as cartoon characters are called. Toons, and this goes for Roger, are childish and impulsive and do about anything without much consequence. They can be flattened by a steamroller and pop right back into shape, which is quite beyond humans. In fact, Eddie's brother didn't get up at all when he was hit by a piano pushed by toons from a high place.

Valiant resents this sort of thing, but he's always worked Toontown and that's the way it is. "The setting is Los Angeles," Vincent Canby wrote in the *New York Times,* "and the time is 1947 when the production of cartoon shorts for theaters was still profitable and Hollywood's biggest stars included, in addition to Gable and Tracy and Davis, the mouses (Mickey and Minnie), Donald Duck, Daffy Duck, Dumbo, Tweety Bird, and Roger Rabbit, among others."

Roger finds himself accused of bumping off the live chief of Maroon Studios, who allegedly has been having an affair with Roger's unbelievably gorgeous wife, who, not to confuse matters, is an animated human. Valiant takes the case, and thus begins one of the movies' most unusual relationships.

It was particularly tough for Hoskins to interact with an animated rabbit who is never with him in the shot. The animation was created separately and mixed with the live action later by Industrial Light and Magic, which worked with Disney on the project. So Hoskins was acting to thin air. "It was like shooting the ultimate buddy picture, maybe *48 Hours,* except Eddie Murphy never showed up," said Jeffrey Katzenberg, who was chairman of the Walt Disney Studio at the time.

Teeming with sophisticated animated characters, the film took three years to make. The animation ate up six hundred drawings per second. Katzenberg tells of walking into the optical department in London and seeing a stack of animation cels eight feet high, which amounted to thirty seconds of film.

Back on the live action side of things, Hoskins honed his approach to the noirish detective in the snap-brimmed fedora. A short, heavy-set man, he was accustomed to playing rumpled criminal types in movies like *The Long Good Friday* and *Mona Lisa.* Here he decided he had enough problems without attempting a physical makeover. "I realized if I was actually going to make a relationship with Roger, I had to see him and there was nothing there for me to see," he told Harmetz in the *Times.* He soon realized he had to become part cartoon himself. "I spent hours with my three-year-old daughter, playing games with her imaginary friends," he said. "As an adult, your imagination is pushed to the back of your head. I forced my imagination to the front. By the end of the film, I started to lose control. I would be talking to a friend and see a weasel."

Disney made the picture with Steven Spielberg's Amblin Entertainment, noted for pioneering new technology. Spielberg was taken aback by the difficulties of merging the two elements. "Every single shot presented a whole agenda of impossibilities," he told Harmetz. "Problems had to be solved a thousand times."

On-screen, Hoskins's Eddie Valiant finally becomes cartoonlike, getting spread-eagled across a ceiling and surviving a twenty-story fall. Zemeckis gives his film a *Chinatown* flavor, with the villainous Judge Doom plotting to get rid of Los Angeles's quaint trolley car system in favor of an expressway. Spielberg got Warner Brothers to lend characters like Bugs Bunny and Porky Pig for cameo roles. Max

Fleischer's Betty Boop also makes an appearance, along with Snow White, Goofy, Woody Woodpecker, and a hippo from *Fantasia*.

Roger was framed, all right. Eddie Valiant centers his investigation on the voluptuous Jessica, a singer at the Ink and Paint, a club that features toon entertainers. (Donald and Daffy Duck get into a twin-piano routine that turns raucous.) But Jessica, it turns out, has been faithful and stands by her husband. "I love you more than any woman has loved a rabbit," she tells Roger.

"A movie of such pure, dizzy enchantment that one watches it from start to finish with a smile so wide that the facial muscles ache," Canby wrote. Very true, but there are some darker elements, too. The Ink and Paint is modeled after the Cotton Club in Harlem, and there are some racial intonations to the disdain between humans and toons. Judge Doom mixes up a toxic concoction for melting down toons he catches, which isn't dwelled upon but could upset small children. Otherwise, despite a noirish patina and frequently grown-up repartee, the film is fine for everybody from about five up. Rumors about Jessica notwithstanding, she has only been playing "patty-cake" with the Maroon studio chief. So we have no sex per se, nor profanity.

98. THE WINSLOW BOY

Nigel Hawthorne, Guy Edwards, Rebecca Pidgeon, Jeremy Northam, Gemma Jones, Matthew Pidgeon, Colin Stinton

DIRECTED BY DAVID MAMET
1999. 104 minutes. G

David Mamet knew he had a natural. "It's just one of the few instances of work I've done with absolutely surefire material," he said in an article in the *New York Times*. In Victorian England in

1912, thirteen-year-old Ronnie Winslow (Guy Edwards) stands outside his house in a cold rain. In his hand is a letter from the British admiralty that expels him from naval school for stealing a five-shilling postal order.

His father, Arthur Winslow (Nigel Hawthorne), takes the boy to his study with a perfectly balanced sense of stern patriarchy. Arthur simply and quietly asks his boy not to lie. "If it's a lie I shall know it," he says. "Did you steal the postal order?" He asks twice, and twice Ronnie says no.

We're off and running in a celebrated court case that took place in real life in 1910 and became the basis of Terence Rattigan's acclaimed play written in 1946. Mamet wrote this screen adaptation, and it is truly a departure for a Pulitzer Prize–winning playwright and prolific screenwriter of tough dramas like *The Verdict, House of Games* (his directorial debut), *Homicide,* and *Glengarry Glen Ross,* among others. It's also odd to think of Mamet as the director of a film suitable for children, but in this case so he is.

Certainly there is nothing to suggest that he was aiming in this direction. The story is about a child, of course, and one from a genteel, strong, and close-knit family. That's good for kids to see, but this is also a story of consummate sophistication couched in airs and conventions, not to mention conversation, that may seem alien and intimidating to children. True, kids can certainly appreciate the idea of a schoolboy touching off a case that stands the country on its ear. "John Bull Can't Get His Work Done Because of the Winslow Situation," reads a headline in the papers. But instead of the action a young audience expects, we get Mametian suggestion. For example, the father's inquiry "is staged with enough cool understatement to lend a shade of ambiguity to Ronnie's denial, and to the maneuverings that follow," Janet Maslin wrote in the *Times.*

In other words, Ronnie could be lying after all. Kids don't need Mamet's ambiguity to weigh that possibility. The film is full of subtle suggestion that will be lost on most children, but there is a parallel universe in this film that is accessible to many kids. To begin with, they will love its looks, grandly photographed by Benoit Delhomme. Most of all, there are large, graspable characters. Catherine Winslow (Rebecca Pidgeon), Ronnie's strong-willed, intelligent suffragist sister, will interest many kids. So will Sir Robert Morton (Jeremy Northam), the renowned attorney and member of Parliament who agrees to take on Ronnie's case.

In a very nice touch of realism, Morton and his aides continually weigh his own fortunes and whether changing winds in the case warrant the next step or a speedy exit. Strongest of all is the father, Arthur Winslow, a Liverpool bank manager who comes close to losing everything he has in the fight to defend his son. Most kids will be engrossed in this drama. One reason they will stay on board is that Mamet directs the film with a kind of stripped-down approach that favors young viewers. "The trick of directing melodrama," he said in the *Times,* "is that it's the hardest form to act because it's so easy to become sententious. Everybody's intention has got to be absolutely perfect and absolutely honest all the time. You cannot play the sad scenes sad and the happy scenes happy. If you lean into the material, if you help it along, what you get instead of melodrama is bathos." Which is to say the kind of sappy, overwrought junk kids often are fed on the screen today.

Mamet gives them something simpler and more real here: a young boy in trouble, with a loving family determined to do what it takes to help him and a nice sense of tension and suspense kids will appreciate. Ronnie's healthy perspective sets a good example for young viewers. Kicked out of one school, he starts right out doing well at another. Who needs the naval academy anyway? When the verdict arrives, the country is in an uproar, but Ronnie isn't around. He's gone to the movies.

Depending on the child, eleven and twelve are the best ages to start with this film, though sharp ten-year-olds can keep up. The thing is to hook them at the start. Some briefing beforehand will help, and they should be prepared to listen. There is no violence, sex, or profanity.

99. THE WIZARD OF OZ

Judy Garland, Bert Lahr, Jack Haley, Ray Bolger, Margaret Hamilton, Billie Burke, Clara Blandick, Charlie Grapewin

DIRECTED BY VICTOR FLEMING

1939. 101 minutes. No rating

In Aljean Harmetz's book *The Making of the Wizard of Oz*, Yip Harburg, who wrote the lyrics to "Over the Rainbow," observed that Dorothy's life is messed up in Kansas and she has to run. In its nostalgia "the song has to be full of childish pleasures. Of lemon drops," he said. As is true with innumerable movie children, she must break from the past to go on her adventure down the yellow brick road, meet new allies, and sort out reality from illusion in the land of the humbug. "I thought that the rainbow could be a bridge from one place to another," Harburg said. "A rainbow gave us a reason for going to a new land and a reason for changing to color" (scenes in Kansas being in black and white and in Oz in vibrant Technicolor).

Kids figure somewhere in all the explanations of the screen adaptation of L. Frank Baum's book, though like most great films, this one is caught up in knotty theorizing. We have the Freudian take, the Marxist element, the feminist thrust. For dysfunction there are the supposedly brainless scarecrow, heartless tin woodman, and a sleepless lion who says he's so cowardly he won't count sheep because he is scared of them.

In his essay "Out of Kansas," Salman Rushdie wrote that the film's "driving force is the inadequacy of adults, even of good adults, and how the weakness of grown-ups forces children to take control of their own destinies." Certainly Dorothy's drab life with her hard-pressed Auntie Em (Clara Blandick) and Uncle Henry (Charlie Grapewin) suggests that a change is in order, especially after the cranky Miss Gulch (Margaret Hamilton), who will become the Wicked

Witch of the West across the divide in Oz, threatens to have the dog Toto done in.

But home is the center of things for most children and the loss of that, as happens to Dorothy when she is displaced by the tornado, obviously is a terrifying prospect. Then again, landing in strange territory offers adventure and new friends who can help, which kids realize once the fear factor is subdued. Adults may continue to be disappointments, as witnessed by a very mortal wizard who can't deliver on his promises, but then the film teaches that authority figures usually are no more reliable than the rest of us. Besides, one can rely only on oneself. As for there being no place like home, as Dorothy exclaims on her return, that's true, but only as far as it goes. Kansas is still Kansas.

Harburg said that it took him a while to think of "somewhere" to precede "over the rainbow" and fill the first two notes of Harold Arlen's music. The song will live forever, but it took exactly one sneak preview for Louis B. Mayer, the head of MGM, to try to kick it out of the movie. In the 1930s the studio was a huge operation employing scores of producers, and they often went to one another's previews. Mervyn LeRoy, the *Oz* producer, was an outsider from Warner Brothers and subject to attack. MGM people carped that Dorothy wouldn't sing in a barnyard.

Well, why not? "Those ignorant jerks," Harburg complained to Harmetz. Under threat of losing the film's defining moment, not to mention derailing American movie history, *Oz*'s associate producer Arthur Freed, also MGM's impresario of musicals, finally persuaded Mayer to restore the song.

"Money rules the roost," Harburg said. "The artist is lucky if he can get a few licks in." But in the heyday of the big studios, commerce and the mechanics of mass production might have put the artistic side in peril, but that didn't necessarily extinguish great movies. *Casablanca*, after all, was a studio assembly-line affair (see page 54). In the midst of making *Oz*, MGM pulled the director Victor Fleming off the film and put him on another of the studio's projects, *Gone With the Wind*. In 1939, and without too much angst, the movies also turned out *Stagecoach*, *Wuthering Heights*, and *Mr. Smith Goes to Washington* (see page 191).

As for *Oz*, according to Rushdie, "a film that has made so many audiences so happy was not a happy film to make." The shoot was grueling and chaotic. Ten writers had a hand in the script. The first, Herman J. Mankiewicz, had the film spend much more time in Kansas than Baum did in the book because he thought, as did other writers, that it was important to establish Dorothy in reality before sending her into a fantasy.

"The generation of newspapermen-turned-screenwriters to which Mankiewicz belonged wrote scripts at breakneck speed," Harmetz wrote. In four days he had produced an incomplete fifty-six-page script, only to be removed in favor of Ogden Nash, who was replaced by Noel Langley, who eventually created enough to be credited with the screenplay but not without pushing and pulling by many others along the way. This was the MGM system. "It was customary for three, four, or even five writers to be assigned to write for the same film at the same time," wrote Harmetz. "One treatment or script would be accepted, the others discarded and their writers sent to write treatments for some other film."

Directors were somewhat less numerous. Four of them worked on *Oz*. Richard Thorpe, a competent journeyman, began the film and lasted two weeks before it was decided he wasn't up to directing a fairy tale. George Cukor was brought in for three days, long enough to get Judy Garland to drop a blond wig and sugar princess routine and start acting like a real little girl from Kansas. Fleming was considered a man's actor (*The Virginian, Treasure Island, Captains Courageous*), but he was a competent studio man and guided *Oz* for four months before moving on to the elaborate sets of *Gone With the Wind*, where Clark Gable was at loggerheads with that film's first director, George Cukor.

Casting was more settled. Shirley Temple was considered for Dorothy. Deanna Durbin was long-legged and pretty, but not vulnerable enough. Garland was thirteen when MGM signed her as a contract player in 1935. The studio, Harmetz wrote, had bought an "extraordinary voice unfortunately attached to a mediocre body and a badly flawed face. In the next seven years the voice would be trained, the teeth capped, the nose restructured, the thick waist held in by corsets, and the body reshaped as well as possible by diet and massage."

Garland would come to an unhappy end in 1969. Jack Haley, the Tin Man, said she was "as lighthearted a person as I have ever met in my life." She was certainly real, as real as Kansas. "She carried the picture with her sincerity," Haley said.

Small children may be upset by Dorothy's separation from home and alarmed at the wicked witch and her brigade of flying monkeys, but there are really no drawbacks to perhaps the most beloved family film ever.

100. YELLOW SUBMARINE

With Sgt. Pepper's Lonely Hearts Club Band

DIRECTED BY GEORGE DUNNING
1968. 85 minutes. G

Paul McCartney had the idea in 1966, but it was for a song called "Yellow Submarine," not an animated feature. The movie concept belonged to Al Brodax, a producer of *Beatles Cartoons* on ABC in New York. The Beatles hated cartoons, but they were obligated to make another movie and were bored at the prospect of doing another live one like *A Hard Day's Night* (see page 118) and *Help!* So they agreed to do animation. Just don't make it look like Disney.

Animation in London was a cottage industry at the time, but it certainly rose to the occasion. The smartest thing the producers did was hire the German artist Heinz Edelmann to produce an incredible range of images, rendered with great blasts of color, from Warholian pop and op art, the comics, psychedelic photography, surrealism. Everything was "so blatantly derivative that it's an amusing catalogue of twentieth-century graphic design," wrote the critic Pauline Kael.

The script has been described as open-ended Rorschach filled with Joycean puns. Various writers had a hand in it, including Erich Segal, author of *Love Story*. Edelmann altered the visual style every five minutes, and the story is every bit as changeable. There is no plot in a conventional sense. The film begins with an assault by the Blue Meanies on all that is musical and colorful in the world. From their hilltop position, the Meanies rain blue artillery shells down on genteel Edwardian folk, who turn to black and white as the music from bandstands fades and dies. A flying blue glove with sharklike teeth is sent in to finish off any survivors, but one white-haired old sea dog escapes to a yellow submarine. We are off under the sea and through the air here, there, and anywhere through fanciful recesses and around constructions of every description.

Somewhere in here cartoon images of the Beatles, representing Sgt. Pepper's Lonely Hearts Club Band, begin to appear to complement "Eleanor Rigby," "Lucy in the Sky with Diamonds," and "All You Need Is Love," to name a few of the dozen Beatles songs. In the film the Lord Mayor tells the Beatles they look so real they could impersonate the real thing. "We are the real thing," John Lennon replies. In the movie they really aren't, though. The boys were supposed to dub the voices themselves, but they never seemed to get around to it so, with production being delayed week after week, soundalikes were hired. George Harrison was the hardest to duplicate. Eventually the producers found someone suitable in a barroom.

The movie generally meanders toward the ultimate conversion of the Meanies into fun music lovers. The submarine disappears for long stretches as the boys wander in and out of various wildly colored realms posing questions and testing notions of peace, love, and harmony. The Beatles describe the movie as an odyssey. Dinosaurs, Frankenstein, King Kong, and all manner of threats appear only to be greeted and disarmed with interest and respect.

"*Yellow Submarine* is a family movie in the truest sense," the critic Renata Adler wrote in the *New York Times*. "Something for the little kids who watch the same sort of punning stories, infinitely less nonviolent and refined, on television; something for the older kids, whose musical contribution to the arts and longings for love and gentleness and color could hardly present a better case; something for parents, who can see the best of what being newly young is all about."

Kids these days might not get too excited about the Beatles, but they are welcome anytime. An animated film doesn't date them as a live feature might. The songs are glorious. Two years ago the movie was completely refurbished for DVD and a revival in theaters. Six-channel sound replaces the old monaural sound track, a process carried out by EMI's Abbey Road Studios in London. "Remixes have a revelatory freshness that even Beatles purists may find surprising," the critic and Beatles buff Allan Kozinn wrote in the *Times*.

For the film itself there were tears to repair, crooked splices to fix, and faded colors to restore. It looks grand. Tell the kids the movie even got its own postage stamp.

No violence, sex, or profanity. As they say, perfect for children of all ages.

Addams Family Values. Raul Julia, Angelica Huston, Dan Hedaya, Elizabeth Wilson, Christina Ricci, Christopher Lloyd, Joan Cusack, Carol Kane. Directed by Barry Sonnenfeld. 1993. 93 minutes. PG-13

The Adventures of Milo and Otis. Narrated by Dudley Moore. Directed by Masanori Hata. 1989. 76 minutes. G

A.I.: Artificial Intelligence. Haley Joel Osment, Frances O'Connor, Jude Law, Sam Robards, Brendan Gleeson, William Hurt. Directed by Steven Spielberg. 2001. 145 minutes. PG-13

Airplane! David Zucker, Jerry Zucker, Robert Stack, Lloyd Bridges, Peter Graves, Julie Hagerty, Robert Hays, Leslie Nielsen. Directed by Jim Abrahams. 1980. 86 minutes. PG

Aladdin. With the voices of Robin Williams, Scott Weiger, Linda Larkin, Jonathan Freeman, Frank Welker, Gilbert Gottfried. Directed by John Musker and Ron Clements. 1992. 90 minutes. G

All the President's Men. Robert Redford, Dustin Hoffman, Jason Robards, Martin Balsam, Hal Holbrook, Jane Alexander, Ned Beatty. Directed by Alan J. Pakula. 1976. 138 minutes. PG

American Graffiti. Ron Howard, Richard Dreyfuss, Paul LeMat, Charles Martin Smith, Candy Clark, Cindy Williams, Harrison Ford, Mackenzie Phillips, Wolfman Jack. Directed by George Lucas. 1973. 110 minutes. PG

An American in Paris. Gene Kelly, Leslie Caron, Oscar Levant, Georges Guetary, Nina Foch. Directed by Vincente Minnelli. 1951. 115 minutes. No rating

Anne of Green Gables. Megan Follows, Colleen Dewhurst, Patricia Hamilton. Directed by Kevin Sullivan. 1985. 195 minutes. No rating (television movie)

Annie. Albert Finney, Carol Burnett, Bernadette Peters, Aileen Quinn, Anne Reinking, Geoffrey Holder, Edward Herrmann. Directed by John Huston. 1982. 128 minutes. PG

Antz. With the voices of Woody Allen, Sharon Stone, Sylvester Stallone, Gene Hackman, Christopher Walken, Anne Bancroft. Directed by Eric Darnell. 1998. 83 minutes. PG

Around the World in 80 Days. David Niven, Shirley MacLaine, Cantinflas, Buster Keaton, Robert Newton, Robert Morley, John Gielgud. Directed by Michael Anderson. 1956. 167 minutes. G

Auntie Mame. Rosalind Russell, Forrest Tucker, Coral Browne, Fred Clark, Roger Smith, Peggy Cass, Joanna Barnes. Directed by Morton DaCosta. 1958. 143 minutes. No rating

Bad Day at Black Rock. Spencer Tracy, Robert Ryan, Anne Francis, Dean Jagger, Walter Brennan, Ernest Borgnine, Lee Marvin. Directed by John Sturges. 1955. 81 minutes. No rating

Bananas. Woody Allen, Louise Lasser, Natividad Abascal, Jacobo Morales, Miguel Ángel Suárez, Carlos Montalban. Directed by Woody Allen. 1971. 82 minutes. PG

The Bank Dick. W. C. Fields, Cora Witherspoon, Una Merkel, Evelyn Del Rio. Directed by Eddie Cline. 1940. 74 minutes. Black and white. No rating

Batman. Michael Keaton, Jack Nicholson, Kim Basinger. Directed by Tim Burton. 1989. 126 minutes. PG-13

The Borrowers. John Goodman, Jim Broadbent, Mark Williams, Hugh Laurie. Directed by Peter Hewitt. 1997. 83 minutes. PG

Brian's Song. Billy Dee Williams, James Caan, Jack Warden, Judy Pace, Shelley Fabares. Directed by Buzz Kulik. 1971. 73 minutes. G

The Bridge on the River Kwai. Alec Guinness, Jack Hawkins, William Holden, Sessue Hayakawa, Geoffrey Horne, James Donald. Directed by David Lean. 1957. 161 minutes. No rating

Brigadoon. Gene Kelly, Van Johnson, Cyd Charisse, Elaine Stewart, Barry Jones, Hugh Laing. Directed by Vincente Minnelli. 1954. 108 minutes. No rating

A Bug's Life. With the voices of Julia Louis-Dreyfus, Kevin Spacey, Dave Foley, David Hyde Pierce, Phyllis Diller. Directed by John Lasseter and Andrew Stanton. 1998. 94 minutes. G

The Caine Mutiny. Humphrey Bogart, José Ferrer, May Wynn, Fred MacMurray, E. G. Marshall, Lee Marvin, Tom Tully, Claude Akins. Directed by Edward Dmytryk. 1954. 125 minutes. No rating

Calamity Jane. Doris Day, Howard Keel, Allyn McLerie, Philip Carey. Directed by David Butler. 1953. 101 minutes. No rating

Captains Courageous. Spencer Tracy, Lionel Barrymore, Freddie Bartholomew, Melvyn Douglas, John Carradine, Mickey Rooney. Directed by Victor Fleming. 1937. 116 minutes. Black and white. No rating

Charlotte's Web. With the voices of Henry Gibson, Debbie Reynolds, Paul Lynde, Agnes Moorehead, Charles Nelson Riley. Directed by Charles A. Nichols and Iwao Takamoto. 1973. 93 minutes. G

Citizen Kane. Orson Welles, Joseph Cotten, Agnes Moorehead, Everett Sloane, Ray Collins. Directed by Orson Welles. 1941. 119 minutes. Black and white. No rating

City Lights. Charlie Chaplin, Harry Myers, Hank Man, Virginia Cherrill. Directed by Charlie Chaplin. 1931. 86 minutes. Black and white. No rating

Coal Miner's Daughter. Sissy Spacek, Tommy Lee Jones, Beverly D'Angelo. Directed by Michael Apted. 1980. 125 minutes. PG

A Connecticut Yankee in King Arthur's Court. Bing Crosby, Rhonda Fleming, William Bendix, Henry Wilcoxon, Cedric Hardwicke. Directed by Tay Garnett. 1949. 107 minutes. No rating

The Court Jester. Danny Kaye, Glynis Johns, Basil Rathbone, Angela Lansbury, Mildred Natwick, Cecil Parker. Directed by Norman Panama and Melvin Frank. 1956. 101 minutes. No rating

Dances with Wolves. Kevin Costner, Graham Greene, Mary McDonnell, Rodney A. Grant, Floyd Red Crow Westerman, Larry Joshua, Wes Studi. Directed by Kevin Costner. 1990. 181 minutes. PG-13

David Copperfield. Freddie Bartholomew, Frank Lawton, W. C. Fields, Madge Evans, Lionel Barrymore, Edna May Oliver, Elsa Lancaster, Basil Rathbone. Directed by George Cukor. 1935. 130 minutes. No rating

Doctor Zhivago. Julie Christie, Omar Sharif, Tom Courtenay, Geraldine Chaplin, Alec Guinness, Siobhan McKenna, Ralph Richardson, Rod Steiger. Directed by David Lean. 1965. 197 minutes. No rating

The Empire Strikes Back. Mark Hamill, Carrie Fisher, Harrison Ford, Billy Dee Williams, Anthony Daniels, voice of James Earl Jones. Directed by Irvin Kershner. 1980. 124 minutes. PG

Fantasia. Leopold Stokowski and the Philadelphia Orchestra. Narrated by Deems Taylor. Directed by Ben Sharpsteen. 1940. 120 minutes. No rating

Father of the Bride. Spencer Tracy, Elizabeth Taylor, Joan Bennett, Billie Burke, Leo G. Carroll. Directed by Vincente Minnelli. 1950. 93 minutes. No rating

The Flamingo Kid. Richard Crenna, Matt Dillon, Hector Elizondo, Jessica Walter, Janet Jones, Fisher Stevens. Directed by Garry Marshall. 1984. 100 minutes. PG-13

The 400 Blows. Jean-Pierre Léaud, Patrick Auffay, Claire Maurier, Albert Remy, Jeanne Moreau. Directed by François Truffaut. 1959. 99 minutes. French with English subtitles. Black and white. No rating

Friendly Persuasion. Gary Cooper, Dorothy McGuire, Anthony Perkins, Marjorie Main. Directed by William Wyler. 1956. 140 minutes. No rating

From Russia with Love. Sean Connery, Daniela Bianchi, Lotte Lenya, Pedro Armendariz, Robert Shaw. Directed by Terence Young. 1963. 118 minutes. No rating

Funny Girl. Barbra Streisand, Omar Sharif, Anne Francis, Kay Medford, Walter Pidgeon, Gerald Mohr, Lee Allen. Directed by William Wyler. 1968. 155 minutes. G

The Gods Must Be Crazy. Marius Weyers, Sandra Prinsloo, N!xau, Louw Verwey, Michael Thys. Directed by Jamie Uys. 1981. 108 minutes. PG

Grease. John Travolta, Olivia Newton-John, Stockard Channing, Jeff Conaway, Didi Conn, Eve Arden. Directed by Randal Kleiser. 1978. 110 minutes. PG

Here Comes Mr. Jordan. Robert Montgomery, Evelyn Keyes, Rita Johnson, Claude Rains, Edward Everett Horton. Directed by Alexander Hall. 1941. 93 minutes. Black and white. No rating

His Girl Friday. Cary Grant, Rosalind Russell, Gene Lockhart, Ralph Bellamy, Helen Mack, Ernest Truex. Directed by Howard Hawks. 1940. 92 minutes. Black and white. No rating

Homeward Bound: The Incredible Journey. Robert Hays, Jean Smart, Kim Greist, Veronica Lauren, Benj Thall; with the voices of Michael J. Fox, Sally Field, Don Ameche. Directed by DuWayne Dunham. 1993. 84 minutes. G

Honey, I Shrunk the Kids. Rick Moranis, Marcia Strassman, Kristine Sutherland, Thomas Brown, Matt Frewer. Directed by Joe Johnston. 1989. 93 minutes. PG

Hoosiers. Gene Hackman, Barbara Hershey, Dennis Hopper, Sheb Wooley. Directed by David Anspaugh. 1986. 114 minutes. PG

The In-Laws. Peter Falk, Alan Arkin, Nancy Dussault, Richard Libertini, Penny Peyser. Directed by Arthur Hiller. 1979. 103 minutes. PG

In the Heat of the Night. Sidney Poitier, Rod Steiger, Warren Oates, Lee Grant, Larry Gates, Scott Wilson. Directed by Norman Jewison. 1967. 109 minutes. No rating

The Jungle Book. With the voices of Sebastian Cabot, Phil Harris, George Sanders, Sterling Holloway, Louis Prima. Directed by Wolfgang Reitherman. 1967. 78 minutes. No rating

Lean on Me. Morgan Freeman, Beverly Todd, Alan North, Robert Guillaume, Robin Bartlett, Lynne Thigpen, Michael Beach. Directed by John Avildsen. 1989. 109 minutes. PG-13

Little Big Man. Dustin Hoffman, Faye Dunaway, Richard Mulligan, Martin Balsam, Chief Dan George, Jeff Corey, Alan Oppenheimer. Directed by Arthur Penn. 1970. 139 minutes. PG

The Long Walk Home. Sissy Spacek, Whoopi Goldberg, Dwight Schultz, Ving Rhames, Dylan Baker. Directed by Richard Pearce. 1990. 97 minutes. PG

The Maltese Falcon. Humphrey Bogart, Mary Astor, Sydney Greenstreet, Peter Lorre. Directed by John Huston. 1941. 100 minutes. Black and white. No rating

A Man for All Seasons. Paul Scofield, Wendy Hiller, Robert Shaw, Leo McKern, Orson Welles, Susannah York. Directed by Fred Zinnemann. 1966. 120 minutes. No rating

The Man Who Would Be King. Sean Connery, Michael Caine, Christopher Plummer, Saeed Jaffrey. Directed by John Huston. 1975. 129 minutes. PG

The Mask of Zorro. Antonio Banderas, Anthony Hopkins, Catherine Zeta-Jones, Stuart Wilson, Matt Letscher. Directed by Martin Campbell. 1998. 136 minutes. PG-13

Mister Roberts. Henry Fonda, James Cagney, Jack Lemmon, William Powell, Ward Bond, Betsy Palmer. Directed by John Ford and Mervyn LeRoy. 1955. 123 minutes. No rating

The Mouse That Roared. Peter Sellers, Jean Seberg, David Kossoff, William Hartnell, Leo McKern, Monty Landis. Directed by Jack Arnold. 1959. 83 minutes. No rating

Mr. Deeds Goes to Town. Gary Cooper, Jean Arthur, Lionel Stander, George Bancroft, Douglas Dumbrille. Directed by Frank Capra. 1936. 115 minutes. Black and white. No rating

Murder on the Orient Express. Albert Finney, Lauren Bacall, Martin Balsam, Ingrid Bergman, Jacqueline Bisset, Jean-Pierre Cassel, Sean Connery, John Gielgud, Wendy Hiller, Vanessa Redgrave, Colin Blakely, Michael York. Directed by Sidney Lumet. 1974. 127 minutes. PG

Mutiny on the Bounty. Charles Laughton, Clark Gable, Franchot Tone, Herbert Mundin, Donald Crisp, Spring Byington, Ian Wolfe. Directed by Frank Lloyd. 1935. 132 minutes. Black and white. No rating

My Brilliant Career. Judy Davis, Sam Neill, Wendy Hughes, Robert Grubb, Max Cullen, Pat Kennedy. Directed by Gillian Armstrong. 1979. 101 minutes. G

My Life as a Dog. Anton Glanzelius, Tomas von Bromssen, Anki Liden, Melinda Kinnaman. Directed by Lasse Hallström. 1985. 101 minutes. Swedish with English subtitles. No rating

My Man Godfrey. William Powell, Carole Lombard, Alice Brady, Gail Patrick. Directed by Gregory La Cava. 1936. 95 minutes. Black and white. No rating

Norma Rae. Sally Field, Ron Leibman, Beau Bridges, Pat Hingle. Directed by Martin Ritt. 1979. 113 minutes. PG

The Nutty Professor. Jerry Lewis, Stella Stevens, Del Moore, Kathleen Freeman, Med Flory, Howard Morris. Directed by Jerry Lewis. 1963. 107 minutes. No rating

Oklahoma! Gordon MacRae, Shirley Jones, Rod Steiger, Charlotte Greenwood, Gloria Grahame, Eddie Albert, James Whitmore, Gene Nelson. Directed by Fred Zinnemann. 1955. 145 minutes. G

Oliver! Ron Moody, Oliver Reed, Mark Lester, Shani Wallis, Jack Wild. Directed by Carol Reed. 1968. 149 minutes. G

Paper Moon. Ryan O'Neal, Tatum O'Neal, Madeline Kahn, John Hillerman, P. J. Johnson, Randy Quaid. Directed by Peter Bogdanovich. 1973. 102 minutes. Black and white. PG

The Phantom Tollbooth. Butch Patrick, with the voices of Hans Conreid, Mel Blanc, Candy Candido, June Foray, Les Tremayne, Daws Butler. Directed by Chuck Jones, Abe Levitow, and David Monahan. 1969. 90 minutes. G

The Philadelphia Story. Cary Grant, Katharine Hepburn, James Stewart, Ruth Hussey, John Howard, Roland Young. Directed by George Cukor. 1940. 112 minutes. Black and white. No rating

Private Benjamin. Goldie Hawn, Eileen Brennan, Armand Assante, Robert Webber, Sam Wanamaker, Barbara Barrie. Directed by Howard Zieff. 1980. 100 minutes. R

The Producers. Gene Wilder, Zero Mostel, Kenneth Mars, Dick Shawn, Lee Meredith. Directed by Mel Brooks. 1967. 88 minutes. No rating

Rain Man. Dustin Hoffman, Tom Cruise, Valeria Golino, Jerry Molen, Jack Murdock. Directed by Barry Levinson. 1988. 133 minutes. R

Rebel Without a Cause. James Dean, Natalie Wood, Sal Mineo, Jim Backus, Ann Doran, William Hopper. Directed by Nicholas Ray. 1955. 111 minutes. No rating

Red River. John Wayne, Montgomery Clift, Walter Brennan, Joanne Dru, John Ireland, Noah Beery Jr., Paul Fix. Directed by Howard Hawks. 1948. 133 minutes. Black and white. No rating

Return of the Jedi. Mark Hamill, Carrie Fisher, Harrison Ford, voice of James Earl Jones, Billy Dee Williams, Anthony Daniels. Directed by Richard Marquand. 1983. 131 minutes. PG

The Right Stuff. Ed Harris, Sam Shepard. Scott Glenn, Dennis Quaid, Fred Ward, Barbara Hershey, Kim Stanley, Veronica Cartwright, Kathy Baker. Directed by Philip Kaufman. 1983. 193 minutes. PG

Roxanne. Steve Martin, Daryl Hannah, Rick Rossovich, Shelley Duvall, John Kapelos, Fred Willard, Max Alexander. Directed by Fred Schepisi. 1987. 107 minutes. PG

Sabrina. Humphrey Bogart, Audrey Hepburn, William Holden. Directed by Billy Wilder. 1954. 113 minutes. No rating

The Searchers. John Wayne, Vera Miles, Jeffrey Hunter, Ward Bond, Natalie Wood, John Qualen, Harry Carey Jr. Directed by John Ford. 1956. 119 minutes. No rating

Searching for Bobby Fisher. Joe Mantegna, Max Pomeranc, Joan Allen, Ben Kingsley, Laurence Fishburne. Directed by Steven Zaillian. 1993. 110 minutes. PG

The Sixth Sense. Bruce Willis, Haley Joel Osment, Toni Collette, Olivia Williams, Donnie Wahlberg, Glenn Fitzgerald. Directed by M. Night Shyamalan. 1999. 107 minutes. PG-13

The Skin Game. James Garner, Louis Gossett, Susan Clark, Brenda Sykes, Edward Asner, Andrew Duggan. Directed by Paul Bogart. 1971. 102 minutes. PG

Stagecoach. John Wayne, Claire Trevor, John Carradine, Andy Devine, Thomas Mitchell, Louise Platt, George Bancroft. Directed by John Ford. 1939. 96 minutes. Black and white. No rating

Stand by Me. Wil Wheaton, River Phoenix, Corey Feldman, Jerry O'Connell, Kiefer Sutherland, Casey Siemaszko, John Cusack, Richard Dreyfuss. Directed by Rob Reiner. 1986. 87 minutes. R

To Catch a Thief. Grace Kelly, Cary Grant, Jessie Royce Landis, John Williams, Charles Vanel. Directed by Alfred Hitchcock. 1955. 106 minutes. No rating

Tootsie. Dustin Hoffman, Jessica Lange, Teri Garr, Dabney Coleman, Charles Durning, Bill Murray, Sydney Pollack, Geena Davis, George Gaines. Directed by Sydney Pollack. 1982. 116 minutes. PG

Topper. Constance Bennett, Cary Grant, Roland Young, Alan Mowbray, Billie Burke. Directed by Norman Z. McLeod. 1937. 97 minutes. Black and white. No rating

A Tree Grows in Brooklyn. Dorothy McGuire, Joan Blondell, James Dunn, Lloyd Nolan, Peggy Ann Garner, Ted Donaldson. Directed by Elia Kazan. 1945. 128 minutes. Black and white. No rating

Tuck Everlasting. Margaret Chamberlain, Paul Flessa, Fred A. Keller, James McGuire, Sonia Raimi, Bruce D'Auria. Directed by Frederick King Keller. 1981. 100 minutes. No rating

12 Angry Men. Henry Fonda, E. G. Marshall, Lee J. Cobb, Jack Warden, Jack Klugman, George Voskovec, Robert Webber, Edward Binns, Joseph Sweeney. Directed by Sidney Lumet. 1957. 95 minutes. Black and white. No rating

Uncle Buck. John Candy, Amy Madigan, Jean Louisa Kelly, Gaby Hoffman, Macaulay Culkin, Elaine Bromka. Directed by John Hughes. 1989. 100 minutes. PG

Wallace & Gromit: The First Three Adventures. Claymation tales from Nick Park: *The Wrong Trousers, A Close Shave,* and *A Grand Day Out.* Directed by Nick Park. 1999. 85 minutes. No rating

What About Bob? Bill Murray, Richard Dreyfuss, Charlie Korsmo, Julie Haggerty. Directed by Frank Oz. 1991. 99 minutes. PG

Yankee Doodle Dandy. James Cagney, Joan Leslie, Irene Manning, Walter Huston, Rosemary DeCamp, Richard Whorf. Directed by Michael Curtiz. 1942. 126 minutes. Black and white. No rating

Young Frankenstein. Gene Wilder, Peter Boyle, Marty Feldman, Teri Garr, Madeline Kahn, Cloris Leachman, Kenneth Mars. Directed by Mel Brooks. 1974. 105 minutes. PG

Index

Buscemi, Stephen, 188, 190
Busey, Gary, 48, 49–50
Busfield, Timothy, 93
Butch Cassidy and the Sundance Kid,
   51–53, 218
Buttons, Red, 175
Byrne, Gabriel, 171
Byron, Marion, 265, 267

Cabot, Bruce, 142
Cagney, James, 5
Caldwell, Zoe, 151
Calhern, Louis, 78, 80
Callan, Michael, 57
Callow, Simon, 134
Campbell, Cheryl, 59, 60
Canby, Vincent, 19, 41, 73, 88, 90, 100,
   101, 263, 280, 297, 299
Canemaker, John, 29, 214
Cannon, Damian, 3–4
Canonero, Milena, 73
Canutt, Yakima, 276
Capra, Frank, 6, 45, 130–33, 179–81,
   191–94
Capra, Frank, Jr., 193
Captain Blood, 5
Carr, Charmian, 256
Carradine, David, 40
Carrere, Tia, 151
Carroll, Leo G., 210
Carroll, Pat, 164
Casablanca, 6, 7, 54–56, 303
Caselotti, Adriana, 249
Cassel, Jean-Pierre, 278, 279
Cat Ballou, 57–59
Cavanagh, Megan, 149
Chakiris, George, 293
Chamberlain, Richard, 278, 279
Chaney, Lon, 2
Chaney, Lon, Jr., 1, 2–3
Chanslor, Roy, 57, 58
Chaplin, Charlie, 105–8, 268
Chaplin, Geraldine, 278, 279
Chariots of Fire, 59–62
Charisse, Cyd, 246, 247, 248
Charleson, Ian, 59, 60
Chase, Daveigh, 151, 259
Chester, Vanessa Lee, 167, 169
Chicken Run, 63–65
Christopher, Dennis, 42, 43

Clavell, James, 110
Clements, Ron, 164, 166
Close Encounters of the Third Kind,
   66–68, 69, 71, 224
Clueless, 85–86
Coates, Anne, 148
Coburn, James, 108, 182, 183, 188
Cocteau, Jean, 27–28, 29
Cohen, Roger, 236
Cohn, Harry, 126, 132, 192, 193
Colbert, Claudette, 130, 131, 133
Cole, Nat King, 57, 58
Colgan, Eileen, 238, 239
Collete, Toni, 85, 86
Collodi, Carlo, 216, 217
Colman, Ronald, 179, 180
Coltrane, Robbie, 121
Columbia Pictures, 132, 192, 193
Columbus, Chris, 121–24, 194–97
Comden, Betty, 248
Connery, Sean, 175
Connick, Harry, Jr., 127, 128
Connolly, Walter, 130–31
Conreid, Hans, 212, 214
Cooper, Gary, 124, 125, 126, 192
Cooper, Merian C., 142–45
Corcoran, Kevin, 275, 276
Corey, Wendell, 225
Costello, Lou, 1–3
Costner, Kevin, 4, 93, 94, 95, 96
Courtenay, Tom, 43
Courtney, Jeni, 238, 239, 240
Cox, Brian, 231, 232
Cox, Ronny, 40
Coyote, Peter, 88, 89
Crane, Norma, 91
Crisp, Donald, 204, 205
Cromwell, James, 13, 14
Cross, Ben, 59, 60
Crossette, Barbara, 101
Crowther, Bosley, 257
Crystal, Billy, 188, 191, 221
Cuaron, Alfonso, 167–70
Cukor, George, 77, 171, 203, 304
Cumming, Alan, 85, 87
Cunningham, Liam, 167, 168
Currie, Finlay, 112
Curtis, Tony, 58, 252–55
Curtiz, Michael, 3, 4, 5–6, 54, 55–56
Curwood, James Oliver, 23–24

About the Author

PETER M. NICHOLS has written about film and video for *The New York Times* since 1988 and the "Taking the Children" column since 1994. The father of three children, he has had long experience leading them and packs of their friends into, and occasionally out of, every kind of movie situation, from the highly recommended to the not so advisable. He lives in New York.